J

MW01094173

A.L. Sadler (1882-1970) was Professor of Oriental Studies at the University of Sydney for 26 years, as well as Professor of Japanese at the Royal Military College of Australia. Among his other works are *Shogun: The life of Tokugawa Ieyasu, Japanese Tea Ceremony: Cha-no-ya,* and *Japanese Architecture: A Short History.*

Paul S. Atkins is Associate Professor of Japanese at the University of Washington, Seattle. Born and raised in Brooklyn, New York, he was educated at Stanford University, where he completed a Ph.D. in Japanese. His field of expertise is premodern Japanese literature, drama, and culture. Professor Atkins is the author of *Revealed Identity: The Noh Plays of Komparu Zenchiku* and numerous articles on medieval Japanese theatre, fiction, poetry, poetics, and literary history.

Japanese Plays

Classic Noh, Kyogen and Kabuki Works

A.L. SADLER
with a new foreword by
PAUL S. ATKINS

TUTTLE PUBLISHING
Tokyo • Rutland, Vermont • Singapore

Published by Tuttle Publishing, an imprint of Periplus Editions (HK) Ltd., with editorial
offices at 364 Innovation Drive, North Clarendon, Vermont 05759 U.S.A. and 61 Tai Seng
Avenue, #02-12, Singapore 534167

Library of Congress Cataloging-in-Publication Data

Sadler, A. L. (Arthur Lindsay), b. 1882.
  Japanese plays : Noh, Koygen, Kabuki / translated by A.L. Sadler ; with a new foreword
by Paul Atkins.
    p. cm.
  ISBN 978-4-8053-1073-1 (pbk.)
1. Japanese drama--Translations into English. I. Atkins, Paul S. (Paul Stephen), 1969- II.
Title.
  PL887.S3 2010
  895.620822--dc22

                          2009030878

ISBN 978-4-8053-1073-1

Distributed by

North America, Latin America & Europe
Tuttle Publishing
364 Innovation Drive
North Clarendon, VT 05759-9436 U.S.A.
Tel: 1 (802) 773-8930; Fax: 1 (802) 773-6993
info@tuttlepublishing.com
www.tuttlepublishing.com

Japan
Tuttle Publishing
Yaekari Building, 3rd Floor
5-4-12 Osaki, Shinagawa-ku
Tokyo 141 0032
Tel: (81) 03 5437-0171
Fax: (81) 03 5437-0755
tuttle-sales@gol.com

Asia Pacific
Berkeley Books Pte. Ltd.
61 Tai Seng Avenue, #02-12
Singapore 534167
Tel: (65) 6280-1330
Fax: (65) 6280-6290
inquiries@periplus.com.sg
www.periplus.com

13   12   11   10   6 5 4 3 2 1

Printed in Singapore

TUTTLE PUBLISHING® is a registered trademark of Tuttle Publishing,
a division of Periplus Editions (HK) Ltd.

CONTENTS

FOREWORD

Arthur Lindsay Sadler's volume of translations *Japanese Plays* was originally published in 1934 by Angus & Robertson of Sydney, Australia. It contains English versions of forty plays from the traditional noh, kyogen, and kabuki theaters. The original edition is difficult to obtain, having been out of print for many years, so this reissue by Tuttle is a very welcome development.

The three dramatic forms represented in this volume may be grouped together under the category of premodern, classical, classic, or traditional Japanese drama, but they are quite different genres. Noh is the oldest, being amply documented from the fourteenth century. It is renowned for its unique staging, which includes the use of masks that are regarded in their own right as works of art; a spare and carefully polished stage made of cypress wood; stylized gestures and movement; and pacing that is typically far slower than the modern theatregoer is accustomed. Some noh plays move quickly, especially at the end, but in most cases it takes ninety minutes or more to perform ten pages of text. This is due to the long dances, pauses between the various parts of the play, and the common use of an interlude between the two acts to allow the principal actor to change masks. Noh music, which requires at minimum a chorus of eight to ten singers, a flutist, and two drummers (a third if a taiko drum is used), forms its own branch of traditional Japanese music. Sadler included few stage directions in his translations of the noh plays (the kyogen and kabuki plays seem more heavily annotated in this regard), suggesting that he may have regarded them more for their literary, as opposed to dramatic value.

Next in length of pedigree is kyogen, a comic form that developed alongside the somber noh. Kyogen actors appear in noh plays as villagers or in other minor roles, but they have their own repertory of delicious farces, the plot of which often involves an inversion of social hierarchies. A servant outwits his master, or a husband tries to deceive his domineering wife. In the end, all is revealed, and the scoundrel is chased off the stage.

Lastly, the kabuki theater, which largely attained its current form in the seventeenth century, is characterized by its sense of visual spectacle and over-the-top acting techniques. As in noh, female roles are played by male actors (although female actors have appeared at times in both genres over the centuries). In the noh, the male actor makes little effort to appear female, but in kabuki, one can hardly tell one is looking at a man at all. The large orchestra, the rotating sets, and the *hanamichi* (a strip of the stage that runs through the audience) all contribute to the thrills of watching kabuki. Such elements are enhanced by a style of acting that often emphasizes stylized bravado. It climaxes periodically when actors assume *mie*, fixed poses (which sometimes entail crossing the eyes) that are held for a few seconds as connoisseurs in the audience shout out the actor's sobriquet.

The Second World War is one of the fault lines in the history of Japan. Sadler wrote this book before the war, during a time when Japan was under the control of right-wing military nationalists, but before it joined Nazi Germany and Fascist Italy in the Axis Pact. Needless to say, much has changed since then. Noh, which has almost always been highly regarded, has been enshrined as one of the defining traditional Japanese art forms both inside and outside Japan and has become an indispensable element of world theater. Kyogen too has benefited, enjoying in recent years a boom in popularity thanks to the charisma and hard work of some star performers. Kabuki has managed to survive the competition of film and television and, although its audiences are not as large as they were in Sadler's day, its prestige has risen; like opera, it is no longer theater for the masses. Distinguished actors from all the traditional forms receive public stipends and the official status known commonly as Living National Treasure. Noh, kyogen, and kabuki troupes regularly tour overseas, typically with heavy governmental sponsorship, contributing to the cultivation of Japan's "soft power."

Sadler's choices of plays are intriguing. Although the volume is titled simply *Japanese Plays*, all of the works included are from premodern genres; there are no plays from the emerging *shingeki* (New Drama) movement that originated in the late nineteenth century during the period of intense cultural contact between Japan and the West. But, to be fair, modern Japanese drama did not really hit its stride until after the Second World War.

The decision to exclude works of the bunraku, or puppet, theater (also known as jōruri) is also interesting, as is the inclusion of only later kabuki plays, from the early twentieth century. All of the four kabuki plays included were written by either Takayasu Gekkō (1869-1944) or Enomoto Torahiko (1866-1916). Moreover, the selection seems to reflect Sadler's personal inclination toward medieval Japanese culture, as reflected in his other volumes of translations. His kabuki protagonists tend toward master craftsmen, elegant recluses, tea masters, and other persons of exquisite taste and accomplishment.

Of the three genres represented in this book, it seems that noh plays have received the most attention from translators over the past few decades, yet five of the dozen noh plays here have still never been translated anywhere else. Eight of the twenty-four kyogen plays have never been translated elsewhere either, and a few more have not been translated since Sadler. It seems that all of the kabuki translations are unique as well. Anyone wishing to sample readable translations from noh, kyogen, and kabuki may read this volume with profit and delight, but it is simply indispensable for reconstructing, to the extent possible, the respective canons of these dramatic forms in English translation.

Even the works that have been translated elsewhere are very much worth reading in Sadler's renditions. His literary style is elegant, robust, and of another age; he also clearly knew Japanese quite well (the same cannot be said for many in the early generation of Japanese-English translators), making for a rare combination of gifts. Earlier translations from Japanese literature possess an inimitable patina in English that is especially fitting to the tone of the original and is especially effective in the lyrical noh drama. One hears verbal music in even the most mundane lines of dialogue, as when in *Tadanori* the woodcutter describes the toil of finding wood to burn to make salt: "To feed it I must tramp to fetch the fuel." Such lines can no longer be written in

English without irony or archaism. The lines that still seem con-
temporary to my ear are also often superb, as in *Tomoe*, when the
ghost of the title character sings,

> *The falling flowers confess the vanity of things,*
> *The water flows indifferent to our fate,*
> *Yet is a symbol of the lucid mind.*

Paul S. Atkins

INTRODUCTION

This small collection of translations of dramas belonging to the three types which such compositions assume in Japan was put together with a view to supplying some material for those interested in the subject and which perhaps does not exist in the compass of one volume. The specimens presented are, I think, fairly representative, though several of them were translated more from interest than any other reasons. So far as I am aware only one or two of these Noh texts have been previously rendered into English, namely, *Hatsu-yuki*, very admirably and accurately done by Waley in his volume of Noh translations, and *Kakitsubata* and *Tamura* which are to be found in that of Fenollosa and Pound, but in a version which, though elegant in parts, bears little relation to the Japanese text, as was only to be expected considering the circumstances under which the book was compiled. I have tried to make all the translations as literal as may be, though it is impossible to reproduce the verbal embroideries of the Noh, depending as they do on puns and homophones peculiar to the structure of the Japanese language. Moreover, they largely consist of devices such as the telescope word, reception of the same sound within in the space of two or three words, and the intertwining of two sentences in one that are rather unpleasing in English. Gilbert's writing sometimes contains just this sort of device that the Noh authors delight in; e.g. this passage:

But each a card shall draw,
And he who draws the lowest
Shall (so 'twas said)
Be thenceforth dead—
In fact, a legal 'ghoest
(When exigence of rhyme compels
Orthography foregoes her spells
And ghost is written 'ghoest!).

Where the commentator would be able to point to the double meaning of "spells" and the propriety of the extra letter in ghost since he (or she) is one who "ghoest." And when Gilbert referred to himself, as he is said to have done, "as a hard-boiled egoist," he was indulging in the adroit overworking of one syllable of a word, which may be found on every page or two of the Noh texts. Perhaps it is the national feeling for economy that makes Japanese writers so fond of this trick. The style of the Noh is archaic and conventional, but not very difficult after some familiarity has been gained with it, owing to the repetition of the same phrases and devices. A Japanese commentator describes it as made up of famous excerpts from classical literature of all periods from the most ancient times up to the civil wars of the twelfth century, representing on the one hand the aesthetic feelings, and on the other the philosophy of these past ages, since it is mainly composed of poetical matter embellished with Buddhist discourses. But these Buddhist quotations, too, are somewhat circumscribed, and like the Chinese texts were doubtless familiar enough to the literate of all periods, while on the other hand they were a source of information to those who were not quite so literate. And the study and chanting of the texts or Utai, quite apart from their performance on the Noh stage, is a favorite hobby among the educated of Japan today as it has been in the past. And people do not go to see a performance of Noh unless they have taken lessons in it or otherwise studied it, and even then they take the text with them and follow it. As Noh stages are only to be found in big cities, and boxes in them must be taken for a period, comparatively few can see the full performance, but everywhere there are readers of Utai so that the texts are well known.

The Noh performance is somewhat the equivalent of opera, though it avoids the artistic defect of this form of entertainment, the attempt to combine first-class singing with acting of the same grade and at the same time fitness for the part. Thus one does not find in the Noh a middle-aged and far from slender person taking the part of a young heroine because he or she has the required fine voice that seems seldom separated from a well-developed figure. The use of the mask and the measured chant, somewhat like plain-song, obviated this discord, while the performers in the

Noh, as in all other dramatic performances in Japan, are all male. Perhaps the Noh is more like an oratorio in which the singers dress for their parts, though there are only three or four of them assisted by the chorus, and supported in its turn by the efforts of one flute and a drum and two "tsuzumi."*

The diagram of the Noh stage will explain the arrangement, and this is no more than the Kagura stage still to be seen in front of the Great Shinto Shrines, such as Isumo, Kasuga, and Itsuku-shima, where the Miko or dancing-girls of the Deities posture before them on festivals and other occasions, since they appreciate this kind of entertainment as much as their worshippers. As is demonstrated by the story of the first dramatic performance given by a certain goddess on an upturned tub in order to bring forth the Sun-goddess from the cave into which she had retired owing to the rude conduct of her brother, thus plunging the world into darkness and the rest of the divinities into perplexity. It will be observed that actresses have been confined to this Kagura or divine drama ever since.

To this stage is attached a dressing-room connected with it by a covered way on which some of the performance takes place, for as soon as the players emerge from the green-room on to this gallery they are liable to begin to posture and chant. For their guidance, three pine-trees are planted along this covered way in the court outside. As the stage was usually built in the courtyard of a mansion facing the Great Reception Chamber it continued to have its own separate roof, and the distinguished audience, after paying their respects to their host as he sat in state on the dais, would then turn round and watch the performance across the courtyard through the opened-out side of the apartment.

As to the origins of the Noh, there had existed from early days both the Dengaku or Rice-field Dance, a rhythmic posturing and song given by the farmers to lighten the labor of planting out the rice-shoots, and also the Sarugaku,† an earlier form, part of which was humorous. From these elements were derived much of the chant and movement, while the stories were supplied by

---

* Hand-drum.
† Noh is merely an abbreviation of Sarugaku-no-Noh, or performance of Sarugaku.

the Heike ballads sung to the accompaniment of the "biwa" or lute, the Genji Monogatari, Chinese texts, and the myths and histories that centered in the shrines and temples. The first Noh were compiled from these sources in the days of the Ashikaga Shogun Yoshimitsu (1367-1408) by the actor-composers Kwan-ami Kiyotsugu, his son Se-ami Motokiyo, his son-in-law Komparu Ujinobu, and others. From this time onward the Noh pieces continued to be selected and composed until the early Tokugawa era about 1600, when its canon was definitely closed. The last Noh extant must be that entitled *Toyokuni Mode*, describing respect paid to the deified dictator Toyotomi Hideyoshi by envoys from the sovereigns of his own country and of China. The performance of these dramas was entirely restricted to the Five Families of Komparu, Kwanzei, Hosho, Kongo, and Kita, of which Komparu claims the greater antiquity. These houses were originally engaged in the production of the Sarugaku given at the two Great Shrines of Kasuga at Nara, and Hiyoshi on Mount Hiei near Kyoto, and the tradition in the house of Komparu is that they were descended from an official appointed by Prince Shotoku (d. 621), to play the Dengaku which he wrote. The first Kwanzei also descends from a Shonagon or Court Councillor Tomonobu, himself fifth in line from the Emperor Kwammu, and Tomonobu is the ancestor of Kwan-ami Kiyotsugu. This house of Kwanzei was in the early seventeenth century made chief of the Five Families and official Noh teacher to the Shogun by the fifth Tokugawa Shogun Tsunayoshi, a great enthusiast for this and other arts. Thus it is apparent that the atmosphere of Noh is entirely aristocratic and largely Shinto.

Shinto is the national cult, which consists in the stimulation, and also the organization of the reverence for, and interest in, the founders of the nation, and particularly in the Imperial House. All the great military leaders and administrators, the sages, loyalists, and thinkers have their shrines or places of remembrance in public just as the family ancestors have theirs in private. Were matters organized on these lines in England there would be more or less standardized shrines to all her heroes from the gods of our Scandinavian ancestors, King Arthur and his companions, King Alfred, Hereward, Robin Hood, and so on to Drake and Raleigh and the other great Elizabethans to Nelson, and the moderns and the Cenotaph. All these are celebrated with us in historical novels, with the exception of such cases as Shakespeare's few historical plays, or in poems, mostly modern. These are not lacking in Japan either, but it is the drama that has been a more powerful influence in this ancestral cult. But as the Shinto of these days was an ally of Buddhism, since the Buddhist ecclesiastics, with admirable shrewdness and insight, did not oppose the ancient national cult but preferred to go shares with it, it follows that the Noh has almost as strong a flavor of Buddhism as of Shinto, though the number of pieces with the former as its motive is very much less. Thus the introducing character of Deuteragonist is as often as not a Buddhist monk with his characteristic phrase, "Shōkoku Ikken no sō nite sōrō"– "I am a priest traveling round the sights of my country." It is the Buddhism of the older type, Nara, Shingon, and Tendai, and of the Amida sects, such as would be congenial to the Court and military circles.

The resemblance of the Noh to the Greek theater has often been made the subject of comment. There is the same chorus, which was the original ballet, from which two or three performers detached themselves to take the principal parts while the rest remained to comment. And the Protagonist, etc., do not really identify themselves with the character, but remain detached from it. There is a similar restriction of the performers to men, and the subject to past history and largely tragedy. There is also the same absence of scenery, use of masks, emphasis of gesture, posture, and clear articulation, the same view of emotion as a thing to be suppressed by properly heroic people, and the same view of the drama as an outlet for repressed feelings. But there is no dependence of the one on the other or any connection at all, it seems. Both must have proceeded independently from the same practical type of mind, well endowed with a sense of form and of the value of history as an education and a State cult.

It is probably unique that in Japan all the elements from which the dramas have grown are still to be seen. The Kagura or Sacred Dance, the Folk Dance, the Biwauta or Minstrel Ballad, the Noh, the Joruri or Gidayu or Popular Ballad, the Puppet Theater and the Kabuki all flourish owing to the support and protection afforded them by the unchanging condition of the national institutions.

One noticeable characteristic of the Noh is its strong appeal to local patriotism, a very potent element in the national variety. Almost all the plays are intimately connected with famous scenes, and abound in moving descriptions of their beauties as well as of their historic associations. With their well-known love of nature, Japanese have always been given to traveling around their country on one pretext or another, often religious, and do so still, greatly to the profit of the national railways. A very convenient handbook entitled *Yokyoku Meisho Meguri*, or *A Tour Bound Scenes of the No Drama*, enumerates a hundred and seventy of these places arranged under their districts and with full information about railways and vehicle routes and distances. These scenes are scattered all over the country, but seventy-seven of them lie between Kyoto and Tokyo in the Tokaido provinces, while the Sanyo district between Kobe and Shimonoseki by the Inland Sea has fifteen; twenty are in the Kansai region round Nara, Yoshino and Kii province, while the opposite Sanin coast facing Korea has only five. Kyushu has ten and the northern Tohoku district fourteen. Thus it will be seen that most of these places are in parts easily accessible and likely to be well known, while the fact that a very important function of temples was, and is, to be used as rest-houses, making pilgrimage easier and more comfortable. That this national feeling is not confined to Japan, though better organized there than anywhere else, is clear from such a very understanding statement as the following, made in a well-known work on England, where, speaking of Tintagel and the Arthurian legend, Thomas Burke observes: "Here is something older than Canterbury, perhaps older than Stonehenge and with more meaning for us. For these tales, whether true tales of figures with a strange past or the fancies of inspired minstrels and chroniclers, make the real Talmud, Koran, or Bible of England. The average Englishman's personal religion, whatever he may be taught or choose to believe, is not an imported religion of Eastern mysticism. It is the religion of honor, courage, right acting, and right thinking; and the hastiest observation of the English character shows that the average Englishman is more ashamed of falling short of Kipling's 'If' than of falling short of the Sermon on the Mount. His working pattern is not the sweet saint, but the gentleman whose origin is found, not in any church, but in the knights of that king whose birthplace this is said to be." When one reflects on the amount of boredom children might have been saved if the parish church had been like the Shinto Shrine, or even if the miracle play had been retained in it, we may see perhaps some reason for Japan's reputation as a "paradise for the young."

As to their classification, an examination of the one hundred and ninety-seven plays given in the Yokyokushu or Noh Corpus shows that fifty-three are stories from Japanese ancient history and legend; forty more are from the Heike Monogatari which is of the same type except that it relates to the civil wars of the later twelfth century; six are from the Genji Monogatari representing Court life of the tenth century; another forty-seven have definitely Shinto motives, and twenty Buddhist, while Chinese history supplies the background for twenty-one; eight are stories of metamorphoses of plants and animals; two are simply auspicious compositions; one is combined Buddhist-Shinto, and one is a straight-out ghost story. It will be seen from this rough analysis that Japanese historical themes are very much in the ascendant, for practically a hundred and fifty are of this nature, while of the rest quite a few are intimately connected with it.

And the Noh in its turn gave rise to the Kabuki or theater of the people. Seeing that the Noh-players were salaried and employed by the aristocracy, there was until the seventeenth century little opportunity for ordinary people to see it or any other dramatic performance. Only when there was a Kanjin Noh, which was the name given to one held to raise money for a temple or a shrine, was there room for any but a select few. For this Benefit Noh a special stage was erected surrounded by a high fence with gates—and an entrance fee charged, a thing quite unknown in the ordinary Noh, which was entirely non-commercial. Later on in the Tokugawa era this Benefit was given by order of the Shogun to raise an honorarium for the family that gave it. It was held eight times during this era, six times for the Kwanzei house and twice for the Hosho. It must have been an ideal ben-

efit, for a batch of tickets was allotted to each ward of the city
and had to be bought by the ordinary people, while there was
no escape for the great nobles from buying boxes. And by command of the Shogun all other entertainments were closed while
the Benefit Noh was on.

It was this stage, with its two-storied loges on each side for
the great, and seats on the ground in front for the multitude,
that developed into the Kabuki or popular theater about the end
of the sixteenth century, roughly about the time the same in-
stitution arose in England. The long passage across the Kabuki
theater from the back of the house to the stage is evidently the
gallery of the Noh adapted to an audience that sits on both sides
of it, though even now the best seats in a theater are those that
face this passage on the right-hand side. This passage, known
as the "Flower-path," and the revolving stage, are conveniences
that allow for more spacious effects than does the more limited
arrangement of the European theater, as is indicated by the adop-
tion of these devices in the very modern houses to obtain those
intimate relations between actors and audience that the Japanese
theater has always possessed.

The Noh stage has no scenery of any kind and was standardized in that those built by the nobles in their mansions both in
town and country had to be constructed by craftsmen of the
house of Gora, the Shogunal stage architect, in the same style,
lest they coincide with that in the castle at Edo which was slightly
different. But there were small "models" placed on it to suggest
scenery, sketchy gates and boats and trees and turrets and cot-
tages in outline to indicate the required atmosphere.

The Kabuki Theater on the other hand went in for realism and
melodrama instead of elegant and restrained convention, and
its audience was almost confined to the citizens or "mere street
people," since the military gentry did not patronize it, except occasionally incognito. As the *Legacy of Tokugawa Ieyasu* observes:
"There are different kinds of music and drama for samurai and
officials and the lower classes. They must be performed by each
class within the prescribed limits." Actually one of these incognito visits of a lady-in-waiting in the Shogun's castle in the early
eighteenth century had a considerable effect on the world of Ka-

buki, when she went on the quiet to the theater instead of the temple, spending there the money that should have been given to the priests, and even having the effrontery to ask the priests to buy her tickets. And not content with just going, she stayed to make merry and get drunk, and to drop liquor from an upper box into the eye of a samurai who was sitting below, who was naturally affronted and complained to the authorities, with the result that they inflicted exemplary penalties on the lady and her friends the actors, and a set of hampering rules on all the theaters.

And just as their clientele was not distinguished, so the Kabuki actors had no social standing, though they soon formed families on the lines of the Noh artists and other specialists into which a player must be born or adopted in order to enter theatrical circles. And they remained male too, but since no masks were used in Kabuki there was instituted a woman impersonator type who made it his business to play female parts.

Though treated differently, the subjects of the Kabuki were just the same as those of the Noh. In fact, the first recorded Kabuki plays are episodes in the life of Yoshitsune, the hero of the Gempei wars of the twelfth century. They are all stories of the great and usually sad deeds of the past. For it seems that the Japanese have always sought the drama as an escape or a diversion, and evidently they do so still, for quite recently a magazine article complained that it was a great shame to see a worthy modern play left unacted, while on the other hand a new output of works taking the audience back to the Kamakura, Toyotomi, or Tokugawa periods (1200-1870) is always sure of recognition and appreciation from manager and public alike. Evidently, this is the complaint of a writer who finds it difficult to compete with the past. The three hundred and eighty-five plays of Mokuami and other older types, for instance, have dominated the stage since he produced them during his not very remote days (1816-93).

Mokuami was what is called a "sakusha" or a writer attached to a theater to put into suitable form any story that actors might fancy. Hence his considerable output. Three of the Kabuki plays here translated, *Raizan*, *Kakiēmon*, and *The Village of Drummakers* owe their form to one of the sakusha, Enomoto Torahiko; the last of these writers indeed, for he died only in 1917. The play

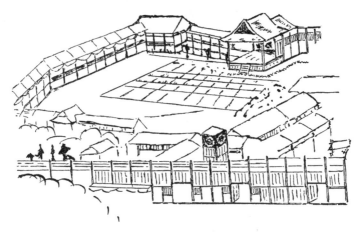

Origin of the Kabuki Theater. Enclosure for the benefit of Noh.

Kakiēmon is considered his masterpiece, and was written for the veteran actor Kataoka Nizaemon, who takes the principal part in it, as also that of Haiya Shōyu in *The Cherry Shower.* These four Kabuki plays were chosen as dealing with aesthetic matters and being less tragic than most, and therefore more pleasing to Western taste. This latter play is the work of Takayasu Gekko, a talented writer who is famous for his presentations of the old type of drama in more modern language and shorter form, and without the lengthy interpellations of the chorus, which has been retained in the older Kabuki just as in the Noh. This chorus has remained a persistent feature of the Japanese stage and has maintained itself in an attentuated form even in the cinema-house in the person of the "benshi" or movie orator, who keeps up a stream of comment on the picture or a translation if it be a foreign specimen. And he has found a place, too, in the English talkies to which he adds a translation, no doubt very instructive to students of the language. But these foreign films, of course, play only a minor part, for the Japanese cinema is as much devoted to the past, as is the theater. Devotion to the past, which in Japan is not so very long past, has never apparently excluded living quite effectively in the present. This fact is no longer hidden even from the English industrialist. For it will be noted that the Noh also dealt with the past. The civil wars of the twelfth century and the joys and sorrows of Genji and

Ono-no-Komachi, and others in the tenth century and earlier ones were long past to those of Ashikaga days. And the Noh deals with little later than the twelfth century.

Anyhow, the present day Japanese does not seem to care to sit in the theater and pay a high price for what he can get for next to nothing in the newspaper, or for a few cents in the hall of the public story-teller, who still flourishes and can provide an admirable one-man drama ranging from sentiments of the loftiest patriotism to scenes of rather improper farce, and all in the space of an hour or so. The desire to see something out of the ordinary was advanced by a Japanese critic as a reason for this preference for the tales of bygone days. His countrymen certainly possess it in a superlative degree. They have always realized, and tried to avoid, the monotony of life by studying it as an art and by cultivating the asymmetric and the suggestive. And yet owing to their practical appreciation of economy and dislike of the superfluous, they have for centuries practiced standardization, and these qualities are to be seen very clearly marked in their dramatic forms, in the uniform structure of the pieces, and their variety of detail.

It must not be forgotten either that during the Tokugawa period any use of historical material of that era was strictly forbidden, so that all plays had to be staged in the days previous to their rule. The famous *Chushingura*, or *Story of the Forty-seven Loyal Retainers* (excellently translated by J. Inouye) is an example of such a play, for since the deeds it celebrates took place in 1702, it had to be fitted out with a hero and villain and motive borrowed from Ashikaga days, and though so arranged it has been performed at least yearly on the anniversary ever since. Known as "The Mirror of Bushido," and foreigners often refer to it as "The Bible of Japan," its influence has been deep and lasting, and by its standard, thought and action still is, and long will be, justified or condemned. Considering all these things, it is clear that as an educational control over the thoughts of the nation the influence of the various forms of drama has been incalculable.

Most of the characters in the Kabuki plays are historical, with the exception of those in the *Village of Drum-makers*. Hon-ami Koetsu, like Kakiēmon, is well enough known to art lovers of

Europe and America for the products of his Village of Craftsmen which he established at Takagamine just outside Kyoto on a piece of land given him by Tokugawa Ieyasu. His hereditary business, still carried on by his family, was that of a sword-connoisseur to the Court, but he was master of all the arts. With him and another Konoe Ozan was reckoned as one of the Three Pens or Calligraphists of the time. Haiya Saburobei or Sano Shoeki, as he is usually called, lived a long as well as an elegant life, surviving Yoshino for many years and dying at the age of eighty-one in 1692. He, too, was a poet and author as well as a potter and tea-master, and it is to him that we owe perhaps the most vivid sketch of Koetsu in the memoirs that he wrote called *Nigiwai-gusa, or Pages from a Busy Life.* The tearoom he designed is still to be seen in the precincts of the Kodaiji Temple at Kyoto as is also another built for his wife, and both are fine monuments to their fastidious taste.

Konishi Raizan belongs to the next generation for he was born in 1635 at Sakai near Osaka, the birthplace of many famous aesthetes including Sen-no-Rikyu. He was a connection of Konishi Yukinaga the "Christian General" who won fame in the Korean campaign under Hideyoshi, and lost his head later on for opposing Tokugawa Ieyasu. Raizan's book of poems, the "Ima-miya-gusa," ranks high among the literary works of that time, and his villa, the Jumando, is still preserved in the village to which he retired, now a suburb of Osaka. Characteristic of him is the verse he made on his deathbed:

Raizan died because he was born.
What need of resentment or any other emotion.

The Kyogen or Comic interlude owing to its nature needs rather little explanation. It is composed of matter that was separated from the original Sarugaku when this was expurgated and edited to make it more dignified to suit the taste of the Ashikaga age. It is given in the intervals between the five pieces of Noh* that

---

* The order of these five pieces should be according to the convention, Shin, Gun Jo, Kyo, Ki. God, Warrior, Woman, Madness, Devil. It is explained that Japan is the country of the Gods, while warriors have always been there to support them. Women solace the

normally make up a performance as a relief from the austerity of the latter. The actors are specialists who confine themselves to it, for it is quite outside the province of the Noh performer.

The Kyogen pieces are classified according to the subject, as Peasant, Deformed Person, Drunkard, Thief, Quack, Bridegroom, Governor, Priest, Wandering Friar, Daimyo, Page, Old Man, Woman, and God and Devil pieces, and are remarkable in Japanese older literature, though they have no literary value, as being the only examples of writing dealing with the ordinary people, whose existence is only assumed as taxpayers and providers of supplies in the background for the courtiers, warriors, and ecclesiastics whose doings alone are important enough to be chronicled. But in the Kyogen these people are shown behaving as they did in the everyday life of the Ashikaga period, to which these compositions belong, and in the colloquial dialect of which they are written. It is about the only survival of the medieval colloquial and interesting as such, for it does not differ so very widely from the modern Kyoto and Osaka dialects.

Some of these interludes are a parody of the Noh with its ghost-hero such as Tsu-en, which is modelled on Minamoto Yorimasa's fight at Uji, a place that became later on famous for its tea. The *Cuttle-fish* is another of this type, and there are many more. The others emphasize those aspects of human nature in both high and low that neither religion nor discipline exactly approve of, but which in Japan are regarded probably with less intolerance than in many countries as long as they do not interfere too much with efficiency. As the proverb observes, even the austere warrior-monk Benkei, a sort of gigantic Japanese Galahad-the-Wake, was not without his one romance, and considered the more interesting therefore. Yet the text of the Kyogen is always quite decorous and free from any coarseness. And it is not remarkable that the Buddhist clergy should not be spared, seeing the little regard the educated and ruling classes in Japan have ever had for the non-producing ecclesiastic with his medieval heaven and

---

warrior in the intervals of his activity. Madness is presumably interesting as a variation, while devils must not be omitted. But in practice this order is not necessarily adhered to, e.g. Noh of an auspicious or duty or propriety type often being substituted, especially for the last two.

hell. The ideal of the warrior was to fear nothing, and it is very noticeable how in stories of collision between this "bushi" and the supernatural powers, the latter usually get the worst of it. With the Shinto Deities people were on terms of good humored, though not always very well informed, respect.

Of the individual Noh here translated, *Murōzumi* and *Kamo-no-Chomei* are Buddhist, the former founded on the tradition of the temple of that name and the latter on Chomei's well-known book, to which here a rather quaint happy ending is added. *Hatsu-yuki* and *Kakitsubata* are characteristic of the metamorphosis Noh. *Tadanori* and *Tomoe* are famous episodes from the Heike tales, while *Oyashiro* and *Kokaji* are of Shinto complexion, and *Tamura* combines Buddhism with the history of the first authentic Shogun. *Shōjo* is Chinese, and also auspicious, for it ends in a Japanese patriotic refrain sung by all the well-inebriated. *Iwabune* too celebrates the happiness of peaceful commerce.

This introduction is merely intended to give a very brief explanation of the text, and those who require more detailed elucidation may find it in the introductions to G. B. Sansom's translations of Noh in the *Trans. As. Soc. of Japan*, Vol. 28, or in A. Waley's *No*, F. V. Dickins's *Primitive and Medieval Japanese Texts*, Lombard's *Japanese Drama*, and, in German, in Gundert's *Der Schintoismus im Japanischen No-drama*.

In Japanese I have used Owada's *Yōkyoku Tsukai* and *Yōkyoku Hyōshaku*, while I have found extremely useful a small work entitled *No to Utai no Kōwa* by the late Professor Takahiko Amanuma, as also *Meisaku Yōkyoku Shinsaku* by Nomoto Yonekichi, kindly presented to me by Lieutenant-Commander T. Onitsuka; and for the Kabuki theater Goto Keiji's *Nikon Gekijo-shi*.

I owe very much also to Professor Hirotaro Hattori of the Imperial University of Tokyo and the Gakushuin, for his great kindness in so often lending me his box at the Kwanzei No theater, whereby my knowledge and appreciation were very much increased.

A. L. S.

NOH PLAYS

TADANORI

PROTAGONIST	*IN THE FIRST ACT AN OLD WOODMAN;*
	IN THE SECOND ACT TAIRA TADANORI
DEUTERAGONIST	*IN BOTH ACTS, A TRAVELING PRIEST*
TIME	*THE THIRD MONTH*
PLACE	*SUMA*

ACT I

PRIEST: I am one who has seen the vanity of this world. Even the flowers and the moon viewed through the clouds no longer attract me. Formerly I was a retainer of the Lord Shunzei, but when my master died I forsook the world and put on this priestly garb, and since I have never visited the western provinces, I bethought me to make a pilgrimage to those parts. So now I have come to the neighborhood of the capital, and look on the ruins of palace and mansion that have passed away, impermanent as a journey where there is no abiding-place. We who must mix with the filth of this world and yet have abandoned all its ties are too sad even to listen to the sighing of the wind in the trees or the sound of the rippling of the waves. The boom of the distant bell awakes us to the vanity of this world as it arouses the traveler from his rest.

WOODMAN: A hard life it is that I lead. When I am not carrying sea water for salt I am laden with wood to boil it, and what with one and the other my garments are never dry. Like the ceaseless cry of the birds is the hoarse voice of the fisherman at his nets. This shore of Suma has a name for loneliness, as the poet Narihira wrote:

"How I spend my days,
Should my friends chance to inquire,
You may tell them this.
On the lonely Suma beach,
I am cutting wood for salt."

On the hills near Suma there is a cherry tree that recalls the memory of one long dead, and when in spring it puts forth its flowers, and I happen to go that way, I break off a branch as an offering to the departed spirit.

PRIEST: Ha, old man! And are you one of the woodmen of these hills?

WOODMAN: It may be that I am a fisherman on that beach.

PRIEST: But if you were a fisherman your dwelling would be by the sea, and I take you for a woodman because your occupation seems to be in these hills.

WOODMAN: How else should I get wood to boil my salt water?

PRIEST: True, true. And so we see the smoke go up at eve.

WOODMAN: To feed it I must tramp to fetch the fuel.

PRIEST: By various paths to hamlets far away,

WOODMAN: By Suma beach are people rarely seen.

PRIEST: But in the hills behind,

WOODMAN: That's where the brushwood is ...

CHORUS: That's where the brushwood is, and so he goes for fuel to boil his salt.

WOODMAN: Indeed your words are not a little simple, priest.

CHORUS: In truth the bay of Suma is not as other places, for flowers dislike the boisterous mountain breezes that sweep down from the hills and send them flying. But here 'tis otherwise, for Suma's mountain cherry was smitten by a blast that blew from seaward.

PRIEST: See now, old man, the day is drawing to a close. I pray you give me lodging for the night.

TADANORI

WOODMAN: The shadow of this cherry tree is all the lodging I can offer.

PRIEST: Indeed it is a very bower of blossom. And who can be the host, I wonder.

WOODMAN:
"Now the daylight dies,
And the shadow of a tree
Serves me for an inn.
For the host to welcome me
There is but a wayside flower."

He who wrote these lines lies deep beneath the moss, but even we poor fishers often gather to say a requiem for him, so why do not you, a priest, take the opportunity of acquiring merit by repeating a prayer in passing?

PRIEST: That verse is Satsuma-no-kami Tadanori's, is it not?

WOODMAN: Indeed it is. And when he fell in the battle that was fought hard by some friend planted this tree in his memory.

PRIEST: How strange a chance. For I am of the House of Shunzei.

WOODMAN: His master and beloved fellow poet.

PRIEST: So here I stay tonight.

CHORUS: So let him hear the blessed sound of prayer, and may he take his seat on heaven's flowery terraces.

WOODMAN: I am most grateful for these prayers said for me, and do rejoice that thereby I grow in enlightenment.

CHORUS: How strange his words! It seems that this old man takes to himself these holy prayers and is much comforted. How can this be?

WOODMAN: 'Twas for the prayers of this priest that I came hither.

CHORUS: And now sleep soundly 'neath this cherry tree, and in a dream you shall be told the message I will have taken to the capital. (*And suddenly he disappears none knoweth whither.*) Yes, hurry hence back to the capital and tell these things to Teika, Shunzei's son. Now the moon rises high, sadly the sea birds flit. The sea breeze scarcely sighs, soundly the traveler sleeps, by Suma's ancient strand where once the guard-house stood.

ACT II

PROTAGONIST AS TADANORI'S SPIRIT: Now in this place where I was slain again I take my former shape that I may declare all that is in my mind, for there is one thing above all that draws me to this world and holds me back from the Buddha realm, and it is this:

For when my verse was chosen by Shunzei,
And placed in the Imperial Anthology,
Since I was then a rebel 'gainst the throne,
My name was not attached,
But it was signed "A verse by one unknown."
This was the most Shunzei could do for me.
And now that he is dead,
Do you go back and tell his son from me
That my name must be written.

CHORUS:

Born of a house so skilled in native verse
How reasonable his wish!
He was a lord of very great renown,
Of equal skill in war and literature,
And when our Sovereign the Retired Emperor
Ordered this anthology to be made,
The Lord Shunzei, Courtier of the Third Rank,
Was chosen to compile it.

And when this Tadanori went from home
To fight the Genji by the Western Sea,
He came to bid his master first farewell
And ask him to include a verse of his.
And this he did, but could not have it signed,
Because the Heike, Tadanori's house,
Were rebels against the throne,
And in the battle that was fought by Suma beach
The Heike, routed, scattered to their ships.

TADANORI:

And as I rode away to get on board,
Okabe Tadazumi of the Genji house
With six or seven retainers challenged me.
At him I rode and threw him from his horse
And grappled him and would have had his head,
When one of his retainers, creeping around behind,
Cut my right arm through with a single blow.
Then seeing all was lost I drew aside
To say the death prayer, and Okabe's sword
Took off my head with the last syllable.
"Alas," he said, "we warriors must slay,
But this was certainly no common foe.
His armor gay like autumn's tinted leaves,
His robes and surcoat all of gold brocade
Show him to be a Taira lord at least."
And so he searched to find out who I was,
And in my quiver there was stuck the verse.
Above it was the title, "Last Night's Bivouac"--
　　"Now the daylight dies,
　　And the shadow of a tree
　　Serves me for an inn.
　　For the host to welcome me,
　　There is but a wayside flower."
And so he knew 'twas Tadanori's head
For that none other could have written this.
Now you know all, and so, as falls the flower,
I go again back to the dark abode.

KAKITSUBATA

PROTAGONIST	*A WOMAN WHO IS THE SPIRIT OF THE IRIS*
DEUTERAGONIST	*A TRAVELING PRIEST*

TIME	*THE FOURTH MONTH*
PLACE	*PROVINCE OF MIKAWA*

PRIEST: I am a priest who is traveling round all the provinces of the Empire, and thus far I have visited the capital and viewed all its famous spots and places of ancient memory and now I propose to continue my journey to the eastern country.

PILGRIM-SONG:
For every eve my lonely pillow changes
As every day I seek another lodging,
Through Mino and Owari lies my weary journey,
And now I reach the province of Mikawa.

CHORUS: Yea, pressing on I soon have reached Mikawa. And over there is a pool with great clumps of iris in full bloom, so I will go thither and view them closer. Ah, how the year flies by, for spring's no sooner past than it is summer, and though some may say that trees and grasses have no mind, they never forget to array themselves in the proper hue for the season, and truly do they call the iris the flower of the fair face. (Kaoyohana.) How beautiful it is!

SPIRIT: Well, priest, and who are you? Why are you lingering here?

PRIEST: I am one who is visiting all the provinces of the Empire, and the loveliness of these irises attracted me. What may this place be called?

SPIRIT: This is Yatsubashi in the province of Mikawa, a place of great renown for these very irises. Consider them well for they are no ordinary blossoms. Mysterious is the affinity of their deep purple hue. 'Tis strange indeed you should not know of this.

PRIEST: Ah yes, there is some ancient verse that speaks of the iris of Yatsubashi in the province of Mikawa. Can you then tell me who it was who wrote it?

SPIRIT: It's in the Tales of Ise. Because the river here flows in eight rills they call it Yatsubashi. Eight bridges cross the streams, and all around between them the flowers grow, a charming checkered pattern. And when he saw it the poet Narihira wove an acrostic on the five syllables of the word Kakitsubata to express his longing for the capital:

"Ah happy is the garment	*Kara-koromo*
Of antique Chinese fashion	*Ki-tsutsu nare ni shi*
That holds my love within it,	*Tsuma shi areba*
While I am far away	*Haru-baru kinuru*
Unable to approach her."	*Tabi wo shi zo omou.*

PRIEST: Ah, how charming! And did Ariwara-no-Narihira then travel as far as these distant provinces of the eastland?

SPIRIT: Indeed much farther. He journeyed through the country, viewing its famous places until he came to Mutsu, remote in the far northland. 'Tis strange you did not know it.

PRIEST: However far one journeyed through many a distant province, never could one forget the iris of Mikawa, the streams of Yatsubashi. And so this be loved purple hue remains—

SPIRIT: To keep alive the memory of him—

PRIEST: Who once was Narihira.

CHORUS:
And as these purple blossoms never fail
To keep their tryst with him in this place,
Do you, O wandering monk, repeat the holy texts
To further his enlightenment and mine,
For as I muse on these events long past,
I long to hear them.

SPIRIT: There's something too I wish to say.

PRIEST: And what is that?

SPIRIT: 'Tis a poor place enough, but in this hut of mine I pray you pass the night.

PRIEST: I shall be most glad to do so.

SPIRIT: Behold this diadem and robe!

PRIEST: What does this glittering robe and courtly diadem in such a humble dwelling?

SPIRIT: This is the robe you read of in the poem, the robe of Princess Taka: and this, the diadem that Narihira wore at the great court festival in the eleventh month. I wear them in their memory.

PRIEST: The robe and diadem. Ah yes, but who are you then?

SPIRIT: I am the spirit of the iris. You may have read in ancient verse how there was a woman who was transformed into an iris. And Narihira, now in Paradise, is a celestial Bodhisattva who protects the art of poetry. For poems are but holy Buddhist texts, by which all flesh may gain enlightenment, and trees and flowers, and all creation too.

PRIEST: It is a wondrous grace to this our world that to the trees and flowers inanimate it should be given to hear the Buddhist law.

SPIRIT: In days of old the dance of Narihira was stately as a Buddhist ritual.

PRIEST: And he, the Bodhisat of poetry, leaving his Paradise of Quiet Light, was here reborn and wandered everywhere to save mankind. But yet while everywhere he wandered his heart was ever in the capital.

SPIRIT: These Tales of Ise, of whom then were they written?

CHORUS: These tales of love and longing, of wanderings through the Empire, beginning not nor ending...

SPIRIT:
> Of old there was a man,
> Wearing the hat of manhood,
> Who went to hunt at Nara,
> Kasuga's ancient city,
> On lands he owned there.

CHORUS:
> They say 'twas in the reign
> Of Emperor Nimmyo,
> And by Imperial edict—
> With reverence be it spoken—
> He was appointed envoy
> To the spring festival
> Of the Kasuga Shrine.
> And granted his first head-dress,
> The hat of early manhood.

SPIRIT: And by special grace of His Majesty.

CHORUS:
> The ceremony of assuming it was held in the palace,
> An honor of very rare occurrence.
> But since good fortune in this world of ours
> Is ever followed by adversity,

He fell on evil days,
And from the capital
Was sent to wander forth
Through all the eastern provinces.
Along the coast of Ise and Owari
He drifted on like a cloud,
With nothing to look at
But the sullen billows,
His heart full of regrets
For what he had left behind.
Until at length he came
To the peak of Asama in Shinano
And viewed its smoky pall.
Now in Shinano
See the cloud of smoke arise
From Asama's peak,
Those who view it from afar
Might mistake it for a cloud.
Then he went on his journey
Till he reached the province of Mikawa,
Where is the famous Yatsubashi,
With its clumps of iris blossoms
And there it was he remembered his spouse
Far away in the ancient capital.
He who was beloved of so many ladies,
As you may read in the Tales of Ise.

SPIRIT:

But though thus gaily he lived and died
And passed into darkness at dawn of day,
And the light of the moon was not so serene
Or the spring quite the same as the springs of yore,
Yet still is he the Narihira of old,
The God of Poetry and the Buddha-mind.
Be in no doubt of this, O wayfarer!
Before the flowers the snow-flake butterflies!
Over the willows bush-warblers like gold!
Still in this place there flowers the purple iris,

The orange blossom wafts its clinging perfume.
The flag, so like the iris, flutters in the breeze
And on the bough in sheen of old brocade
Shrills the cicada.
While 'gainst the purple clouds of iris shines
The snow-white Deutzia.
Thus all these flowers and trees together gain enlightenment.
And like the earth itself attain the Buddha-mind,
And so are here no longer.

IWABUNE[*]

PROTAGONIST	THE DRAGON SEA GOD
DEUTERAGONIST	AN IMPERIAL ENVOY

TIME	THE NINTH MONTH
PLACE	SUMIYOSHI IN SETTSU

ENVOY: The Empire is at peace on every side. No barriers stay our progress through the land.

CHORUS: I am one who humbly serves in the court of our Sovereign. And so wise and benevolent is his rule that no rough wind of adversity stirs the tranquility of his people, who sleep secure with their doors all unbarred. And as he has issued an Imperial edict that a market be established on the beach of Sumiyoshi in Settsu, to the end that his people may buy the precious merchandise of China and Korea, I am this day on my way to Settsu in the province of Tsu.

PILGRIM-SONG:
All things go as we wish.
On the four seas of our land
The waves lap soundlessly.
Akitsushima's bounds
Are happy and secure.
Now are we come to Tsu
Where always without fail
Arrive the tribute-ships
From China and Korea.

---

[*] Iwabune. The rock-stout ship. Sumiyoshi and Sakai, two of the most ancient ports in Japan were Shinto Shrine property, the Deities of which protected and throve by trade, both native and foreign.

CHORUS:
    The town of Sumiyoshi,
    Where softly blows the pine-breeze,
    We enter.
    This town whose farthest limits
    Our Sovereign's grace embraces.

DRAGON GOD: His grace is wide extended, and here in Sumiyoshi, a place full good to live in, the God of Sumiyoshi adds his protecting favor. May our Lord live forever, and rule his prosperous people, unchanging as the pine-trees. I am the Dragon God of the Waters of Akitsushima, who dwells in this world reverencing the great Deities and protecting the Sovereign of the land.

CHORUS: As it has been from the Age of the Gods—

DRAGON GOD: I go forth in the Empire—

CHORUS: As guardian of the treasure ships of the Mikado.

DRAGON GOD: Greatly to be revered is the Imperial command. And his great ship—

CHORUS: Bearing his treasure let the waves lap gently—

DRAGON GOD: Bearing it on its way.

CHORUS: A zephyr appears in the sky—

DRAGON GOD: With gentle rhythm the wavelets—

CHORUS:
    Roll splashing round its bosom, while from fair Sumiyoshi
    Blow soft the pine-bough breezes.
    The full tide sweeps it onward.
    Eight Dragon Gods arise.
    From out the heaving billows

They haul upon the cables.
They bring it safe to shore,
To Sumiyoshi's strand.
And pearls and gold and silver
And myriad precious treasures,
Tribute for the Mikado,
Rejoicing hands unload.
May the Gods guard forever
Our land's Imperial Sovereign
Ruling his prosperous Empire.

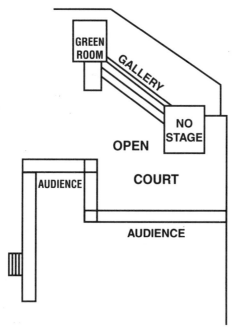

Arrangement of the Noh stage adjoining the reception hall
of the main castle of the shogun at Edo.

TAMURA

PROTAGONIST	*IN THE FIRST ACT A YOUTH. IN THE SECOND SAKA-NO-UE NO TAMURA MARO*
DEUTERAGONIST	*A PRIEST FROM THE EASTERN PROVINCES*
TIME	*THE THIRD MONTH*
PLACE	*KYOTO*

ACT I

PRIEST: Through many a country town I have pursued my journey, and now I haste to the Nine-fold Capital. I am a priest from the eastern provinces, and since I have never yet beheld the capital, this very spring I have determined to visit it. 'Tis now the season of early April, and calm is the shadow of the circling sunbeams. The mists drift yonder o'er Mount Otowa, and gently murmurs the fall of its water, for now we approach to Kiyomizu. Now we draw near to its well-known temple. Indeed we have come to the end of our journey, for this is Kiyomizu well known in the capital. And see! Its cherries are all in blossom. Let us then find someone whom we may ask about it.

YOUTH: Spring of its bounty thus makes its offering, and lays its flowers before the Gongen. Though many are the places whose flowers are famous, by the radiance of the grace of the Goddess Kwannon this spot is indeed surpassed by none. By the blossoming spring of her great compassion, the autumn moon of her thirty-three revelations shines clear in the water of the five impurities and makes fragrant this world of the ten transgressions. Snow white as the palaces of the mighty Deities, like the masses of cloud that spread o'er the hills are the full-laden boughs of the blossoming cherries, manifold as the clustering courts of the Imperial Palace. Embosomed thus in its encircling hills decked with these lovely blossoms, how seasonable is the spring scene of our ancient capital.

PRIEST: Ah, here is one of whom I may inquire.

YOUTH: And what is it then that you wish to know?

PRIEST: And you who ply your broom so gracefully beneath the trees. Are you the Flower-warden, may I ask?

YOUTH: I am indeed one who thus serves the Goddess here. And since in the season of flowers I sweep beneath these trees, you may call me the warden of the flowers, as also I am styled the servant of this shrine. And my attachment to it is most strong.

PRIEST: Ah, so it seems. And do you then tell us all its history.

YOUTH: Know then that this Temple of Kiyomizu was founded in the second year of the era Daido through the vow of Saka-no-ue no Tamura Maru. Long ago the monk Kenshin of the Temple of Kojima in the province of Yamato prayed earnestly that he might behold the real form of Kwannon, and seeing one day a golden light shining from the upper waters of the Kozugawa, he made his way towards it and there found an old man who addressed him thus: "I am called Gyō-en Kōji. Do you seek out a beneficent donor and with his assistance build a great temple;" and with that he suddenly vanished in the direction of the eastern hills. And this Gyō-en Kōji was indeed a revelation of the Goddess Kwannon.

CHORUS: And this beneficent donor whom he was to seek, it was none other than Saka-no-ue no Tamura Maru. Ah! How gracious is the vow of the all-embracing Kwannon of the Thousand Hands of this most famous fane of Kiyomizu, deep and constant as its perennial waters, that offers salvation to all men without exception, so abundant is her overflowing mercy. Yea, unutterable is her divine condescension in leaving Paradise to appear in the flesh in this world of sorrow.

PRIEST: How happy are we to meet with one whose words are so entertaining. No doubt these spots we see around us are all famous in story. I pray you, sir, tell us what you know about them.

YOUTH: I'll tell you all I know. Pray point them out.

PRIEST: There toward the south there stands a pagoda. What is that place called?

YOUTH: That is Uta-no-nakayama Seiganji that looks over toward Ima-kumano.

PRIEST: And that temple to the north from which we hear the sound of the bell of eve?

YOUTH: Ah, that is Washi-no-o. But look! From out of the high peaks of Otowa the moon emerges, and floods with its clear light the cherries of our temple. How beautiful it is!

PRIEST: True. For such sights in spring is every moment precious. For we would gaze on them the livelong day.

BOTH TOGETHER: One hour of an evening in spring is worth a thousand gold pieces. The fragrant scent of the flowers and the silver orb of the moon!

YOUTH: Indeed that sum were well lost for an evening such as this.

CHORUS:
　　How lovely is the scene of our temple's flowery precincts,
　　The moonbeams filter through the spaces of the blossoms,
　　Gently the petals fall in the evening breeze like snowflakes,
　　And with them calm descends, pervading all our spirit.
　　Far-famed is the spring scenery of the Flowery Capital,
　　And now is it arrayed in its finest attire.
　　Set about with the delicate green of the willow,
　　The white thread cascade and the fall of Otowa

Mingle their murmur with the rustle of even.
By the grace of our Goddess our flowers are the finest!

YOUTH:
In her be our trust, for she will not fail us
Though slight be our faith as the stem of the mugwort.

CHORUS:
In this world our prayers must rise to her only.
Her grace is pure as these waters and ever green as the willows,
And even the withered tree will flower afresh at her bidding.
Constant is her kindness as the flowers of springtime,
Quiet and bright as the moon of the morning,
When the spring heavens flush with the hue of the blossoms.
How happy then is spring! How happy then is spring!

CHORUS: Indeed, when we consider it, this seems to be no ordinary person. Who then can it be I wonder?

YOUTH: Who indeed? Ah, well, if you view my now retreating footsteps with regret, I pray you watch the manner of my going.

CHORUS: He retires but not far. Perchance he hides his traces in these hills.

YOUTH: Though you may think it mysterious, mark well the way that I take!
(*And when they look for him to withdraw from before the abode of the Goddess, instead of descending he goes up the slope* to the *Tamura Shrine, and pushing open the moon-checkered door disappears within it, yea, withdraws into the sacred abode.*)
(*Exit*)

---

* Saka-no-ue.

ACT II

PRIEST: Here all night long, beneath the falling petals of the cherry-trees I will chant the holy Sutras. The wondrous law of the Flower of the Lotus in the clear moonlight that frees from the clouds of illusion.

TAMURA: Ah, how blessed are the holy Sutras! It is the voice of the traveler brought hither by the affinity of a former life, who has drawn deeply from the waters of the one pure river that flows from the waterfall of Kiyomizu. And this affinity is also the effect of the protecting mercy of the Goddess Kwannon.

PRIEST: How strange! See, over there amid a glimmering light a man's form takes shape! What can it be?

TAMURA: Why dissemble further? I am that Saka-no-ue no Tamura Maru who in the august reign of the Emperor Heijo, the fifty-first earthly Sovereign, did smite the demon and subdue the eastern barbarians, and thus by loyal service give peace to the Empire; and that by the divine help of the Deity of this temple. For when at the august command of His Majesty to smite the demon Suzuka of the province of Ise and so restore security to the land, I raised an army. Before I set out I visited this temple and prayed to the Goddess and made my vow. And then I was favored with a gracious revelation, and trusting in her smile of compassion I hasted to smite the power of evil.

CHORUS: And know that there's no spot in earth or heaven where the Imperial mandate does not run.

TAMURA: Passing then swiftly over the barrier of Ausaka I gained the shore of the lake by Awayu and made my way to the Temple of Ishiyama, where is adored the same Goddess Kwannon of Kiyomizu, and there too I offered up a prayer. And right soon then did our horse-hoofs rattle bravely on the long bridge of Seta. And the plum blossom, hardy vanguard of all the flower realm, came out to greet us as a token of victory, and our hearts beat high with martial valor, for every flower and tree is subject to our great Lord's will and lends no refuge to his demon adversaries. And little did the demon Suzuka divine that in serried ranks the Imperial armies, backed by the aid of Buddhas and of Gods, would speedily confront him. And 'tis a portent too that in the holy Suzukawa, Ise's stream, to bathe has been to conquer.

CHORUS: Hark to the roaring voice of the devil! It fills the earth and echoes to heaven! The hills quiver and the forests tremble.

TAMURA: Ho! there, O devil, incline your ear! In former days there was a rebel named Chikata who employed devils to resist the Imperial authority, and heaven blasted them so that they forsook his cause and he was soon overthrown and ceased to be! How, then, do you think to escape your fate?

CHORUS: And now by the plains of Ano by the Sea of Ise, in a whirl of black clouds and lightning the demon transforms himself into thousands of charging horsemen who sweep on like a mountain in movement.

TAMURA: But now see what a miracle takes place.

CHORUS: Indeed 'tis wondrous! For above our army's banners there flash forth the beams of the Kwannon of the Thousand Hands, as she flies through the sky above them, and with each of these hands she lets fly the arrow of wisdom from the bow of compassion. At each discharge there fly a thousand shafts. They fall on the demons who flee in confusion, each one transfixed by an arrow of the Goddess. And so they perish, the whole host of them. Thanks be to the Goddess Kwannon. For those who call on her aid shall see the evil spells and weapons of the demons turned back in their faces. Yea the strength of her Buddha-might shall sweep them away.

TOMOE

PROTAGONIST	*IN FIRST ACT A COUNTRY GIRL. IN THE SECOND, TOMOE*
DEUTERAGONIST	*A TRAVELING PRIEST*

TIME	*THE FIRST MONTH*
PLACE	*THE PROVINCE OF OMI*

ACT I

PRIEST: If only we push on the deepest forest will soon be passed. And thus I now have gained the Kiso Road.

CHORUS: I am a priest who comes from the mountains of Kiso, and never yet have I beheld the capital, so now do I take my way thither.

PILGRIM-SONG:
As on I journey
Kiso's hills grow more distant,
And never knowing
Where the next night will find me
I make my way
Through Mino and Owari,
So by the Omi high road
I hasten to Lake Biwa.

CHORUS:
Thus quickly have I come
To Awazu in Omi,
And here by the lake-side
A while will I rest.

COUNTRY GIRL:

> Calm are the waves,
> And 'tis most pleasant
> At pine-clad Awazu
> To worship the God.
> How hallowed the feeling!

PRIEST:

> How strange! I wonder how it is
> That with such deep devotion
> A country girl comes to this shrine
> With eyes so full of tears.
> What can it mean?

COUNTRY GIRL: Did you speak, priest?

PRIEST:

> I did. I thought it strange
> To see you weep before the shrine.

COUNTRY GIRL:

> Strange, and it may be foolish?
> But you may perhaps remember it is written
> How the monk Gyokyo when he visited
> The Shrine of Hachiman at Usa made a verse—
> "I wonder why it is, I cannot tell,
> But tears of gratitude my eyes o'erflow"—
> So that the Deity himself was moved
> And spread forth the protection of his arm,
> Shadowing the monk with his wide-flowing sleeve.
> And from that time the Lord of Usa came
> And at Otokoyama nigh the capital
> He took up his abode and swore to keep
> Under his protection all the land.
> Think you that strange or foolish?

TOMOE

PRIEST:
  Gentle are women everywhere, but here,
  So nigh the capital, their elegance is famed.

COUNTRY GIRL:
  Then you, O monk, it seems are country-bred,
  And come perhaps from some far province?

PRIEST: I am from the hills of Kiso in the province of Shinano.

COUNTRY GIRL:
  Ah, if you come from a far-off hamlet of Kiso,
  How should you know the name of the Deity of Awazu?
  But it is Yoshinaka of Kiso whence you come,
  Who is worshipped as the Deity of this place.
  I pray you do him reverence, traveler.

PRIEST:
  Indeed I'll clap my hands before his shrine,
  So strange it is to find him here a God!

CHORUS:
  His fame from ancient days
  Still shines bright as the moon.
  On him we may rely
  As God and Buddha too,
  To guard this land of ours.
  We owe him thanks indeed.
  The meeting of two travelers 'neath a tree
  Has been predestined by their former lives,
  So do you spend the night under this pine,
  And read aloud the holy Buddhist texts
  That so may be relieved the Five Defects
  That even the highest suffer.
  How fortunate the chance that brings you here.
  Behind the hills the setting sun sinks low,
  Over the lake the evening bell resounds,
  And all around is silent mystery.
  Should the departed come,
  'Twere well to ask this village girl
  Who it may be.
  (*With this she vanishes.*) (*Exit.*)

ACT II

PRIEST:
>My pillow is the dewy grass.
>The sun has set and it is dusk
>And on Awazu's dreary shore
>I pray for his enlightenment.

TOMOE'S SPIRIT:
>The falling flowers confess the vanity of things,
>The water flows indifferent to our fate,
>Yet is a symbol of the lucid mind.

CHORUS:
>Misdeed and retribution are the fruit
>Of Karma-action in a former life,
>But by the wondrous power of the law
>Shall trees and grass, and even the earth itself,
>Transform themselves at last into the Buddha-mind.
>Much more then shall we men for whom are said
>These efficacious texts of mighty power,
>Sit soon upon the Lotus terraces.

PRIEST:
>What's this I see? The woman who just now
>Spoke with me, but arrayed in warrior's mail.
>Awazu is an eerie place to sleep,
>Haunted it seems by some uneasy ghost.

TOMOE'S SPIRIT:
>I am Tomoe the woman-warrior,
>But since I am a woman I was not allowed
>To die here with my lord,
>And so my smoldering anger keeps me here.

PRIEST: A rancor so long cherished?

TOMOE'S SPIRIT: For long I served my lord.

PRIEST: Yet still this memory rankles.

TOMOE'S SPIRIT:
    To this strand of Awazu I would have followed him
    That we might die together. To my lasting shame
    He would not have it, since I was a woman.
    For is there anyone who is a warrior who would not resent
    Denial of his right to win a glorious name
    By dying for his lord as love and duty bid?

CHORUS:
    Now Yoshinaka had gone forth from Shinano
    With fifty thousand horsemen in his train.
    At Kurikara, Shio, and Tonami-yama
    He won undying fame by mighty victories,
    Surpassed by none, acclaimed by all his peers.

TOMOE'S SPIRIT: Yet when his hour arrived—

CHORUS:
    For even the bravest at the appointed time,
    Must vanish like the dew upon the grass,
    Or fade out like the foam on Awazu's shore.
    And, priest, you were a countryman of his,
    So prithee aid him by your prayers.
    But let us hear how Yoshinaka came to meet his end.

TOMOE'S SPIRIT:
    'Twas in the snowy first month of the year,
    Though here and there the snow had melted,
    When slowly he rode down beside the lake
    Trusting to his good steed to pick his way.
    But on the deep rice-fields the ice was thin,
    And horse and rider plunged in and stuck fast,
    And neither voice nor rein nor whip availed
    To extricate the pair from the morass.
    But when I saw him in this wretched plight,
    I rode up quickly, put my horse right close

Beside him, and when I saw how maimed he was,
I offered to accompany him in death,
And bade him not delay to take his life.
"But you're a woman," said he. "Take this souvenir,
My wadded jacket, to my native land. If you refuse,
Then our relations as of lord and servant are dissolved."
Though they would hold for three existences,
What could I do but weep?
But meanwhile, as I stood before my lord,
A strong force of the foemen galloped up,
And shouting, "Don't let Tomoe escape,
We have the woman-warrior!" on they came.
But without fear I turned to face them,
And charging on them whirled my halberd around
In all directions, so that where it struck,
Their heads and limbs went spinning like the leaves
A sudden blast sends whirling to the ground.
And those who fell not hastened from the field,
And I was left alone. Then back I went.
But when I sought my lord, already he was dead,
And by his pillow lay the wadded jacket.
And overcome by grief I stood and wept,
But then, remembering his last behest,
Although it wrung my heart to leave him there,
I steeled myself, and with a mind composed,
I stripped from off me all my warlike gear,
And taking up the jacket went my way.
And it was here, here on this very spot,
I took my leave of him and of the world,
But still resentment lingers holding me,
Chained to phenomena. Therefore I entreat
Your repetition of the holy texts
That I may be enlightened. Fare you well!

HATSU-YUKI OR VIRGIN-SNOW

PROTAGONIST	*IN THE FIRST ACT THE PRIEST'S DAUGHTER. IN THE SECOND, THE SPIRIT OF THE COCK*
DEUTERAGONIST	*THE LADY-IN-WAITING YU-GIRI*
TRITAGONISTS	*TWO LADY ATTENDANTS*
TIME	*UNCERTAIN*
PLACE	*THE PROVINCE OF IZUMO*

ACT I

TUGIRI: I am Yugiri, a lady-in-waiting to the Princess Roku-no-Miya of the Great Shrine of Izumo. And the Kannushi here has a daughter who is not only good to look on but also gentle in her disposition, and last year someone presented her with a beautiful chicken, a young cock, so white that she gave it the name of Hatsu-yuki, and became exceedingly fond of it. And when I went this morning to see it, as is my custom, I found that it had passed away. Oh, how am I to break this news to her? Your beloved Hatsu-yuki is no more.

PRIEST'S DAUGHTER: Do you say that Hatsu-yuki is no longer with us? Can it be true? Why should he die? How can I bear it! He was so tame and fond of us, and now he's gone and left no trace! Ah, I remember now a dream I had last night. I thought it might be a portent of evil to myself, but now I see it must have been of him.

CHORUS: Whether it is a dream or reality we know not. It may be we should not be thus affected with surprise, but still this unexpected grief burns in our breast like fire. For long will our sleeves be wet with tears. And everything reminds us of our loss, even the written word that suggests the footprints of the beloved.

The pity of it that this bird should thus depart! His plumage was so white that rightly did we call him Virgin-snow. And he became so tame that he was as his mistress's shadow. What contrast here between the Departed Cock so much regretted and the Cock of Departure which in the world of love is so much hated for his tiresome crow at dawn.

PRIEST'S DAUGHTER: Well, 'tis no use lamenting thus.

CHORUS: So dry your tears and turn your minds to higher things. For if, relying on the vow of Amida you say the proper prayers, why should not even this bird be able to attain the Halls of Paradise?

PRIEST'S DAUGHTER: How now, Yugiri? Why this sorrow for Virgin-snow? To mourn is unavailing. Assemble the ladies-in-waiting of our house and bid them that for seven days they say their prayers for this cock.

LADIES: Indeed, indeed, most blessed is this prayer. So with calm minds we ring the bell and chant. Namu Amida Butsu! Amida Nyorai!

ACT II

CHORUS: See now! Look over there! How wonderful! It seemed at first a cloud came floating. It is no cloud. It is our Virgin-snow, who flaps his wings and comes towards us. He goes to the princess and hops around her joyfully. How pitiful a sight!

SPIRIT OF THE COCK: Drawn hither by the power of this prayer, I have been reborn in the Halls of Paradise and am happily sporting by the Lake of All Virtuous Merit. With the wild geese and mandarin ducks for my companions, I sit all day in the branches of the jeweled trees and our pleasures are never-ending.

(*And so he flapped his wings and flew round for a space and at last vanished we knew not whither.*)

OYASHIRO OR THE GREAT SHRINE

PROTAGONIST	*IN THE FIRST ACT A PRIEST OF THE SHRINE. IN THE SECOND, THE DEITY OF THE SHRINE*
DEUTERAGONIST	*IN THE FIRST ACT AN OFFICIAL. IN THE SECOND ACT AN ANGEL*
TRITAGONIST	*IN THE FIRST ACT A SECOND PRIEST. IN THE SECOND THE DRAGON SEA GOD*
TIME	*THE TENTH MONTH*
PLACE	*THE PROVINCE OF IZUMO*

ACT I

OFFICIAL: The land of Izumo where is the Festival of Many Vows is a place I have always wished to visit. For I am an official serving at Court and I have heard that during this month, which is called there the God-present month, all the Deities assemble in the land of Izumo and there are all sorts of celebrations, so I have made up my mind to go thither.

PILGRIM-SONG:
Up betimes in the morning
We start on our far-off journey,
And over many hills
And through the rain and drizzle
Toward the land of Issuing Clouds
To where it is the God-month
We now direct our footsteps.

THE TWO PRIESTS:
"Eight-fold clouds arise,
An eight-fold hedge of issuing clouds

And the bride goes within."
'Tis to this shrine we make our way.

SECOND PRIEST: In the topmost boughs of the pines of Onoe,

TWO TOGETHER: The voice of the Deity calls in the breeze.

FIRST PRIEST:
  Yea, though born in this impure world
  There is a vow to help us.

BOTH:
  For if we serve the Deity
  His mercy will not pass us by.
  And all our springs and autumns will be blessed,
  And all our days and years he'll grant us aid.

CHORUS:
  So quicken we our steps.
  For what place can we find
  Where the God's power is not?
  'Tis on the coasts and peaks
  With pine and cedar clad,
  On river, sea, and moor,
  Rice-field and village too,
  There is no place exempt.
  So to receive his grace,
  That falls on all alike,
  Do many courtiers come.

OFFICIAL: Here now I have come to the Great Shrine of Izumo, and since we do not know how to proceed I will address myself to one of these priests of the shrine.

FIRST PRIEST: Ah, it seems you are a stranger here. And whence have you come?

OFFICIAL: I am one who has little leisure from my service at the Court, but since I have heard that in this God-present month all the Deities of the land assemble here, I begged leave from our Imperial Lord and started on this distant pilgrimage.

SECOND PRIEST: It is a blessed sign that over all the land—

OFFICIAL: Our Deity's and the Emperor's might extends.

FIRST PRIEST: Where'er you go—

OFFICIAL: The Deity's grace extends—

FIRST PRIEST: Where'er the moon shines.

CHORUS:
> The God is reverenced,
> And Izumo's shrine pillars,
> Made fast to the foundation
> Of this firm-rooted island,
> Stand stout and lasting
> As this land of Yamato.
> But see the variegated autumn tints are passing
> And the leaves are falling with the drizzle on the hills,
> For winter is approaching.

OFFICIAL: Now since I know but little about them, tell me, I pray you, all about the mysteries of your shrine.

CHORUS: The Great Shrine of Izumo has within it thirty-eight shrines.

FIRST PRIEST: And here dwell five great Deities.

CHORUS: First is the Sanno Gongen, who manifests himself as Ajika Daimyōjin.

PRIEST: Second comes Minato Daimyōjin,

CHORUS: Who appears here as the Myōjin of Munakata in Kyushu. Third comes the Deity of Hayatama, who is the Myōjin of Kashima in Hitachi.

CHORUS: The fourth is Toya Daimyōjin, who is the Myōjin of Suwo in Shinano. Fifth is the Daimyōjin of the land of Izumo, who is manifested as the Myōjin of Mishima in Iyo. And on the last day of the ninth month—

PRIEST: The Deity of Sumiyoshi comes first incognito. While all the other Gods arrive together at the Hour of the Tiger of the first day of the tenth month. And then begin in these precincts all manner of divine diversions so various that description would be vain.

CHORUS: How blest to hear these things. O'er all the land, even in such an age, the Gods reveal their might.

PRIEST: Yea, on this night of every year the Gods in sportive mood—

CHORUS: Each in his place—

PRIEST: In varied guise—

CHORUS:
   They sway their sleeves in lively dance,
   As if to tear the sacred rope
   And roll against the tasseled fence.
   But then at a divine command
   They file into the sacred court.

ACT II

CHORUS:
   See how the clouds have cleared away
   And now the holy shrine shines out
   Illumined by the moon's bright rays.

ANGEL:

Here I appear in the land of Izumo,
An angel to protect the Buddhist law
And this Imperial realm,
Though in my native India
I am a devil.

CHORUS:

Her face and form are beautiful indeed,
And with what grace she now begins to dance,
Waving her jeweled sleeves in rhythmic measure,
While radiance shines about her.
(*Angel-dance*)

CHORUS:

A matchless dance was that!
Now from the rifting clouds
We see the Gods appear,
Flying down before the shrine
With strains of heavenly music.
The bright moon bids them welcome,
Flooding the courts with radiance.
An awe-inspiring sight!
'Tis by the favor of the Sovereign of this realm
That we can thus receive the favor of the Gods.

PRIEST:

Indeed these Deities, so clearly manifest this night,
Must be a wondrous comfort to these guests of ours.

CHORUS: So thus the Gods in order of their rank.

PRIEST: Sumiyoshi first, then Kashima.

CHORUS: Then Suwo, Atsuta, then all the Deities of the three
thousand worlds, have here appeared and danced before us. How
graceful is the waving of their sleeves!
(*Dance*)

CHORUS:

> Now as the dance is ending once more clouds appear,
> And in the offing on the rising waves comes the Sea Dragon
>   God.

SEA GOD:

> I am the Dragon Deity of the Sea,
> And every year it is my custom
> To put a little dragon in a casket,
> All of fine gold, and offer it to this shrine.

CHORUS:

> Spurning the tide and sweeping o'er the waves,
> The Dragon Deity of the Sea appears.
> The river he ascends, lays down the casket,
> And humbly does obeisance to the God.
> He lifts the lid from off the casket,
> Takes the small dragon out and offers it before the shrine.
> Thrice happy is our Empire,
> Embracing land and sea,
> Under one peaceful rule!

DEITY OF THE GREAT SHRINE: The Four Seas are secure and the
Empire at peace!

CHORUS:

> The Four Seas are secure and the Empire at peace!
> The harvest safely gathered and the people well content.
> So may it be for ever 'neath our Sovereign's happy rule
> Is the prayer of all the Deities as they pass before the shrine,
> Each in his place and wave the white Gohei.*
> Then once again the Dragon seeks the sea,
> While all the Gods rise hovering in the sky.
> And as they vanish each to their own spheres,
> The God himself retires into the shrine.

---

* Symbol of offering.

KO-KAJI

PROTAGONIST   *IN THE FIRST ACT INARI AS A YOUNG MAN.*
                IN THE SECOND INARI AS A GOD
DEUTERAGONIST   *THE SWORDSMITH, KO-KAJI MUNECHIKA*
TRITAGONIST   *THE MINISTER TACHIBANA MICHINARI*

TIME   *UNCERTAIN*
PLACE   *THE PROVINCE OF TAMASHIRO*

ACT I

MINISTER: I am Tachibana Michinari, minister of the Emperor Ichijo-in. This night the Mikado has received a supernatural revelation and has ordered me to bid the swordsmith Sanjo Ko-kaji Munechika forge him a blade.

KO-KAJI: Who is it that comes to the House of Munechika?

MINISTER: By the command of His Majesty Ichijo-in I seek you out! This night the Mikado has had a supernatural revelation and bids me call the swordsmith Munechika to forge him a blade. So haste! Comply forthwith!

KO-KAJI: With reverence I hear the Imperial command! But to forge a blade worthy of the Mikado another must work with me not less skilful than myself, else can it not be finished with success.

MINISTER: Indeed, but there is reason in your speech. But since it was revealed to His Majesty that he should rely on you, I pray you get to work without delay. It is the Emperor, I say again!

KO-KAJI: But Munechika, whate'er betide—

CHORUS: But Munechika, whate'er betide, dares not with mind uncertain forge the blade; for surely then the edge would not be true. And if through that our Sovereign's righteous rule be hindered anywise—'tis that I fear.

KO-KAJI: Oh, beyond words the crisis now I face! Now verily I must resort to God. Inari Myōjin is the Deity of my house, and to his shrine I will direct my steps.

INARI: Is it Sanjo Ko-kaji Munechika who approaches here?

KO-KAJI: What voice is that? 'Tis strange indeed! Who can it be that calls me thus by name?

INARI: His Majesty the cloud-enthroned Mikado sent to you and bade you forge a blade for him to wear.

KO-KAJI: Strange and more strange indeed the portent! Who can so soon have heard the Imperial order when I have but just received it? Most incomprehensible it is!

INARI: Strange it may be. But if one knows a thing full soon will others hear.

KO-KAJI: Heaven speaks!

INARI: Earth echoes!

CHORUS: Walls have ears and rocks have tongues! What is hid will be revealed! So how much less can the flashing of the sword of the cloud-enthroned one be concealed? Only have faith, and by the favor of the Great Lord why should you not forge a good and proper blade?

CHORUS: The three-foot blade of the King of Han subdued the rebellious land of Ts'in. With his sword Kei the Emperor Yang also seized the glory of the House of Chou!

INARI: In after days Chung Ku'ei, the minister of the Emperor Huan Tsung—

CHORUS: By virtue of the sword stood as a spirit beside his lord!

INARI: And all the ghosts and devils feared the flashing blade, and thus could work no evil. Both in China and in our country the might of the sword—

CHORUS: Was truly wonderful beyond all words! Also in the beginning in our own country the Imperial Prince Yamatotaké, receiving a command from the Emperor Keiko his father that he should subdue the eastern barbarians, set out on his journey to the far remote eastern confines. By the sea-beach of Ise and Owari, envying the waves as they rolled towards his homeland, he wondered when he too should turn his face thither.

INARI: Hither and thither in the battles that followed—

CHORUS: In their caves he smote down both men and horses, and poured forth their blood in flowing rivers; wet to the shield in dark-red gore! Thus the barbarians, many times routed, at last laid down their arms and surrendered. And it was from the age of this Mikado that the pastime of hunting was first begun at Court. Once, when the twentieth day of the tenth month, the No-god month, was past, the prince was viewing the light snow on the distant mountains, where the tints of autumn were fading into winter.

INARI: When the barbarians surrounded him on every side and set fire to the parched plains of autumn. Quickly the flames blazed up, and the enemy beat their drums for the onset. But as they kindled the fire around him—

INARI: Then the divine prince drew his blade—

CHORUS: Then the divine prince drew his blade, and suddenly whirled it about him that the flames retreated, slashing down the grass on every side. The spirit in the sword turned into a blast that blew the flaming grasses backward. Earth and sky were filled with the fire, as it blazed and swept against the foe, and the barbarian horsemen perished in myriads. So was the whole Empire at peace under his rule, and the people forgot to bar the doors of their houses. And all this was due to the might of the blade Herbqueller. Go back to your forge with a quiet mind and fashion a no less worthy blade, O son of a line of valiant craftsmen!

KO-KAJI: The might of the sword in our country, and in the land of Han, it is thrice blessed in due season. But tell me, I prithee, to whom I am speaking!

INARI: It matters not if you but have faith. So go back at once to your dwelling and prepare the mound whereon to forge the Imperial blade. Then do you await my coming, for verily I will attend to give strength to your arm. Without fail I will be there to aid you!

(*In the evening clouds over Inari-yama he vanishes, no one knoweth whither.*)

ACT II

KO-KAJI (*Then in obedience to the august order Munechika ascends upon the mound. Around him he stretches the sacred strawrope, sevenfold to banish all impurity. At each of the quarters he sets an image, suspending the white Gohei around him. Gazing up to heaven thus he speaks*): That in the fullness of time I, Munechika, in the august era of Ichijo-in, the sixty-sixth earthly Sovereign, do thus bring glory on my craft, is not by my strength alone. First was the spear with which Izanagi and Izanami, standing on the Floating Bridge of Heaven, groped for the Central Land of Reed-plains. Then from Pashimida Sonja of Sogada in India the art was handed down to Amakuni, and from his descendants we too received it. Now I beseech thee—

CHORUS: Yea, I beseech thee! For not to me be ascribed the glory! At the command of the Heavenly Sovereign I forge it. Ye Deities of the Ten Quarters, countless as sand-grains, I beseech you be present and lend me aid! And so within the suspended Gohei he looks to heaven and bows to earth. Now hear the essence of truth and let the mind be made receptive.

KO-KAJI: Profound is my reverence and lowly my adoration!

CHORUS: Verily heaven knows the time for Munechika to forge as his Sovereign commanded! Have faith and trust! The Deities will aid! A youth ascends the mound!

CHORUS: A youth ascends the mound! He bends the knee to Munechika! He asks for the metal. Munechika with fear and worship in his heart brings forth the iron and swings the hammer. Clang! They strike! Clang! Clang! Clang! They strike. The sound of their hammers echoes to heaven. Thus they forge the Imperial weapon. On the front of the tang he chisels his name, "Sanjo Ko-kaji Munechika," and on the back the divine helper inscribes the words, "Ko-kitsune," "Little Fox."

CHORUS: In the form of clouds is the pattern of the edge. Its name shall be called "Ama-no-Murakumo," "Massed Clouds of Heaven."

INARI: First blade in the Empire—

CHORUS: First blade in the Empire, twice signed is the Imperial sword! And let the land be ruled therewith!

INARI: So do you present to the Imperial messenger this sword, Ko-kitsune Maru, that is the symbol of the Deity of your clan, the God Inari.

(*And with these words he ends his speech and, rising above the clouds, he returns to the peak of Inari in the eastern hills.*)

MURŌZUMI

PROTAGONIST	*FIRST A COURTESAN. SECONDLY, FUGEN BOSATSU*
DEUTERAGONIST	*A TRAVELING PRIEST*
TIME	*UNCERTAIN*
PLACE	*MURŌZUMI IN THE PROVINCE OF SUWO*

PRIEST: I am the Priest Shoku of the Temple of Shosha in the province of Harima, and I have founded that temple and built its halls, wherein, fulfilling an ancient tradition, the chief object of our worship is a cherry-tree, through which we adore Nyoi-rin-Kwannon. And I have, moreover, added thereto a chapel. Now though the sole aim of devotion to the Law of Buddha is the sinking of the Six Senses into the perfect tranquility of Samadhi, I have yet a great desire to behold the manifestation of Fugen Bosatsu, and being directed in a dream to go and meet a certain courtesan of Murōzumi in Suwo, to that place I am now hastening.

PILGRIM-SONG:
His well-loved temple left behind,
That well-known temple left behind,
Over the unknown watery path
He journeys to a far-off shore.
On a moving couch he makes his bed,
The breeze of dawn fills out the sails,
By many a port they plough the waves,
And soon they reach Murōzumi.

PRIEST: Thus quickly have I reached Murōzumi, and now I look to find the lady's house. Ho! I am the Priest Shoku of Shosha in Harima and at the behest of the Deity of my temple have I come to meet you.

LADY: Indeed you are an unexpected guest. But since you are so famed a holy man, I hold myself thrice blessed that I can see you and receive your instruction in the law and thus acquire great merit and enlightenment in the life to come. I pray you tarry here some days to rest yourself. And now the day is drawing to its close, and with the moon the wine-cup too is due.

(*With her own hands she fills his cup, urging the holy priest to sip the fragrant liquor. And so conviviality begins. Then the priest lifted up his voice and sang again and again this refrain*)

"On the Lake of Amida Nyorai the surface of the water is always rippling." When we ponder this, how deep is the saying: Passing strange are the affinities of one who is reborn among men! Though he be reborn again and again as man, he may be reincarnated in the body of a harlot, so that the mist of the Five Infirmities and the Three Obediences obscures the Moon of Truth!

CHORUS: Nevertheless, illumined by the rays of the holy law, Devadatta of the Five Deadly Sins became a celestial Bosatsu, while the Naga maiden of eight years old who presented a wondrous jewel to Buddha was straightway changed in form and became a male, being reborn in the Pure World of the Southern Region. The eternal spring flowers of the sacred mountain waft their fragrance on the winds to the farthest quarters of the world, even as the tranquil beams of the autumn moon of this our land illuminate even the most remote confines. And whosoever will incline the ear and have faith in this wondrous law, even though it be a woman, shall forthwith attain to Buddhahood.

Humbly confessing her guilt before the holy man she tells of all her offenses.

PRIEST: Ah, how admirable is her resolution! Most efficacious is the virtue of this Sutra for all who trust in its power.

FUGEN: And now the cup has circled many times, and being drunken beyond measure she goes to her chamber to sleep away the wine before again talking with her guest. The priest also retires to his room to rest a while.

PRIEST: And as he waits there, from her chamber comes forth she who has been his hostess, but wondrously transformed—diffusing golden rays and strange sweet odors—most marvelous to see, she now stands forth as Fugen Bosatsu, seated upon her white elephant and shining with supernatural light. How blessed was the vision! Then from the sky sweet melodies were heard, and on a purple cloud appeared a host of Bodhisats who floated down to earth playing twelve kinds of celestial music. Stepping down from her seat Fugen danced to the heavenly strains. Marvelous was her divine condescension!

FUGEN: And now the dawn draws near, and the Bodhisats gently float away on the cloud and return on high, while the priest, bowing his head in low obeisance, adores Fugen with tears of joy. He says farewell and departs, and when he has gone a little distance from the gate he looks back again with longing gaze, but now the diadem of jewels and robes of brocade have faded and vanished, and he sees but the form of the courtesan of Murōzumi.

THE SHŌJO AND THE BIG JAR

PROTAGONIST   *IN FIRST ACT A YOUTH. IN SECOND ACT A*
                           SHŌJO
DEUTERAGONIST   *KŌFŪ. OTHER SHŌJO IN SECOND ACT*

TIME   *THE NINTH MONTH*
PLACE   *CHINA*

ACT I

KOFU: I am one Kōfū who dwells at the foot of Mount Kanekin in China. And because I was most filial to my parents I have gradually become more and more wealthy. Now of late a number of youths have come to buy my liquor and I can't think who they may be. So when they come today I intend to ask them their names and whence they come.

SHŌJO (*sings*): See the dawn comes up from the fathomless depths of the ocean!

KOFU: Ah, here come those fellows, though not so early as usual.

SHŌJO (*sings*):
    Ho, ho! How jolly! This is where we go in to drink the lovely
       liquor!
    Lute, and lay, and liquor!
    The friends from which we never want to part!
    Ever most praiseworthy indeed is liquor.
    And to those who love it are we always drawn.
    For the cup goes with the lute,
    And the cup goes with the lay,
    And drinkhards are the only friends we need.
    But quiet now, or we shall be the jape of these townsmen.

KOFU: I pray you tell me who you are, for I wish to know whence you come.

SHŌJO: Now why should we conceal it any longer? We're really Shōjo, the Drinkhard Baboons, who live by the Bay of Jinyo. And because heaven has been touched by your filial conduct, we hereby present you with a perennial liquor-spring. And have no doubt about it.

CHORUS: And now as dusk approaches they bid him farewell and mingle with the people in the streets, and their bright red visages are seen no more, their bright red visages are seen no more.
  (*Exit Shōjo*)

ACT II

CHORUS: Ah, now as for liquor! What fine stuff is liquor! In chilly autumn–the month of chrysanthemums. When autumn tints are glowing, and all the hills are reddened. Then make a fire of maple-leaves and warm the splendid liquor! How comforting it is on a cold autumn evening!

SHŌJO (*sings*):
  Now why is our friend so late?
  'Tis strange that he does not come.
  We'll go to the strand and see
  Why he has not arrived.
  Oh that he soon may come.

CHORUS:
  And now many Shōjo appear,
  And present to Kōfū the jar,
  The perennial source of liquor
  By the shore of the Bay of Jinyo.
  On that autumn moonlight night,
  While the waves lapped peacefully,
  A Shōjo climbed on the jar

And heaved with strength on the bung.
Up welled the generous drink,
The "sake" came gushing forth
A never-ceasing spring,
That poured forth copiously
However much they drew.
Ah how they drank and danced!

SHŌJO:

Hail, the chrysanthemum dew!
The never-failing spring!
We leave it at your inn,
Your never-failing inn!

CHORUS:

And even when he rose,
Thinking that he would wake
From a drunken dream,
The liquor ne'er gave out,
Even when he gathered in,
Everyone he could find,
Both men and women too,
And gave them all their fill,
Until they tottered off with tipsy gait,
Repeating o'er and o'er the glad refrain:
"How blest the tranquil realm of our Great Lord,
Ten thousand autumns may his peaceful reign endure!"

KAMO NO CHOMEI

PROTAGONIST	*KAMO NO CHOMEI*
DEUTERAGONIST	*A MAN OF THE CAPITAL*
TRITAGONIST	*HIS COMPANION*
A YOUTH	*THE COMPANION OF CHOMEI*
TIME	*THE THIRD MONTH*
PLACE	*THE PROVINCE OF YAMASHIRO*

MAN OF THE CAPITAL: I am one who resides in the lower district of the capital. And now that spring has come I intend to invite a congenial companion to go out to the hills with me that we may enjoy the flower-viewing, as is my custom. And today I think of visiting Hinoyama at Daigo to see its blossoms.

PILGRIM-SONG:
The cherry blossoms,
Though every spring we view them,
They never pall
Though every spring we view them,
They never pall.
Nay, every year,
They seem to flower finer.
And thus from hill to hill
We satisfy our senses
Taking deep draughts of beauty
Until we come to Daigo,
So far renowned for flowers,
To Toyama by Hino.

CHORUS: As we have lost no time on the way, so soon are we arrived at Toyama in Hino, and here we will rest for a while.

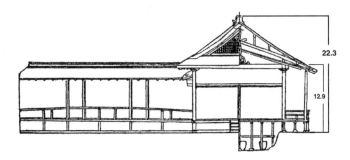

NOH STAGE IN THE NISHI HONGWANJI, ORIGINALLY PART OF
HIDEYOSHI'S PALACE. Late sixteenth century. Jars are placed under the
floor to increase resonance.

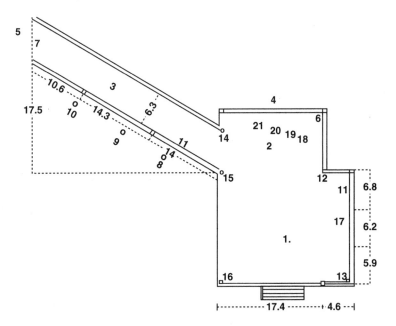

PLAN OF THE NOH STAGE IN THE NISHI HONGWANJI 1, stage; 2, cross
floor; 3, gallery; 4, dressing-room (Gakuya); 5, green-room (Kagami-no-ma);
6, door; 7, curtain; 8, first pine; 9, second pine; 10, third pine; 11, balustrade;
12 flute pillar (Fue-bashira); 13, deuteragonist pillar (Waki-bashira); 14, Kyogen pillar; 15, protagonist pillar (Sh' te-bashira); 16, censor pillar (Metsuke-
bashira); 17, seat of the chorus; 18, flute; 19, small hand-drum (Tsuzumi); 20,
large hand-drum; 21, big drum.

COMPANION: But see! There is a small hut over there, which I think must certainly be the ten-foot square cell of Chomei. "Would it not be well to go there and rest a while?

WAYFARER: It would indeed. Let us proceed then, and I will give notice of our presence.

CHOMEI: Ceaselessly the river flows, and yet the water is never the same, while in the still pools the shifting foam gathers and is gone, never staying for a moment. The impermanence of this life is like foam on the water. Like the dew on the morning glory is its evanescence. Ah, how transient is this world of ours!

MAN OF THE CAPITAL: Do you then announce me to him who is within.

COMPANION: And who are you then?

MAN OF THE CAPITAL: I am one from the lower district of the capital who has come to view the flowers, and I would stay a while in this hut.

COMPANION: I will announce it to the master of the cell. Within there! We are people from the lower district of the capital, and we have come hither to view the flowers. I pray you let us rest in your hut a while.

CHOMEI: I would do so, but this hut is very small and so there is no room for anyone to rest in it. Do you say thus to your companion.

COMPANION: I will. He says it is a very little hut, and there is thus no room for you within.

MAN OF THE CAPITAL: So he may say, but I have heard that in the ten-foot cell of Vimalakirti of Bihar there was space made for thirty-two thousand lion thrones.

CHOMEI: Ah, that was Vimalakirti's mystic power. But I am a mere hermit.

MAN OF THE CAPITAL: But even the whole universe of ten thousand worlds attains enlightenment at last.

CHOMEI: You may say so.

CHORUS: This matchless gate of entrance to the Buddhist law is thus forced open by this city-dweller. Let him enter here. These cherry-blossoms of Daigo Temple, like clouds that hang over Toyama Hill, like snow they seem when scattered by spring breezes. 'Tis said in ancient story an angel from on high has scattered them on earth.

MAN OF THE CAPITAL: Indeed I thank you. This spot, so far removed from human habitation, it is more fit than any in our Empire to lodge a holy hermit. How long have you been here? And pray relate the manner of your coming.

CHOMEI: I will. I am a man of the village of Kamo, and by the time I reached the age of forty I had experienced all the terrors of whirlwind, fire, and earthquake, wherefore I was thus convinced of the impermanence of life. And when I was fifty I abandoned the world and retired, and since I had neither wife nor child, it was not difficult for me to leave it, nor had I any rank or revenue to be a tie to hold me. And so I have come to spend I know not how many useless years hidden in the mists of Mount Ohara. And thus, not far from the capital, at the age of sixty, I am spending here my last remaining years.

MAN OF THE CAPITAL: Your life has been no ordinary one. But tell me more about these natural calamities.

CHOMEI: In the third year of the era Angen and the twenty-eighth day of the fourth month the wind blew a gale in the evening and a fire started in the southeast of the capital and was carried over to the northwest. And everything as far as the

Shujaku Gate, the Daikyoku Hall, and the Academy and Office of Internal Affairs was reduced to ashes in a single night. They say it started at Higuchi Tominokoji in a temporary structure used as an infirmary. And as the flames came on they spread out like an opened fan and devoured everything. And the precious treasure that was lost is beyond reckoning. Then again in the fourth year of the era Jisho from the vicinity of Naka-no-Mikado and Kyogoku a great whirlwind blew even to Rokujo. For the space of near a quarter of a mile it raged, and of the houses within its reach there was none, great or small, that it did not overthrow. And in the Waterless month of the same year the capital was suddenly changed and all the inhabitants, from His August Majesty the Mikado and the ministers and great nobles of the Court, had perforce to remove to the new one. And the mansions that had stood so proudly side-by-side now from day to day became more ruinous. They were broken up and floated down the River Yodo, while their splendid gardens were turned into rice-fields. And the minds of the owners too were changed, so that everyone took to riding on horseback like a man-at-arms, and none used the courtier's ox car. And it happened at this time that I chanced to go down myself to the new capital in the province of Settsu, and the site was too narrow to lay out a proper city. For on the north the mountains towered over it while on the south the sea hemmed it in, and the noise of the billows and the smell of the brine were beyond measure painful. And the palace was but a log-hut edifice as befitted such a rustic city. And most of the site was still unused for few dwellings had so far been built. Nothing had the air of the ancient capital, and the inhabitants looked like a lot of yokels. Indeed the troubles of the people were many, and there was a feeling of unrest on all sides. So that by the winter of the same year, the capital was moved back to its ancient seat. Then in the era Yōwa there were two years of famine, and a very terrible experience indeed it was. And not long after a pestilence followed, and by the walls and in the highways everywhere lay the bodies of those who had died. But the priest Ryugyo of the Temple of Ninnaji—

CHORUS: Filled with compassion led a number of monks round the city and wrote on the foreheads of the dead the syllable "A," that they might enter the Heaven of Amida. And within the space of two months they counted forty-two thousand three hundred corpses within the city. And the number in the regions without it was beyond counting. Then in the second year of Genryaku there was a great earthquake. And it was indeed no ordinary one. The hills crumbled and filled the rivers, while the sea surged up and overwhelmed the land. The earth split asunder and water gushed out. The rocks broke away and rolled into the valleys. People walking on the roads stumbled and fell, and houses as well as monasteries and temples were overthrown, and the roar of their falling was like thunder. And the terror of these scenes was beyond the power to imagine or, describe.

CHOMEI: But now you must be weary. Pray take a rest after this long narration.

MAN OF THE CAPITAL: An admirable suggestion. And how about some liquor? The time seems suitable. Boy! Serve the reverend hermit.

YOUTH: I will most willingly.

WAYFARER: When thus we listen to these tales of old, we must reflect that a cup of liquor in this life has more savor than a great name in history.

CHOMEI: 'Tis very true. And you remember that in ancient China the recluse Hui Yuan retired to Tiger Valley and vowed never to leave it. But his friends Tao Yuan Ming and Liu Hsiu Ching came to see him, bringing a keg of liquor ... and though to drink liquor is contrary to the precepts of Buddha, yet he who has never been moved by it is less than a beast or devil ... and so the three friends drank together.

CHORUS:
> And as is their wont when old friends meet over the "Parrot"
>   cup,
> Merry with drink he went to see his comrades on their way
> And unwittingly wandered out of his place of retirement.
> And the drink they drank was but muddy liquor,
> By no means as fine as this "sake" of ours,
> That sparkles so bright and clear in the cup,
> As the youth bears it round unceasingly
> Circling about like the sun in springtime.

YOUTH:
> The petals of the mountain cherry floating in the breeze
> Are like the snowflakes falling when the wind is very still.

WAYFARER: Now we're well flushed with wine, let the youth dance.

YOUTH (*dances*): The petals of the mountain cherry, etc.

CHORUS:
> And so in this symposium the hours pass by
> Till even in these lengthy days of spring
> The sun is now declining in the west.
> Though this hut may be an imitation of that of the Saint Vi-
>   malakirti,
> One virtue does not even equal that of the stupid Panthaka.
> (*So murmuring an unavailing invocation to Buddha, they take
> their leave and part from Chomei, and as he stands looking after
> them he gazes at the sky, and as he re-enters his hut he mutters
> the verse*):
> > Sad am I at heart
> > "When the moon's bright silver orb,
> > Sinks behind the hill.
> > But how blest 'twill be to see
> > Amida's perpetual light.

DŌJŌJI

PROTAGONIST	*A SHIRABYOSHI.* IN THE SECOND ACT A DRAGON
DEUTERAGONIST	*THE ABBOT OF THE DŌJŌJI*
ASSISTANT DEUTERAGONIST	*A PRIEST OF THE DŌJŌJI. TWO SERVANTS OF THE TEMPLE.*
TIME	*THE THIRD MONTH*
PLACE	*THE PROVINCE OF KII*

ACT I

ABBOT: I am the abbot of the Temple of Dōjōji in the province of Kii. Now for a certain reason we have for long had no bell in this temple, but lately we have had another cast and today, it being a day of good omen, we intend to hold the inauguration ceremony. Ho! You fellows there! Get the bell hoisted up into the belfry.

SERVANTS: We will indeed! See now how we have hung it in its place.

ABBOT: Now while we hold the ceremony for this bell for certain reasons women are forbidden to approach. So see that none enter. Take good care!

SERVANTS: We will, your reverence!

SHIRABYOSHI: The evil that I did must be wiped out! The evil that I did must be wiped out! So I will go to the inauguration of

---

* Shirabyoshi, literally "White rhythm maker." A medieval female dancer, whose measures were one element of the Noh.

DOJOJI

the bell. Indeed I will set out for the Temple of Dōjōji that I may
find some pretext to take part in the ceremony.

PILGRIM-SONG:
    Over the waves the moon has disappeared,
    And on the pine-clad beach the salt spray dashes.
    So quickly do I hasten on my way,
    To reach the temple while the sun is high.
    To reach the temple while the sun is high,
    Before they may begin the service for the bell.

SERVANTS: Whence, woman, do you come? You cannot enter
the enclosure here.

SHIRABYOSHI: I am a Shirabyoshi who lives near this province, and as you are holding this inauguration ceremony I have come to dance at it. I pray you let me enter the precincts.

SERVANTS: Indeed we should much like to allow you, but there is the matter of what the abbot would say. For he gave us strict orders that no woman was to enter. Still we might let you in of our own accord. So now we will let you pass, and pray entertain us with a lively dance. Here is a hat of ceremony. Pray take it and dance in it.

SHIRABYOSHI: Ah, I am grateful to you, and I will dance my very best.
(*Putting on the elegant ceremonial hat of a courtier she begins her rhythmic measure*) —
"Beside the blossom there is only the pine
As the twilight falls we await the boom of the bell!"

ABBOT: Because this temple was one of those built by the Lord Tachibana*-no-Michinari it was called Dōjōji.

CHORUS:
If you come and visit the mountain temple in spring
At the sound of the evening bell when falls the twilight,
The petals of the blossoms flutter down.

ABBOT:
And so the boom of many temple bells sounds forth ...
And as the moon sinks the song of birds ...
The sky is filled with snow ... The full tide ebbs,
The fishing-fires shine mournfully by the river hamlet ...
And now if sleepy 'tis a good time to drowse.
(*And as she dances nearer to the bell, fixing her gaze upon it as if to strike it, she seems to slip her hand upon the dragon-head by which it swings and. take it off and put it on her head, and so she vanishes.*)

---

* Michinari's name was not Tachibana, but the author could not resist the jingle of "tatsu" = "build" with Tachibana, especially as Tachibana-no-Mi=the fruit of the orange-tree, which is the meaning of Tachibana.

ACT II

SERVANTS: Ah! It has fallen!

ABBOT: Why, what has fallen?

SERVANTS: The bell has fallen from the belfry.

ABBOT: What? You tell me it has fallen?

SERVANTS: Indeed it has.

ABBOT: And how can that be?

SERVANTS: Indeed we took all care, but it has fallen.

ABBOT: And can you then think of nothing?

SERVANTS: There is one thing. There was a Shirabyoshi who lives not far away who came and asked us if she might enter these precincts, and though we told her that women were forbidden, when she promised us to dance we let her in. Could she have done this thing?

ABBOT: Too terrible for words it is; It was because I knew of this I gave such strict command no woman be admitted. And how have you transgressed it! But come hither. And have you never heard why it is that no woman must come near this bell?

SERVANTS: Indeed we have not.

ABBOT: Then I will tell you.

PRIEST: Yes, kindly do so.

ABBOT: In ancient days there lived here a man called Managono-Shōji who had one daughter. And there was a wandering monk, a Yamabushi, who came from the north and would go to

Kumano. And Shōji took him in and gave him lodging. And often he would come to this temple. And Shōji's daughter fell in love with him, and he with her. And when he told her, not quite seriously, that he would marry her, it seems that she believed him. So when he went again to stay at Shōji's house, when all was still at dead of night, she went into his chamber and entreated him: "Let me stay with you always! Take me away with you." But the Yamabushi in great amazement slipped away from her and fled at once to this temple, earnestly praying to be hidden. But as there was no place where he could be hidden, the bell was lowered down upon him and so he stood concealed. But soon the girl pursued him, and just then this Hidaka River rose high in flood and flowed over all the country, and this maiden, turned to a dragon in her hate, came riding on its waves right to this temple, and searching everywhere at last became suspicious of the bell thus lowered on the ground. Gripping its dragon-boss between its teeth the dragon wound itself seven times around the bell, and lashed it with its tail and spat fire from its jaws, until at last the mighty heat melted the bell to water and the monk beneath it. A fearsome tale indeed. Is it not so?

PRIEST: Too terrible for words. I never heard the like.

ABBOT: That fierce desire of hers is not assuaged, but still clings round this bell and seeks to harm it. But let us, therefore, show the power of the Buddhist prayers and all the merit of our austere lives. Come let us to it!

PRIEST: Indeed we will.

ABBOT: The waters of the Hidaka River may be dried up and the sand by its banks taken away, but who can put bounds to the power of an anchorite's prayers?

PRIEST: Together be our voices lifted up!

ABBOT: On the east Gozanze Myo-o!

PRIEST: On the south Gundari Yasha Myo-o!

ABBOT: On the west Dai-itoku Myo-o!

PRIEST: On the north Kongo Yasha Myo-o!

ABBOT: In the center Dai-nichi Daijo Fudo!

CHORUS:
> Movable or Immovable with his rope!
> Namaku Samanda Basarada!* Senda Maka-Roshana.
> Soba-haya Untara Takan-man!
> He who hears shall obtain great enlightenment,
> And he who understands shall straightway become a Buddha!
> And if thus we pray over the dragon—

ABBOT: How can she still harbor wrath?

CHORUS: It moves! It moves! Pray now your hardest! A mighty heave with all your thousand arms, O Goddess Kwannon! The Gatha of the saving grace of Fudo! Pray till the sparks fly from his halo and the black smoke goes up to heaven! And now the bell, unstruck by any hand begins to echo! Untouched by man it rises up. By the might of our prayer it is heaved up into the belfry! But see! The dragon now appears! Give ear, ye Dragon Kings! On the east the Green Dragon Shōjo! On the west the White Dragon Byakutai! In the center the Yellow Dragon Otai! Give ear, all ye Dragon Kings of the three worlds, countless as the sands of the Ganges River, for if ye hear our prayers why should we fear this dragon?

> (*Thus conjuring and being conjured the dragon rises and confronts the bell to strike at it once more, but her fierce intent spontaneous turns to flames which burn her up, and turning back she plunges into the waters of the Hidaka River. Sated with the sight the anchorites retire within their cells.*)

---

* These words are Sanskrit-Chinese-Japanese. Darani or Buddhist spells, mysterious and therefore potent.

KYOGEN OR
COMIC INTERLUDES

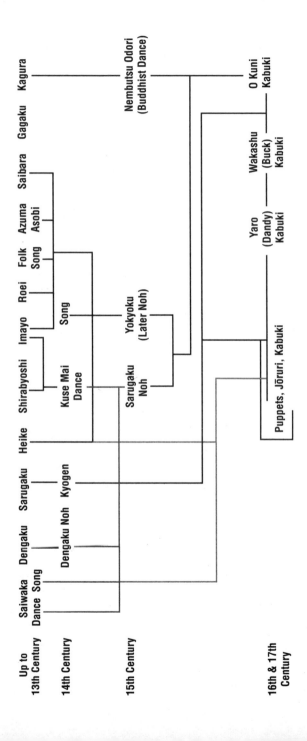

SCHEME OF JAPANESE DRAMA

THE BAG OF LEAVE-TAKING

MASTER: I am a man of these parts. And I have a woman living with me who is not at all good to look at and who stays in bed late in the morning, and when she does get up is always drinking tea and talking scandal about people, and what is more she is also given to taking too much to drink and getting tipsy and she is such a trouble that I have for long thought I would get rid of her, and now she has gone off yesterday to visit her home, so I think I'll take advantage of the opportunity to send her a letter to that effect. I'll just call Taro Kwaja and give him the job. Hi, Taro Kwaja!

TARO KWAJA: Here I am

MASTER: What I have to say is this. You know what a great nuisance that woman's goings-on are and that I am quite unable to put up with her any longer. Well, I am going to send her away, so please take her this letter to inform her of the fact. That's what I want you to do.

TARO KWAJA: Very much at your service, sir, as usual, but that woman is something quite out of the common, and what she is likely to say will not, in my opinion, be pleasant, so I beg you to excuse me.

MASTER: Oh, that's all right. Don't you worry. All you have to do is to leave it and say there's no answer needed.

TARO KWAJA: Yes, sir, perhaps, but ... any other errand I shall be very pleased to do if only you will excuse me this one.

MASTER: Oh, I see, you're more frightened of her than of me, are you. Well, whether you like it or not you've got to go now. (*Lays his hand on his sword-hilt.*) Now will you go or not?

TARO KWAJA: Oh, yes. I'll go. I'll go.

MASTER: Then off with you at once. Take this and say I want no reply. And come back immediately.

TARO KWAJA: Certainly, sir.

MASTER: Then hurry up.

TARO KWAJA: Yes, sir. Oh dear, what a troublesome business this is that he has thrust on me. I can imagine what she'll say to me. What a temper she'll get into when she sees this letter.

PILGRIM-SONG:
Well at any rate
It's my master's order,
So I must obey.
But I'll hand it down,
To my grandchildren's children,
Never go to service
In a noble's household.
Ah, well, here I am. Within there!

WOMAN: Hullo, that's Taro Kwaja's voice. I expect he's come to escort me back again. Ah, Taro Kwaja, so you've come to take me back. I expected you before.

TARO KWAJA: Oh … yes … well, I've got a letter for you.
(*Hands it to her. She reads it.*)

WOMAN: Yah! Yah! You devils! Here's this beast of a man of mine sent me my dismissal! And you're a nice one to bring such a thing! You're as bad as he is! You stinkard! You devil! I'll tear your eyes out! I'll kill you!

TARO KWAJA: Oh, I say, look here, do let me explain a bit. I told him I couldn't do it at first, and then he threatened to kill me if

I didn't, and so I had to. It's no affair of mine. I didn't have anything to do with it.

WOMAN: Well, well, perhaps you didn't, for all I know. So you can just go back and tell him that I'll come along after you. I've got some business there. Now then, hurry off!

TARO KWAJA: But he said he didn't want any answer.

WOMAN: I don't care what he said. I tell you there's something I must do there. Off you go. I'll be there soon.

TARO KWAJA: Certainly. Just what I thought. I suppose there's nothing for it but to go back and do as she says. Well, here we are.

MASTER: Is that Taro Kwaja back again?

TARO KWAJA: Yes, master. She got into a frightful rage … and she'll be here directly.

MASTER: What does she want here? After I told her there was no answer.

TARO KWAJA: Yes, I gave her that message all right; but she said she had some urgent business here, and so she must come.

WOMAN: Yes, you devils, it's enough to make anyone angry! D'you think I'm going to be taken in by a fellow like that? You could kick two or three like him out of the bushes any day of the week. Here, where's that bag? I want it. I'm fairly on fire with rage. Now you dirty beast, what do you mean by sending me that letter? Let me get hold of you! I'll bite you to bits! You …

MASTER: Get out! What do you mean by coming back here after you've been dismissed? What d'you want? Eh?

WOMAN: Bah! It wasn't for love of your charms that I came back! There's something of mine here I want, that's all.

MASTER: And what's that?

WOMAN: Something I can get into this bag.

MASTER: If that's all, you're welcome to it. What is it?

WOMAN: That.
  (*Points behind him.*)

MASTER: What? I can't see anything.

WOMAN: That, d'you see, over there. That's what I want.

MASTER: What d'you mean?

WOMAN: Why this.
  (*Throws the bag over his head as he is looking in the opposite direction.*)

MASTER: Here! What are you up to? I can't see! You're throttling me! Let me go!

WOMAN: Let you go, eh? Not a bit of it! You'll come with me. I need you!

MASTER: Oh! You're hurting me! Curse it, I can't get out. Let me go, I tell you!

EBISU AND DAIKOKU

MAN: I am a man of the province of Tsu who wishes to become wealthy, and to that end I intend to pray to Ebisu Saburo Dono of Nishinomiya and to the three-faced Daikoku Dono of Mount Hiei, so I will choose a day of good omen and offer supplication, and perhaps may obtain a divine manifestation. Now this is a most fortunate day, so I will put up the sacred Shimenaw* and purify my house and so to prayer.

EBISU and DAIKOKU appear: We are the Gods Ebisu and Daikoku, and here we have many precious things to enrich mankind.

MAN: Now who are these who appear shedding brightness all around?

EBISU and DAIKOKU: Nishinomiya Ebisu Saburo and Hieizan Daikoku Dono, whom you worship so faithfully, at your service.

MAN: How thankful I am. Pray come this way.

DAIKOKU: Indeed I will make you wealthy on account of your great faith in me.

MAN: I am most grateful.

EBISU: And I too shall be delighted to favor you also.

MAN: I am deeply obliged to you. And there is something I should like to request of you, and that is that you would relate to

---

* Straw rope.

me your origin that I may have the more faith in you, for so far
I do not know it.

EBISU: What! You don't know who I am. Well, that is somewhat
remiss of you, but I will tell you. When Izanagi and Izanami became man and wife in the Heavenly Rock-cave they proceeded
to beget the Sun-goddess, the Moon-goddess, Hiruko, and Susa-
no-o-no-mikoto. And Hiruko is myself. Being thus the younger
brother of the Sun-goddess, Ama-terasu-o-kami, I was revealed
in glory as Ebisu Saburo Dono of Nishinomiya. Yea, verily am I
not the mighty Ebisu Saburo, the tutelary Deity of riches who
giveth wealth to the needy?

MAN: I am most grateful for your divine condescension, and now
may I beg of Daikoku to impart his history also?

DAIKOKU: Now Mount Hiei is a most august and revered mountain, and Dengyo Daishi prayed that it might not be without a
tutelary Deity. So I, Daikoku, deigned to reveal myself there. And
Dengyo Daishi made a vow that if I would maintain for one day a
thousand of the three thousand priests who lived on that mountain I should certainly become the tutelary Deity of all the three
thousand. Then suddenly I manifested myself with three faces
and six arms and Dengyo was greatly impressed, and forthwith
appointed me as the Deity of the mountain. And so it is that the
Law of Buddha is still prosperous. And do you trust in me and I
will make you rich.

MAN: I am most grateful.

DAIKOKU and EBISU (*dancing*): Yes, we now confer wealth upon
you. By our favor your business will prosper. With the fish-hook
of a myriad blessings you shall catch the fish of fortune.
   (*So Daikoku advances and confers on him the bag of a myriad
treasures, and the mallet that strikes out the precious things of
the earth, after which the august pair deign to withdraw their
presence.*)

THE SECOND-CLASS MASTER-BLINDMAN* AND THE MONKEY

BLINDMAN: I am a second-class blindman of this district. The cherry-trees of the eastern and western hills are now all in blossom, and my wife always tries to coax me to take her to see them every year, but since I cannot see them myself I have always refused so far, and this has made her exceedingly vexed, so this year I think I will take her, and amuse myself by smelling the flowers at any rate, even though I can't see them. Hi! Are you there, wife?

WIFE: What do you want?

BLINDMAN: Oh, only to tell you that I will go with you to view the cherry-blossoms this year as you have always wanted to go so much, and while you view them I will smell them.

WIFE: Oh, how nice. That will be delightful. But flowers are things to look at. Surely you can't care to smell them only.

BLINDMAN: Oh no, not at all. It will be quite easy to smell them. You know the verse:
"Though he may forget
That the early spring has come,
Yet the wayfarer
As he trudges on the road
Marks the fragrance of the flowers."
And so you see the scent is not to be overlooked.

---

* Jap. Kōtō. There were originally two ranks of Master Blind-men, Kengyo and Kōtō, which were instituted by the Emperor Kokaku in 1547, for blindmen of superior attainments such as musicians and scholars. Later on in the Muromachi era this was increased to four, Kengyo, Betto, Kōtō, and Zato, this last term being commonly used to denote all Master Blindmen. There was also So-Kengyo or Chief Kengyo, chief of all the Master Blindmen of one district.

WIFE: You're quite right. Well, then, come along. Let's go.

BLINDMAN: Take my hand then.

WIFE: All right.

BLINDMAN: Ah, to go out hand in hand like this is really much nicer than any flower-viewing, isn't it?

WIFE: Hush! Don't let anyone hear you talking in that sentimental way.

BLINDMAN: There seem to be a lot of people going to view the flowers.

WIFE: So there are.

BLINDMAN: I say, you didn't forget the bamboo bottle, did you?

WIFE: Oh dear no. I sent it on in front of us to the Kiyomizu Temple grounds.

BLINDMAN: Excellently managed.

WIFE: Well, here we are at the temple.

BLINDMAN: Then let us find a quiet place.

WIFE: Yes. I think this will do. And there are a lot of fine blossoms too.

BLINDMAN: That seems quite good. You sit down just here by me. Let's have a drop now. Where's the bottle?

WIFE: Here.

BLINDMAN: Then pour me out some liquor from it. Ah! That seems all right.

WIFE: Another brimmer?

BLINDMAN: Ah! This is something different from drinking at home. It tastes far better. You have some too?

WIFE: Thanks.

BLINDMAN: I'll pour you out one. And now for a lively song.

BOTH: Za-an za! The sound of the pines by the shore goes za-an za.

WIFE: Well, will you have another?

BLINDMAN: I don't mind if I do. Pour it out. Ah! The more one drinks the better it tastes. Let's have another verse.

MONKEY SHOWMAN: I am a strolling showman who goes round the city with this monkey, and today I am on the road as usual. Now that the cherries are in blossom I think I will go to Kiyo-mizu to see them. So here we are, and what a fine lot of blossoms. Why how funny, there's a blindman who has come to view them with his wife. A fine woman she is too! Yes, indeed she is. I think I'll have a word with her.

WIFE: Did you speak to me? What is it?

MONKEY SHOWMAN: I say. Is that your husband with you?

WIFE: Oh yes, that's my dearly beloved all right.

MONKEY SHOWMAN: Dear me, dear me, what a shame that such a good-looking woman should be the wife of a blindman. Why I'm sure I could arrange a much better marriage for you than that.

WIFE: Could you, really? Well, perhaps I shouldn't object, but this old love-of-my-youth, he might, you see.

BLINDMAN: Here, wife, where have you got to?

WIFE: Oh, I'm just here.

BLINDMAN: That won't do! Come here! I want another drink. Pour it out!

WIFE: All right. There you are. How's that?

BLINDMAN: Ah! That's good, I tell you. I'll have another. Ah! You have one too.

WIFE: I shall be tipsy in a minute. Oh well, all right, here goes. And as there is no one by we might have another little dance as an accompaniment.

BLINDMAN: Oh, yes, if you'd like to. We're tipsy ... and we'll dance.

WIFE: Yes, how jolly. We certainly will.

BLINDMAN:
Come on then (*dancing and singing*):
The Empire is at peace,
The ocean waves are still,
By favor of our Gracious Lord
We go where'er we will,
No rebels dare to hinder us
Or work us any ill.

MONKEY SHOWMAN: Ha! Ha! How quaint! Look at the blindman dancing! I say! One moment.

WIFE: Well, what is it?

MONKEY SHOWMAN: Look here, won't you run away with me? I can find you a much better match.

WIPE: That doesn't seem a bad idea, but are you sure you can arrange a really good match?

MONKEY SHOWMAN: A really fine one, I tell you. A splendid fellow.

WIFE: Then I think I'll risk it.

BLINDMAN: Wife, wife! Wherever have you got to?

WIFE: I'm here all right. That was a jolly dance, wasn't it?

BLINDMAN: Look here! I don't like your getting up like that. I know what I'll do. I'll tie you up to my sash.

WIFE: Why, what *are* you doing?

BLINDMAN: Now I feel more comfortable. Let's have another drink.

WIFE: There you are.

MONKEY SHOWMAN: Ah ha! The blindman's a sharp fellow. He's tied her up. He thinks she can't get away, does he? Perhaps he does, but I've an idea. I'll tie him to this monkey instead. I'll slip up to him silently so that he doesn't hear me, and then tie the monkey to him. There, that's done. Very neatly. I say, when I said I'd arrange a good match for you that was not quite the truth. What I meant was that I would take you home with me. I want you for always. Yes, forever and ever. So let's get away from here at once. Quick now. Ah, hurrah! That's splendid.
    (*They run off.*)

BLINDMAN: I want another drink. Here! Pour it out! Here, wife! Why don't you answer? I suppose you're angry because I tied you up. Now, come along.

MONKEY: Kya-aa, kya-aa!

BLINDMAN: Oh, how painful! What d'you mean by scratching me like that, you bad woman!

MONKEY: Kya-aa, kya-aa!

BLINDMAN: Oh! How awful! My wife's grown fur and turned into a monkey! Oh, what shall I do?

MONKEY: Kya-aa, kya-aa!

BLINDMAN: Ow! Let me go you beast!

THE STONE GOD

WIFE: I am the wife of a fellow who is a great drunkard, and when he is in his cups he often beats me. I am very sorry, but I am quite tired of him, so I am leaving him and running away home, but first of all I am going to see the man who was the Go-between when I was married, to tell him all about it, and then I shall go home to my people. It is very unfortunate to have a husband like this, but I suppose it was my fate, though I much regret leaving him after living together for so long. Well, here we are. Hullo there! Are you at home?

GO-BETWEEN: Hullo! Someone is at the door. Who is it?

WIFE: It is I who has come.

GO-BETWEEN: Oh, I am glad to see you. What is the matter?

WIFE: It is about my husband. He is always drunk, and often beats me when he is in his cups, so I have made up my mind to leave him. He is sure to come here to inquire about me, so when he comes, tell him I have been to see you and told you that I am tired of him and wish to leave him, and I am going to perform the Kagura* before a Stone God every day. I won't have any reconciliation, for I can't bear him any longer!

GO-BETWEEN: Well, I am very sorry to hear it, but what you say seems quite reasonable. So if he should come here I will tell him what you say, so pray set your mind at ease.

---

* Sacred dance.

WIFE: That is very kind of you. Please do so. As you can imagine, it is not at all pleasant for me to go away like this. Well, I must be going now. Good-bye.

GO-BETWEEN: Good-bye.

WIFE: Ah, how sad it is to part after living together like this! And now I will go on home.

HUSBAND: I am a man of these parts, and my wife is now a Miko who goes round praying. When I was in my cups I said something or other she did not like, and so she ran away home. No doubt she went to the Go-between who arranged our marriage on her way, so I am just going to see him and make inquiries. Really women are great fools! Fancy taking anything seriously that I said when I was in liquor, and then running away! How stupid! Well, here we are. Hullo there! Is anyone in?

GO-BETWEEN: Who's there?

HUSBAND: It is I who have come.

GO-BETWEEN: Pleased to see you. And what can I do for you?

HUSBAND: Oh, it is nothing particular, but I had a few words with my wife, and she has run away from me, and as she has no doubt been here, I should be glad if you can tell me anything you know about her.

GO-BETWEEN: Ah, indeed? I am very sorry to hear that. I haven't seen her myself, but I have heard on the quiet that she is tired of you and has run away, and that she is going every day to perform Kagura before a Stone God and pray that she may be quit of you.

HUSBAND: Oh indeed, is that so? Then I will go to the Stone God and meet her there, and see if I cannot make it up with her and bring her home.

GO-BETWEEN: Yes, that is right. Do so as quickly as you can.

HUSBAND: Yes, I will. I'll be off now.

GO-BETWEEN: Good luck.

HUSBAND: Ha, I have a good idea! She goes to this Stone God every day, so I'll get myself up as the Stone God, and then I'll give forth an oracle. Ah, here we are. I'll just prepare myself before she comes.

WIFE: Well, I'll go and pray to the god as usual. If I go and pray like this every day, I am sure to get rid of that husband of mine. Now I will begin my Kagura.

HUSBAND: Chō-yō! Guard us from all harm! Guard us from all harm and give us long life! Far out in the offing there is another stone. It is the seat of Ebisu, the God of Good Fortune!

WIFE: Why, if that isn't that husband of mine! You rascal! To get yourself up like a god and try and deceive me! What do you mean by it?

HUSBAND: No, no, it's nothing. Please forgive everything and come home again. Do, please!

WIFE: I won't! I won't come back whatever you say! I mean it! I'll not forgive you!

HUSBAND: Oh, do please!

HANA-KO

DAIMYO: Is the Kwaja* there?

KWAJA: At your service, my lord.

DAIMYO: If I don't go and see Hana-ko she will think it strange, and hold me fickle, will she not?

KWAJA: She certainly will, my lord.

DAIMYO: Well, there is something I want you to do for me, as I am going to visit her tonight.

KWAJA: Oh, there is some new duty for me, is there? I am at your command, as always, my lord.

DAIMYO: Ah, that's good. You see I have just hoodwinked the old lady so that I can get off. I have told her that I am going to sit in meditation for seventeen days, so she must not come near me all that time, for I wish to be undisturbed, and I have got her to consent. So I shall go off to see Hana-ko, and smooth out some of my wrinkles. Now what I want you to do is to sit down covered up in this Cloak of Meditation until I come back, and if the old lady should come in, whatever she may say you must remain covered up without uttering a word, and not show your face on any account. D'you understand?

KWAJA: That'll be a pretty troublesome job. The mistress will just about kill me if she does find out who it is. Really I don't think I can do it.

DAIMYO: You don't think you can do it? What? Are you more afraid of your mistress than you are of me? Sit up! I'll cut your head off!

KWAJA: Oh, please wait a moment, my lord! I'm more afraid of you than of the mistress! I'll do as you wish, whatever happens.

DAIMYO: Indeed? You're sure?

KWAJA: Certainly I will. Why should I tell you a lie?

DAIMYO: Well, well; you're a good fellow, and I like you very much. I didn't really mean anything; it was only because I wanted to see Hana-ko so much. So I trust you to manage it all. Now let me see you put on this Cloak of Meditation. There; so. That's better. Now I'll be off. Be sure you don't utter a word! Farewell. I won't be long.

KWAJA: Pray come back soon, my lord!

DAIMYO: All right. Be careful!

KWAJA: My lord! If I might presume so far, would you be kind enough to remember me to the maid Kogai, if you should see her when you visit her mistress?

DAIMYO: Oh, certainly. And next time I will take you with me so that you can see her yourself; so that will be a treat for you to look forward to.

KWAJA: Ah, what a kind master!

DAIMYO: Now I must hurry off to Hana-ko. How delightful!

LADY: My lord has declared that he will sit in meditation for seventeen days, and will not even take a bath all that time, as he wishes to be left quite alone; but I think he is much to be pitied, and though he has told me not to come and see him during this period, I cannot bear to leave him in that state, so I will just go and take a peep at him. Dear me! To be muffled up in that cloak must be very uncomfortable. I say! What Sutra can you need at your age? A young man like you! Your life doesn't depend on it, so wouldn't you like me to bring you something or other? Ah, he makes no answer. He only sits like that, all muffled up! You had better take that thing off a moment. I'm sure it won't matter. Well, I'll do it myself.

KWAJA: Oh dear! Pardon me! Pray pardon me!

LADY: What's this? I thought it was your master. What on earth are you doing here? What d'you mean by it? Where's your master? Tell me at once! I'll have your head off immediately if you don't!

KWAJA: Oh, please don't! I'll tell you everything if you will spare me!

LADY: Well, hurry up! If you don't—

KWAJA: The master has gone to see Hana-ko Sama and—

LADY: What's this? Hana-ko *Sama* do you call her?

KWAJA: Hana-ko-me, I mean. Er … the wench Hana-ko; and he told me to get into this cloak, and I did not want to do it, but he drew his sword and threatened to cut off my head if I did not do as I was told, so I did it willy-nilly. Please spare my life, for I didn't do it on purpose.
    (*Sheds tears.*)

LADY: You're sure you didn't do it on purpose then, but only because he threatened your life?

KWAJA: Yes, indeed, that is the truth.

LADY: Then look here. I have something I want you to do too. Listen to me.

KWAJA: Please tell me. I will do anything for your ladyship, even to the risk of my life.

LADY: That's good. Then put this cloak over me and arrange it just as you were yourself.

KWAJA: That is an awkward thing to ask me; when the master comes home, he is sure to kill me. Please let me off.

LADY: Oh! You're more afraid of your master than of me, are you? I'll show you!

KWAJA: Oh, I'll put it on for you. If you'll spare me, I'll put it on!

LADY: Then make haste about it! Now does it look just like your master's figure?

KWAJA: Exactly like it.

LADY: That's a good boy. Now you go along and see your aunt in the capital, and I'll send and fetch you back when the master has got over it. You had better hurry off at once.

KWAJA: Yes, my lady. It is very considerate of you to let me go now. A pretty fix I've got into! I think I'll be off at once.

DAIMYO (wearing a ko-sode or wadded garment, his hair loose, and his robe tucked up, singing):
    How sweet it is to loose the dainty brocade inner girdle!
    Who could forget her willowy form, her loosely flowing tresses!
    When I think of the grace of her lovely face, as from far she watched me depart;
    So dazzling and shy like the moon in the sky, regret still fills my heart.

Dear me! Here am I singing to myself in my happiness. Taro Kwaja will be tired of waiting. I'll cheer him up a bit when I get home. Ah, ha! It's a fine thing to be one having authority. There he is, nicely covered up, just as I told him. Ho, Taro Kwaja! I've come back. Why doesn't he say anything? It must be rather uncomfortable in that thing. But you will be pleased, too, looking forward to hearing something pleasant. Well, this is how it was. When I reached her house, though she did not know I was coming, strange to say, as I stood listening outside to hear how things were, the sound of her voice came to me from within singing this song: "The lamp burns dim, and all is lonely here, then comes my love to me." Greatly rejoicing I tapped at her door, whereupon she sang again: "When one is held in very high esteem, who is it that knocks at the door in the evening?" At this I replied in an answering verse:

Who is it who would come, dripping wet, on a rainy evening?
Would you reproach me forsooth, if you too long for a meeting?

Then Hana-ko came forth and took my hand and led me into the house. Ah! Then it did not matter about the rain. She took off my upper garments and brought me some fresh ones, and then we had a long chat about all sorts of things, and danced and sang until, all too soon, we heard the cry of the crow that heralds the dawn. It seemed but an hour we had been together before the voice of the crow proclaimed the dawn. And so we had to say farewell. Then Hana-ko sang this stanza:

By a copse beneath the mountains lies my house, and so the crow cries always to the moon.
Let it be midnight ever while you're here.

"Though you may wish it," I replied, "if the day breaks someone may see me, so I must hasten away." When did Hana-ko ever say anything contrary to my wish? "I expect you want to see your wife again," she said. So I sang these lines about my wife:

If you would compare my wife to other ladies,
She is like an old monkey huddled up, wet through with the rain,

which made her laugh exceedingly. And this mantle she gave me as a memento, so I must get rid of it somewhere, for it would never do for the old lady to find it. (*Utai*)–"But I cannot bear to leave it, for whene're I take it up, I see a lovely form appear, and by day and night love overtakes me so that I must weep bitter tears." So I give it to you. Keep it somewhere so that the old lady does not see it. Take off that mantle now. I'll get into it in your place.

LADY: What's that you don't want the "old lady" to see? A fine kind of meditation indeed! The sort of meditation you practice!

DAIMYO: Oh! Oh! What's this?

LADY: Yes, you may well ask what it is!

DAIMYO: Oh, please excuse me. Please overlook it this time.

LADY: No you don't! I won't let you off!

THE SIX SHAVELINGS

FIRST MAN: I am a man of these parts, and I have it in my mind to go on a pilgrimage, and but as I prefer to go in company I think I will call on some of my friends and invite them to go with me. Well, here we are. Is anyone at home?

SECOND MAN: Who is it?

FIRST MAN: It's only me.

SECOND MAN: And what do you want?

FIRST MAN: Today being a fine one it seems to be a suitable occasion to set out on the pilgrimage that I intend to make, as I have already suggested to you.

SECOND MAN: Yes, certainly. And as I think there is someone else who will come too, I will go and invite him, so I will follow you in a short time.

FIRST MAN: Very well.

SECOND MAN: That is done.

FIRST MAN: Then let us go.

SECOND MAN: Certainly.

FIRST MAN: Now when people travel together it is natural that occasionally things should happen that irritate them, so let us agree to keep our tempers at these times.

SECOND MAN: As you say, on such a long journey it won't do to play the fool, so whatever happens we won't get angry with each other.

FIRST MAN: Ah, I'm tired. I feel extremely tired. I fancy there is a small temple by the wayside just here, so I will go in and lie down. How sleepy I feel.

SECOND MAN: He looks very tired, doesn't he?

THIRD MAN: Yes, evidently he isn't used to traveling yet.

SECOND MAN: Look here. He's sound asleep. Well, he said, not long ago, that he would not get angry whatever happened. It would be amusing to tease him and see.

THIRD MAN: Yes, as he was so sure about it, it would. But what shall we do?

SECOND MAN: He's such a heavy sleeper that you could burn him without his knowing it. Let's make a priest of him.

THIRD MAN: Oh, that's too much.

SECOND MAN: Not at all. He said he would not complain whatever happened, and so it's all right. And if he does get angry, well, it will be time then to consider what to do. Have you a razor?

THIRD MAN: No, I haven't.

SECOND MAN: You're a careless sort of fellow. Anyhow, I have, for I thought I should want it to shave myself. Now you hold him.

THIRD MAN: Right. (*The other produces the razor and shaves his head.*) There. That's one side done. Now how are we to manage the other? Ah, I have an idea. They say if you pour some water into anyone's ear when he's asleep, he'll turn over. (*Pours a drop of water into his ear so that he turns over. Then shaves the other*

*side of his head, puts a hood on his head, takes off his outer coat,
and puts a priest's cassock on him instead.*) Well, I think I'll have
a nap too.

SECOND MAN: I, too (*The two of them lie down. The first wakes
up and stares in astonishment at his priestly garments. He goes
and wakes the other two.*)

SECOND MAN: Hullo! What has made you take orders so suddenly?

FIRST MAN: What has made me indeed? Why if this isn't your
doing, whose is it I should like to know?

SECOND MAN: What on earth d'you mean? You think that, do
you? Why, we know nothing about it.
    (*The other abuses them vigorously.*)

SECOND MAN: As you will. But, anyhow, suppose we did. You
know you promised not to lose your temper whatever happened,
so you ought not to go on like that.

FIRST MAN: That may be, but it depends on the ease. How would
you like to be made a priest like this?
    (*After further exchange of compliments the priest goes off. The
other two go on.*)

SECOND MAN: Well, let's get on. What an awful fellow!
    (*They sit down by the Daijin-bashira.*)

FIRST MAN: I shan't be easy till I've paid them out. But how to
do it? Ah, I have an idea. I'll go back again home and see. Hullo!
Is anyone at home?
    (*The two wives of the others appear.*)

WIVES OF FIRST and SECOND MEN: Why, that's his voice. Yes,
he's back again. What is it? Why have you come back?

FIRST MAN: Yes, but I find it difficult to face you again.

WIVES: Why? What is it? Has anything happened to our husbands? Why haven't they come back too?

FIRST MAN: Well, it's like this. I came with the intention of telling you all about it, but I feel so overcome that I can't speak for tears.

WIVES: But we must know more. Do please tell us at once.

FIRST: Well, I suppose I must speak out. The fact is that we were going along the road together, when we came to a big river, a place I think you are hardly likely to know, and those two went to cross it straight away. I warned them that it was probably too deep, and suggested they test it, but they wouldn't listen but plunged in, holding each other's hands, and when they got to the middle they got out of their depth and were swept away by the stream and drowned.

WIVES: Oh dear, how awful! Is it really true?
(*Both weep.*)

FIRST MAN: Yes, I am afraid it is. It was such a shock to me, you see, that I at once became a priest and was on my way to Mount Koya to pray for them, when I remembered that you knew nothing about it and thought you ought to be informed, and so I turned back again to do so.

FIRST WIFE: Ah, then, it is really so. I was thinking it was but a bad dream, but now there is nothing for it but to throw myself into a river and die too.

SECOND WIFE: Yes, I shall commit suicide too.

FIRST MAN: But I think that won't do any good at all. It would be much better to shave your heads and spend your time saying prayers for the welfare of your late husbands. Don't you think so?

WIVES: Perhaps you may be right. I think I will.

FIRST MAN: Yes do. That's excellent.

WIVES: And since there is nobody else we can very well ask, will you shave our heads for us.

FIRST MAN: Well, then, if you really mean it I will.
   (*He shaves them one after the other and they put on cotton hoods.*)

FIRST MAN: Now as I said before I am going on pilgrimage to Mount Koya, so I can take this hair of yours there with me and make an offering of it.

WIVES: That's very kind of you. Please do.

FIRST MAN: Well, so the pair of them have become nuns. That's something accomplished. I feel better after that. I don't suppose those fellows will have got far. I'll follow them up.
   (*Goes on.*)

SECOND MAN: Ah, that fellow wasn't likely to have gone home like that.

FIRST MAN: Hullo! Who are you?

SECOND and THIRD MEN: What d'you mean? Can't you see it's us?

FIRST MAN: It sounds like you certainly, but … It's very odd.

SECOND MAN: What's odd?

FIRST MAN: Why, when I got home I was told that someone had brought word that both of you had been drowned in a river, and I found your wives in mourning for you.

SECOND MAN: What nonsense you talk! I suppose you are telling us that to get even with us.

FIRST MAN: Not at all. I'm quite serious. And your wives were so overcome by grief that they committed suicide in despair.

SECOND MAN: Yah! You can't take us in with that tale.

FIRST MAN: Well, if you won't believe me here is proof of it.

SECOND MAN: What proof?

FIRST MAN: Look here. Look at this hair. Don't you recognize it? That's your wife's, and this is yours.
  (*The two take it in their hands and examine it.*)

SECOND MAN: Ha! Yes, this is short and brown.

THIRD MAN: Yes, and this hair has a kink in it all right. Can it be true?

FIRST MAN: Why should I deceive you? I just came to tell you because I thought you didn't know about it.

SECOND MAN: Ah, yes, now I come to think of it, she always said she wouldn't survive if anything happened to me. It's just what I might have expected. I'm afraid there's no doubt about it. How cruel!
  (*The pair of them begin to weep.*)

FIRST MAN: Well, if you feel it so much, don't you think the best thing would be to pray for their welfare in the after-life?

SECOND MAN: Yes, that is the best thing we can do. We'll become monks and go to Mount Koya.

THIRD MAN: Yes, so we will. Will you shave our heads?

FIRST MAN: Oh, yes, if you wish. (*Shaves them and they put on the hoods and dress of mendicant monks.*) You look well like that. Monks' robes become you. Well, let's get on. But we had better go home on the way.

SECOND MAN: Yes, that would be as well.

FIRST MAN: Well, here we are. And here are your wives. (*They appear.*) And now d'you think it was so clever to play that trick on me?
   (*The four fly into a rage.*)

SECOND MAN: Yah! What shall we do to him? We'll get his wife and shave her head too.

FIRST MAN: Oh, I can't allow that.

SECOND MAN: Who wants you to. We'll do as we like.
   (*They get his wife and shave her head and change her dress. All six now appear as shavelings.*)

FIRST MAN: Carrying a joke too far has always been considered bad form. But this seems to me no ordinary matter. It is very likely a warning to us to seek enlightenment in the future.

SECOND MAN: Yes. That may well be. Life is short and we ought not to fool it away. We ought to be more serious. We must improve on this opportunity to obtain enlightenment.

FIRST MAN: Then let me lead the chorus. Namo-oda!

THREE MEN: Namo-oda!

THREE NUNS: Namo-oda!

ORUS: Namo-oda! Namo-oda! Namo-oda! Toppai! Hyaro! Hi!

ASAHINA

EMMA: I'm Emma-O, the Lord of Hell. I'm Emma-O, the Lord of Hell! And here I am in the guise of a begging monk!

CHORUS: Here indeed is Emma-O, the Great Lord of Hell, for of late men have grown cunning, and what with the eight, yea, the nine, sects of Buddhism, more and more of them have been getting into the Pure Land Paradise of Amida, so Hell has grown quite poverty-stricken and Emma-O has to go out to the Six Roads and see if he can't find some sinners there.

PILGRIM-SONG:
  My well-loved Hell thus left behind,
  My native Hades left behind,
  On foot I jog upon my way,
  And now I've reached the Six Highways.

CHORUS:
  Yes, now he's reached the Six Highways,
  And here he'll wait till sinners come
  That he may haul them down to Hell.

ASAHINA: Here am I, Asahina, as mighty as ever, hastening along to the Dark Road.

CHORUS: Ah, it is Asahina Saburo, suddenly swept away by the wind of impermanence, and now on his way to the Dark Road.

EMMA: Ha! There's a smell of man. That must be some sinner coming. Ah, yes, here's a sinner all right. Hi! You sinner! Hurry up!

ASAHINA: Hullo! I thought I saw something moving here. Who are you?

EMMA: I'm Emma-O, the Lord of Hell!

ASAHINA: Oh, indeed. Well, you make a pretty poor show. They tell us in the Shaba-world that he wears a crown of jade and a girdle of jewels and shines brightly all over, but you're not doing anything of the sort.

EMMA: Oh, in the good old days I used to glitter in gold and jewels all right, but now things have changed and man has got so cunning and gets into the Paradise of Amida in such numbers that Hell is frightfully hard up and I've had to put my jade crown and the rest into pawn and I haven't a single thing left. But come here, my man, and let me torment you and throw you into Hell.

ASAHINA: Yes, I'd like to see you.

EMMA: Come on then. (*Bangs at him with his iron club, but Asahina takes no notice.*) Hullo, what sort of a fellow are you who doesn't turn a hair when Emma-O starts to torment him?

ASAHINA: Don't you know me? I'm Asahina Saburo.

EMMA: Oh, are you? Sorry you have had the trouble of coming so far. I suppose I ought to let you off, but really it's a pity not to torment a stout fellow like you a bit, so I'll have another go at you and then fling you down into Hell.

ASAHINA: Go on then.
   (*He snatches the club and knocks him down with it.*)

EMMA: Well, well, I suppose I'd better give it up. Ah, I've a bright idea. You know all about Wada's wars, of course? Well, I'd like to hear you recite some of them.

ASAHINA: Oh, I know, for I was in the middle of them all. But I must sit down if I am to recite. Bring me a camp-stool.

EMMA: Yes, yes, but go on. (*Asahina pulls away the camp-stool Emma was using.*) Now! What a way to treat the Lord of Hell! A rough fellow!

ASAHINA: See here! These are the seven weapons with which I did my great deeds in those fights.

EMMA: Ah, they smell of blood!

ASAHINA: Now, listen to my tale!

EMMA: Go on, I'm all ears.

ASAHINA: Well then, the origin of the fighting was that Egara-no-Heita was seized by the Shogun at the Usui Toge and taken to Kamakura. So that ninety-three warriors of his house swore to wipe away the shame of his imprisonment, and my father, Wada Yoshimori, again putting his helmet on his white hair, led all our clan against the palace of the Shogun at Kamakura and flung his forces against the south gate with a mighty shout. And just as I was flinging the foe in all directions and doing great exploits my father sent me a message to know why I had not broken down the gate, and to do so at once. So I dismounted from my horse and seized a great beam with which I proceeded to batter at its iron-bound doors and bolts. Though in as fearful a position as the Mount of Swords in Hell I never blenched for a moment, but putting forth all my strength pushed and pulled and heaved with might and main until at last the doors gave way and fell. I then fell on the thirty warriors who were within and slew them. I cut them to pieces so that they were like nothing but a fish salad.

EMMA: Ah, how I would like to cram my mouth with a salad like that!

ASAHINA: A pity you were not there to say so! But as I was saying, one of the palace warriors, Igarashi Kobunji by name, suddenly tried to unhorse me, whereat I, astonished at his impudence, gripped him and pressed him against the saddle-bow, and ground him against it from one side to the other—(*seizing Emma*) —like this; yes, just like this.

EMMA: Oh, oh! I think I've heard enough of the wars of Wada.

ASAHINA: Oh, no, I'll go on.

EMMA: I've heard enough, I tell you.

ASAHINA: Well, then, you shall guide me to the Pure Land Paradise.

EMMA: Oh, if you let me alone, I'll guide you where ever you like.

ASAHINA: Really? (*Glares at him.*)

EMMA: Yes, really.

ASAHINA: And truly?

EMMA: And truly.

CHORUS: So Asahina, with determined mien, loads his rake and bill-hook, and iron club, and all the rest of his weapons on the back of Emma, since he had no servant to carry them, and thus they hurry off to Paradise

THE PERSIMMON-SELLER

MOKUDAI[*]: I am the Mokudai of this province. As I have plenty of money, I am establishing a new market, and whoever will set up a stall in it of whatever kind will have his taxes remitted for a whole year. Herewith I put up a notice to that effect. This may be a suitable place, I fancy. There, that looks all right, so I will return.

PERSIMMON-SELLER: I am a persimmon-seller of Heguri-dani in the province of Tamba. I hear a new market is to be established by some rich man in the capital, so I will make my way thither. I am hoping to set up a stall there to sell these wares of mine, so that I can get my taxes remitted and make a lot of money. Well, I suppose this must be the market. Well, I will go to the head of the market. Persimmons! Persimmons!

MOKUDAI: Ah, I am quite pleased with my market. It seems to be going very well. I think I will just go and have a look around it. Ha! There is a persimmon-seller. Hi! You there!

PERSIMMON-SELLER: What is it?

MOKUDAI: What do you mean, fellow?

PERSIMMON-SELLER: You had better come and see.

MOKUDAI: Here, you! Don't you know who I am?

PERSIMMON-SELLER: No. How should I know?

MOKUDAI: Well, see if you can guess.

---

[*] Deputy governor.

PERSIMMON-SELLER: My trade is to sell persimmons, so I am not good at judging people.

MOKUDAI: Well, you must, whether you like it or not.

PERSIMMON-SELLER: H'm, you seem to be an unreasonable sort of fellow. I must, must I?

MOKUDAI: Certainly you must.

PERSIMMON-SELLER: Well, turn round that way, so that I can have a good look at you. Yes, I see.

MOKUDAI: What do you think I am?

PERSIMMON-SELLER: You are a Satsuma-o.[*]

MOKUDAI: Indeed I'm not. Guess again.

PERSIMMON-SELLER: Then turn round again. That will do. I see.

MOKUDAI: Well, what?

PERSIMMON-SELLER: You seem to be a man who always wears a hakama,[†] so I suppose you are a cook or a go-player, or a chess-player perhaps.

MOKUDAI: No, I am none of these things.

PERSIMMON-SELLER: Oh, then I can't say.

MOKUDAI: I am the Mokudai, the deputy of this province. Couldn't you see that?

PERSIMMON-SELLER: Oh, you are the Mokudai, are you? Then have a persimmon.

---

[*] Meaning unknown.
[†] Divided skirt.

MOKUDAI: Do you think the Mokudai is the sort of person to be seen eating persimmons in the cities or towns of his province?

PERSIMMON-SELLER: I don't see what harm there would be if he did.

MOKUDAI: You don't think it would be of much consequence? Then I'll try one. I say, fellow, these persimmons are nicer than I should have thought. I will have another. Give me one of those in front there.

PERSIMMON-SELLER: All right. But I shall want payment for this one.

MOKUDAI: Very well. I will pay you what you want.

PERSIMMON-SELLER: Ah, then I will give you one.

MOKUDAI: I say, is this one sweet?

PERSIMMON-SELLER: Yes, sweet enough to put your jaw out of joint.

MOKUDAI: Get away, fellow. This is no good!

PERSIMMON-SELLER: What? But it is sweet.

MOKUDAI: Bah! It's too sour for anything. Ugh! It's uneatable!

PERSIMMON-SELLER: Why, what d'you mean? I'm sure it's quite good.

MOKUDAI: Then eat it yourself!

PERSIMMON-SELLER: All right. It is sweet. It's too sweet for words.

MOKUDAI: There's nothing so beastly as bran or sour persimmons. If you eat one you can't whistle, they say. Now whistle, you. Quick!

PERSIMMON-SELLER: All right.

MOKUDAI: Well, why don't you whistle?

PERSIMMON-SELLER: Wait a moment. I will.

MOKUDAI: Hurry up!

PERSIMMON-SELLER: It's so sweet, I really can't whistle.

MOKUDAI: You beastly swindler! The way to treat a fellow like you is take away his persimmons. So.

PERSIMMON-SELLER: Yah! You! Give me them back!

SONG:
    Give them back again!
    Though they be steeped in "sake"
    To take away their sourness,
    Best to leave them on the tree,
    'Twill better bear next year.
    In old times Hitomaru
    Lived beneath a kaki-tree,
    Gazing up into the sky
    And composing verses.
    You provoking knave!
    You had best pull off your lips
    If they cannot whistle.
    And if you are sorry,
    If you've got no "comb persimmons"
    To scratch your head withal,
    Pick up your persimmons
    And take them home again!
    Ho! Gather up your kaki,
    And get you home again.

PINS AND NEEDLES

MASTER: Ho there! Is the page there?

PAGE: At your service, sir.

MASTER: A guest has just come, so go and buy a carp.

PAGE: Certainly, sir.

MASTER: And be quick back again.

PAGE: I will, sir. (*Aside*) From morning till night he does nothing but tell me to go out and buy carp. I will feign illness so that I shan't be able to go. Oh! Oh! How it hurts!

MASTER: Now the– What is it?

PAGE: It's the pins and needles. I get it from my parents! Oh! Oh! It's awfully painful!

MASTER: What's that? Do you say you've got the pins and needles?

PAGE: Yes, sir. Ever since I was quite small, if I thought I would go out, it used to come on suddenly when I least expected it.

MASTER: Then stay at home and rest.

PAGE: Yes, sir.

MASTER: Oh, by the way, someone sent a message to me to ask me to go to an entertainment at his house quite suddenly, and asked me to bring my page too. I'll just tell him that I can come but my page will not be able to come with me this time.

PAGE: I say, master!

MASTER: Well, what is it?

PAGE: If you are going to that entertainment please take me with you.

MASTER: But your pins and needles will prevent you from going out, won't it?

PAGE: If I tell it the reason it will soon go away.

MASTER: Then let's see you do it.

PAGE: All right. Look here, pins and needles, listen to me! If we go with the master to this entertainment at my grandfather's we shall have a fine feast and lots of liquor, so leave me alone, won't you? Yes!

MASTER: Who was that that answered?

PAGE: The pins and needles, I suppose.

MASTER: Well, that's most extraordinary! Is it better?

PAGE: Yes, it's quite well now.

MASTER: What a wonderful pins and needles. Well, get up if you're all right.

PAGE: Please give me your hand and help me up.

MASTER: There, get up, do!

PAGE: Now I'm up; is that all right?

MASTER: Don't you feel any pins and needles now?

PAGE: If I go to the feast with you the pins and needles won't come, however many miles I walk.

MASTER: In that case go and buy the fish I ordered.

PAGE: Oh, then the pins and needles will soon come back. Oh, oh, master!

MASTER: I'll give you something, you rascal! Be off with you!

PAGE: Oh, certainly! Yes, yes, I will!

THE STAG HUNTER

PRIEST: I am a priest who has some business over the hill yonder, so thither am I taking my way.

SAKON: And I am Sakon-no-Saburo, a hunter who lives at the foot of this hill, and today I am going hunting as usual. Aha! That's a disgusting sort of fellow to meet just when you are starting out after some, sport. I'll accost him and have some fun with him. Hi! you priest!

PRIEST: Is it me you want?

SAKON: Indeed it is.

PRIEST: And what may you want?

SAKON: Where are you going?

PRIEST: Oh, just over to that hill.

SAKON: So am I, so we can go together.

PRIEST: But you seem to be a samurai, so I shall hardly be a congenial companion for you. Pray let me go on alone.

SAKON: Oh well, priests and samurai are not so very different after all. Let's go together.

PRIEST: But I am in a hurry, so let me go on.

SAKON: Now look here my priest. You'd better go with me or—
   (*Makes a motion to draw his bow.*)

PRIEST: Oh, oh! Yes. All right.

SAKON: Ha, ha! I was only joking. It doesn't matter.

PRIEST: Well, then, will Your Honor lead the way?

SAKON: Oh, I don't want holy company. You go on.

PRIEST: Thank you. I will.

SAKON: But I say, priest. There's something I want to ask you.

PRIEST: What is it?

SAKON: About fish? Do you eat it?

PRIEST: Oh no. Recluses never eat fish.

SAKON: I think they do.

PRIEST: Oh no they don't.

SAKON: But you have eaten it. Now, haven't you?
  (*Menaces him.*)

PRIEST: Oh yes. Yes I have.

SAKON: I thought so. And look here, priest. I expect you've got a wife.

PRIEST: Oh no, recluses never have anything to do with women.

SAKON: Oh, don't they. Are you sure you don't?
  (*Draws the bow.*)

PRIEST: Oh well. Yes, yes, I do.

SAKON: Ah, well, that's nothing. I think you a very worthy fellow really. In fact, I should very much like to have you for my chantry priest. How about it?

PRIEST: Oh, of course I should be highly honored to have you for my patron. Are you indeed serious?

SAKON: Oh, certainly. I shall be much obliged to you. And so, as my chantry priest, you will be at my service both for this world and the next, won't you?

PRIEST: Indeed I shall.

SAKON: Well then, there is something I want you to do for me now.

PRIEST: What is that?

SAKON: Just take this bow for me for a bit.

PRIEST: Oh, but I have never carried one in my life and I don't know how to handle it.

SAKON: Well, if you don't know I'll teach you. You hold it so.

PRIEST: This way, you mean?

SAKON: Yes, that's right. That'll do very well. Now go on.

PRIEST: All right. Now there's something I should like to ask you too.

SAKON: Well?

PRIEST: Since you have kindly become my patron I should like to know your name so that I can write it in the temple Roll of the Blest Departed.

SAKON: Oh, don't you know. I am Sakon-no-Saburo.

PRIEST: What? The hunter? Why should I carry the weapons of such an unclean fellow.
  (*Drops the bow.*)

SAKON: Hi! What have you dropped my bow for?

PRIEST: It isn't right for a holy priest like me to carry weapons for taking life.

SAKON: Oh, and does Buddha dislike taking life?

PRIEST: Why, of course he does.

SAKON: Well, explain the matter to me then.

PRIEST: Certainly. Recluses must observe the five prohibitions: of taking life, of stealing, of impurity, of lying, and of drinking intoxicants, and of these Buddha particularly emphasized the first.

SAKON: Look here, priest. Your head may be shaven, but there is a lot you don't know. There are texts that allow taking life. For instance, in the Daruma Sutra it says: "Take like, take life, every moment! If you don't you will go to Hell like an arrow." What do you say to that, eh?

PRIEST: Oh, that refers to what is within oneself. There are plenty of texts that consign to Hell those who take life.

SAKON: Yes, but how about this too: "If you don't live in the Universal Mind there is no guilt before the Law." If there is no guilt there is no Law, and if there is no Law there is no Buddha? So it seems to me there is no harm in taking life.

PRIEST: Yah, whatever you say, if you shoot a stag you can't help being reborn a stag.

SAKON: Oh then, if that's so, if I shoot a priest I shall be reborn a recluse.

PRIEST: Don't you dare shoot at me. I have a three-inch figure of Amida on my breast.

SAKON: Then I'll cleave it and see what's inside.

PRIEST: Then you'll be like the fool who split open the Yoshino cherry-tree to find the blossom.

SAKON: Blossom.* Well, you've got one anyhow.

PRIEST: Where?

SAKON: Why, on your face, of course.

PRIEST: How silly. Do go away.

---

* Hana = blossom and also nose.

THE THIEF AND THE CHILD

WET-NURSE: Now then, I'll get it to sleep in the reception-room. Ah, that's fine. Now he's asleep down here I shall have time to go and get a cup of tea.

THIEF: I am a great gambler of these parts. Of late I have had bad luck, for I have lost all my money and even my wife's clothes playing with those worthless fellows whose company I keep, and now I don't know where to turn. So I suppose there is nothing for it but to take what I want from someone who has a superfluity. Well, there is a man not far off who has any amount of money and rice and other things, and tonight I intend to pay him a visit and slip into his house and help myself to what I need to try and retrieve my fortune again with the dice.

PILGRIM-SONG: 'Twould have been better to have taken people's advice and given up this life before. But you always think you are going to make your fortune and take no heed, and so it comes to this pass. Well, here I am, and it is just getting dusk. Ah, he has repaired his house lately it seems, and it looks quite imposing. It's no use trying the front, so I'll go round to the back. Now there's this wall. I cannot reach the top. Still I've got to get over it. Perhaps it can be managed. Let's see. Ah, that's good, I'm over. Now there's a reed-fence. I must break a hole in that. That's awkward, I'm afraid someone will hear. No, it seems not, for no one has come out. That's a good thing. Now I'll creep through the hole. Right. Now if I open this door into the corridor I shall soon be in the reception-room. Ah! There's a lantern burning. It seems they had guests here last night. I wonder whether anyone has heard me. No, it seems not. There are some fine things here. There's a tea-kettle and brazier and a tea-caddy and tea-bowl. Yes, they are excellent. If I can get away with these I shall be quite set up. Ah! There's a wadded coat. Better and better. When I took my wife's clothes to gamble with she wasn't a bit pleased I can tell you, in fact ... well I'll take this for her and it will brighten her up wonderfully no doubt. Well, it's time I took my leave I think. Eh ... what's this? There's a child sleeping in it. Dear me, what a huzzy of a nurse they must have to leave it sleeping here while she goes off to amuse herself. Well ... what a nice child. Ah! It's stuck its hand out. Suppose I nurse it a bit. Yes, I think I will. Ah! That's got it. There's a good boy. Now then, I wonder if it knows any tricks. Bo-peep! Bo-peep! Bo! Ah! He's up to it. How charming. Now, what else can you do. Let's see. Ah! What a clever child. Your parents must be proud of you. Ah! I laughed a bit too loudly. I must have startled him. Well, I will try to get him to sleep. I'll rock him in my arms. So. There–(*sings*)–"The little puppy-dog over the way hasn't yet opened its eyes." Ah! Now he's begun to smile. Now he seems all right.

WET-NURSE: Now I'll just go and see how that child is going on in the reception-room. Bless my soul! There's a thief in there. Here! Here! There's a thief nursing the baby.

MASTER: What's that? Oh, a thief has got in, has he? Just send someone round to the front. Where is he? I'll soon cut him down.

WET-NURSE: Oh, mind! Wait a moment!

THIEF: I am not a thief. I've just come to have a look at your reception-room.

MASTER: That won't do. Don't try to take me in. I'll soon settle you.

WET-NURSE: Oh, do mind the child! You may hurt him!

MASTER: Oh, bother the child! I'll cut him down!

THIEF: Well, if you really mean to cut me down there's the child—(*puts it down*). Now strike—(*slips away*).

MASTER: Where's he gone? I didn't get him. Confound him!

WET-NURSE: Eh, what now! He's dropped the child and run, has he? Now then, darling, come to me and I'll give you some of my milk. Well, I wonder that didn't give me the colic.

THE FOWLER

EMMA: I am Emma-O, the Lord of Hell! I propose to go forth for a while through the Six Ways of Sentient Existence! Yai! Yai! Are my retainers there?

THREE DEVILS: Here we are!

EMMA: If any sinners arrive just pitch them down into Hell and torture them.

DEVILS: We will.

EMMA: But who is there to save the sinners who have done no sin?

SEIRAI: Here stand I, Seirai, a mighty fowler in the Shaba-world. I was intended to live to a good old age, but the Wind of Impermanence swept me away, and here I am on the Dark Road.

SONG:
Regretfully he leaves his old familiar life,
And setting out on the strange road on foot,
Ere long he comes to traverse the Six Ways.

SEIRAI: It seems that I now stand at the crossroads of the Six Ways, and must look about to consider how I may get to heaven.

DEVIL: I smell mankind! Ah! As I thought, here comes a sinner. I must announce the matter. A sinner has arrived, my lord.

EMMA: Then quickly torture him!

DEVIL: Most certainly! Now then, my sinner! Heaven is far distant, but Hell very nigh; so haste your steps. Ho-ho! You differ from the common run of sinners; you seem amused. Who were you when you dwelt among mankind?

SEIRAI: I was Seirai, a mighty fowler in the Shaba-world.

DEVIL: If you were a fowler, you were one who took life both by night and day. Your sins were very great. I certainly must torture you in Hell.

SEIRAI: No, no! My sins were not so great. I pray you let me go to Paradise.

DEVIL: That I cannot. You must come before the King of Hell. My lord!

EMMA: What is it now?

DEVIL: This sinner was a fowler in the Shaba-world; and so I say his sins are great, for he has taken life continually, and must go down to Hell. But he says it is not so. What is to be done?

EMMA: Bring him here to me!

DEVIL: So I will. Come hither now, for Emma summons you.

SEIRAI: At your command.

EMMA: Now then, you sinner! You did nothing but catch birds in the Shaba-world. You are a great rascal, and must go down to Hell.

SEIRAI: 'Tis true I caught them; but this I did only to feed my hawks, and so sustain their life. What harm was there in that?

EMMA: And these hawks; they are birds, too, are they not?

SEIRAI: Most certainly they are, my lord.

EMMA: In that case you are hardly much to blame.

SEIRAI: Indeed 'tis so. The blame is with the hawks, and not with me. So let me go to Heaven.

EMMA: But as I do not yet know the taste of birds, and on this Mountain of Shide there are many of them, do you catch some for me with that pole of yours, and then I will consider your request.

SEIRAI: That will be easy enough. I will soon bring you some.

CHORUS: Lo! Now he goes to catch the birds. From the southern plain of the Mountain of Shide, many flocks of birds come flying, and as soon as he sees them he darts his pole in among them and takes them. Then he roasts them and offers them to Emma.

EMMA: Ha! I will try them. (*Eats.*) How good they are, forsooth!

SEIRAI: Come on, you devils, too!

DEVILS (*eating and smacking their lips*): Good! Good! How tasty!

EMMA: I have never tasted anything I liked better in all my life. So as a reward I permit you to go back to the Shaba-world, and catch birds again for three more years.

SEIRAI: How can I thank you!

CHORUS: Released, he goes back to the Shaba-world, for three years more to catch his birds again. Ducks, pheasants, wild geese, storks, and others, too. For even the small birds he gets specified; and so returns. And Emma, in regret at losing him, gives him the jeweled diadem from off his head. Seirai bows low in gratitude, and starts his journey to the upper air.

THE PRIEST'S STAFF

PRIEST: I, who appear before you, am a priest living in the country. I happened to have some business in the capital, and at the same time I ordered a staff to be made, and as it is now time for it to be finished, I have come today to fetch it. Well, well! So we go along! There's no more pleasant life in this world than a monk's! I think I'll go and pay my respects to some Buddha, and stay there a while before I go back again. Ah, here we are at the maker of staves. Ho, there! Is the master at home?

MASTER: Who is there?

PRIEST: It is I who have come!

MASTER: Oh, is it the monk who ordered the staff?

PRIEST: It is, and is it ready yet?

MASTER: It is quite finished. Please wait a moment, and I will bring it and show you.

PRIEST: Ah, good. Please do so.

MASTER: Here it is.

PRIEST: Well, that's excellent! It is exactly as I ordered it.

MASTER: Indeed, I have taken great pains with it. I may say it is much finer stuff than the ones I showed you before. I must have a joke on this staff, you see.

PRIEST: A very good one too!

MASTER: How very white the wood of it is!

PRIEST: Since it is not lacquered it can't be covered.

MASTER: Capital! Capital!

PRIEST: Can you ornament it in lacquer?

MASTER: When this staff is broken, what will you do then?

PRIEST: I can only think of one thing at a time.

MASTER: Better and better! Really you are exceedingly witty! Now I am carrying on this occupation, but what I have always wished is to forsake the world and become a monk. I pray you come in and partake of my humble meal, that I may enjoy the opportunity of hearing some of your holy teaching. Do, I beg you!

PRIEST: Truly, it is the business of us monks to give exhortation. Yes, I will come in. And kindly bring the staff with you. Here we are.

MASTER: Yes, your reverence, as I have just stated, I should so much like to become a recluse, and I was hoping that you might be able to take me as your disciple, so that we might be able to travel about the country together.

PRIEST: Oh, to forsake the world and shave your head and become my disciple is an easy thing enough, but first you should take counsel with your relations, your brothers, and your wife, for if people become recluses without proper reflection they sometimes repent of it afterwards. For when you become a monk you have to observe the Law of Buddha, and to study the Sutras and Mantras, and—ah—be careful not to misconduct yourself, you know. But if you do the things that you ought to do, you will have a mind quite free from care, and wherever you wish to go you can go, and wherever you wish to stay you can stay! Ah, and if you rid yourself of that nasty, grasping, envious, avaricious desire, your mind will be so devoid of all trouble that you will become just like a Buddha.

MASTER: Ah, how true, how true! But this wish of mine is no sudden one, for I have cherished it for a long time. I quite understand everything, so please make me your disciple at once.

PRIEST: You are sure you quite understand and agree to everything?

MASTER: I am quite sure.

PRIEST: Then I will shave your head. And your relations and your wife are also quite of the same opinion?

MASTER: I consulted with my womenfolk some time ago, and they are quite willing that I should do as I please.

PRIEST: Then that is sufficient! So prepare yourself.

MASTER: Very well! I will have my head shaved.

WIFE: My man seems to have gone out of the house with that monk who came to get the staff he had ordered. I wonder what they are doing! They are a long time about it. I will go and see. Ya-a-a-h! Is that you making yourself into a monk? Whose doing is this? This monk wants to shave your head, does he? I'll teach you, you—!

PRIEST: What does she say? I thought you said your wife was quite willing?

WIFE: Who dares to say so? What d'you take me for? Become a priest indeed! You get off back where you came from, wherever that is! Off with you! You make me mad!

PRIEST: What's this! I didn't persuade him against his will. He said it had always been his secret desire.

WIFE: That's a lie! You dirty, swindling bonze! I'll give you something!

PRIEST: Oh! Oh! Don't! Please excuse me! This is very unpleasant!

WIFE: Yah! You! You thought you would become a monk without saying anything to me, did you? What did you think I was going to do? Eh?

MASTER: Oh, no! It was because this monk told me what a pleasant life it was, and invited me to become one. So I thought I would shave my head.

WIFE: Nonsense! Don't tell me that tale! Well? What now?

MASTER: Oh, I've changed my mind now. So pray excuse me!

WIFE: Get away, you wretch! I won't excuse you!

UNDER THE HAT

PRIEST: Though I think myself a Buddha, what do others think, I wonder?

CHORUS: What do they think, I wonder?

PRIEST: I who thus speak am a noble recluse. And as I have never beheld the capital, I am now making my way thither.

PILGRIM-SONG: Leaving my ancient temple where I have dwelt so long, thus I set out on foot and have come thus far. Hastening my steps I have arrived at this place, and as the sun is setting I would stay a while and pass the night in this house. Ho! Within there!

HOST: Who is it that calls?

PRIEST: I am a traveling recluse, and as dusk is coming on I pray you to give me a night's lodging.

HOST: That would be easy enough, but it is a rule of this house that no lodging shall be given to solitary recluses. So I must decline.

PRIEST: That rule is reasonable enough, but my conduct is not bad like that of some recluses. So please allow me to stop here for one night.

HOST: No, I cannot.

PRIEST: Are you sure you cannot?

HOST: Why, haven't I told you so?

PRIEST: Well, if you won't, don't.

HOST: This priest is too much!

PRIEST: Well, if you won't let me have a lodging, am I to do without one? But I haven't anywhere to go, so I must devise a plan for staying here. Hullo, there!

HOST: Who is it now? Why it's that priest again.

PRIEST: It is. I say, I don't care at all where I sleep, but I want to leave this hat of mine somewhere. Won't you let me leave it here for tonight?

HOST: Oh, I don't mind your hat. You can put it where you like.

PRIEST: But I am very particular about this hat. Please let me leave it here. In the middle of this room.

HOST: H'm, as you please.

PRIEST: Much obliged, I'm sure. Then I will put it down here.

HOST: Very well. Come and get it as soon as you like tomorrow morning.

PRIEST: Thanks. Good-bye. There! I've got my lodging. I'll put this hat on and spend the night under it. Ha, it's time to say the Sutra. To prayers.

HOST: That's strange! It sounds as if someone was chanting the Sutra in that room over there. What can it be? Why, what's this? It's that priest, sitting in the middle of the room with his hat on, looking like a mushroom that has sprouted there. Hullo! Is that you, priest?

PRIEST: It is indeed.

HOST: And who gave you leave to stay there?

PRIEST: I say, mine host, I have something I want to I ask you.

HOST: Well, what is it?

PRIEST: This house; to whom does it belong?

HOST: To me, of course.

PRIEST: And is everything in it subject to your disposal?

HOST: Of course it is.

PRIEST: Whose hat, then, is this?

HOST: It is your hat.

PRIEST: But did you not consent to its being here till tomorrow?

HOST: Yes; the hat only.

PRIEST: The hat is to remain here. Granted. And as what is under the hat is at the disposal of the hat, I have its permission to spend the night under it.

HOST: Well I never! Hear the fine logic of this confounded recluse! And how about what is outside the hat?

PRIEST: Oh, as that's in your room, you can pull it off or shave it off, or do what you like with it.

HOST: Can I really?

PRIEST: Certainly.

HOST: Then this is outside.
     (*Pulls.*)

PRIEST: Yo-ho!

HOST: Yes, and this is outside.

PRIEST: Ha! I see.

HOST: Well, this is an amusing priest, to be sure. So I will give him a lodging for the night. I say!

PRIEST: What is it?

HOST: It is too bad to turn you out now, so you can stay here for the night. Take off your hat and make yourself comfortable.

PRIEST: Ha, mine host, you want to get me to take off my hat, and then you will turn me out.

HOST: No, no. I speak the truth. I swear it by Hachiman the War God!

PRIEST: In that case I will take it off its landlord. Ah, that's better. What a nuisance it was.

HOST: What a humorous priest you are. I will stay here and have a chat with you to-night.

PRIEST: I shall be most honored, I'm sure.

HOST: I say, your reverence, shall we have a drop of liquor?

PRIEST: Thank you very much, but you see I observe the Five Prohibitions, and especially the prohibition against drinking; so I must be particularly on my guard against it. But I am very much obliged to you all the same.

HOST: A most admirable recluse! I never saw such a one. Well, I must take my night-cap by myself then. You're sure you won't join me?

PRIEST: I couldn't think of it! I couldn't think of it! But I say, mine host, what is that dish over there?

HOST: That is bean-curd and sea-weed.

PRIEST: Then I will take a little of that.

HOST: Oh, I beg your pardon. Certainly.

PRIEST: And please pour some "sake" over the seaweed.

HOST: But I thought you were an abstainer?

PRIEST: Oh, "sake" sauce is another matter. There is no need to abstain from that. Put some more on it, please.

HOST: That is rather more than "sake" sauce I fancy.

PRIEST: Well, mine host, you have broken the rule of your house about taking in priests, so I may perhaps break one of the Five Prohibitions. Let us have a drink then.

HOST: Right. We can have a pleasant evening over this liquor. (*They sing.*) And now let us have an additional course. (*They dance.*)

PRIEST: Ah, that's good! That's very charming. That's excellent.

HOST: Won't you give us a dance too?

PRIEST: But I am a recluse, you see, so I don't know how to do anything except chant the Sutras.

HOST: Oh, anything will do. If you will only get on your legs and do something.

PRIEST: All right then, I'll dance.
     (*Dances and sings.*)

HOST: Excellent! Very amusing, indeed!

PRIEST: Now, one more. I say, mine host, it will soon be daybreak, so I will give you another dance if you will be good enough to sing the accompaniment.

HOST: What shall I sing then?

PRIEST: Sing the Jizo dance.

HOST: All right. (*Sings.*) Now we dance the Jizo dance!

PRIEST: The place where Jizo dwells is Mount Karada in the Western Paradise.
   In Hell and in the worlds of Pretas, Beasts, Asuras, and Men,
   Everywhere he wishes to deliver mankind plunged deep in sin.
   With his staff he lifts them up,
   Calmly, quietly he saves them.
   Once in ancient days Prince Shaka,
   He the much-revered Nyorai,
   Stretching out his golden fingers,
   Ah, how blessed! Ah, how gracious!
   Three times stroked the head of Jizo.
   Saying to him, "Now from henceforth;
   To thy care are men committed."
   So on men he takes compassion,
   Wheresoe'er they may have wandered.
   Though no cup of tea we offer,
   He will come into this chamber,
   With a seven "to"* pot of liquor,
   On his festal day especially,
   Twenty-four cups he will tipple,
   Then, his eyes with drink a-glitter,
   Staggering, rolling, striding widely
   From one side unto the other,
   He will dance, the reverend Jizo.
   That is how I like to see him!

---

* Nearly four gallons.

THE OINTMENT VENDOR

FIRST VENDOR: I am an ointment vendor of Kamakura. I consider my ointment the most renowned in the country, but they say there is also a wonderful ointment in the capital, so I am betaking myself thither to see how it compares with mine. And so here I am jogging along. Ah, what a fine day it is! I feel glad to be alive. But it is very lonely to have no companion, so I think I will wait for someone to come along, and then we can journey on together.

SECOND VENDOR: I am the famous ointment vendor of the capital. I fancy there is no more skilled compounder of ointment in the capital than I, but I hear there is a wonderful ointment in Kamakura, so I am on my way thither to try if it is as potent as mine, so here I am. But it is very lonely to travel by oneself.

FIRST VENDOR: Ah, what a smell of turpentine! I wonder what it can be. Ya-ah! You fellow! What are you bumping into me for? Isn't this beach wide enough for you?

SECOND VENDOR: It was you who bumped into me!

FIRST VENDOR: What d'you mean? Whence are you? And whither are you bound?

SECOND VENDOR: I have some business in Kamakura, and so I am proceeding thither. And whither are you going?

FIRST VENDOR: I am an ointment vendor of Kamakura, and I think there is none like mine, but as I have heard there is someone in the capital who has a wonderful ointment too, I am on my way thither to try how it compares with my own.

SECOND VENDOR: Oh, then you are the proprietor of the Kamakura ointment. I have heard of the fame of it, and that is why I have come down to Kamakura.

FIRST VENDOR: Oh, indeed? Yes, my ointment has a long history. I suppose yours has too?

SECOND VENDOR: Yes, mine has also. But I should like to hear about yours.

FIRST VENDOR: Very well, I will tell you all about it. In former days the Shogun Yoritomo had two famous steeds named Ikezuki and Surusumi, and one day, when Surusumi was let out and jumped up into the air, the Shogun cried out to the Daimyos who were with him to stop him, but none of them was able to do so. Then my ancestor of that time stood forth and declared that he could stop him with his ointment, whereupon Yoritomo and all his lords burst out laughing at the idea. "However," said the Shogun, "stop him if you can." Then my ancestor, putting a little of his ointment on the end of his finger, and blowing on it, faced the plunging steed, calling to him to come and smell it. Immediately he did so, the horse stopped its rearing and, attracted by the power of the ointment, came quietly up to him to smell it. Then Yoritomo and all his lords burst forth into exclamations of amazement at the potency of the marvellous compound, and inquired what name it bore. "It has no special name," replied my ancestor, "only, as it draws things, we call it drawing ointment." "But an ointment like this ought to have a name," replied Yoritomo, "so, as it can draw a horse, you had better call it the Finest Horse-drawing Ointment of Kamakura." And since that time there has been no ointment in Kamakura to equal it.

SECOND VENDOR: Yes, that's a wonderful history. And now let me tell you the history of mine.

FIRST VENDOR: Very well. Go on.

SECOND VENDOR: When the Taira Chancellor Kiyomori Jokai was having his garden made, a great rock, to stand as a pillar in it, was dragged by three thousand men from the northern mountains of the capital as far as the gate of his mansion, but they could not get it any farther. Then my ancestor of that time stood forth and said: "If your Excellency wishes to have that stone properly placed, please tell me where you intend to put it, and I will draw it into position with my ointment." At this my lord Jokai and all his attendants burst out laughing at his vain words, but told him to do it if he could, but if he did not manage it they would declare him nothing but a boasting vagabond. So my ancestor, putting a little of the ointment on his finger, blew on it, and, facing the great stone, exclaimed: "Draw that stone!" Whereupon the stone was gradually drawn into place by it. Then Jokai and all his attendants exclaimed in amazement at the marvellous power of the ointment, and asked what its name was. And when they were told that it had no name, but was only called drawing ointment, they said that such a wonderful ointment ought certainly to have a special name, and as it could draw even stones, they gave it the name of the Finest Stone-drawing Ointment in the World. And since that time my ointment has had no equal in the world.

FIRST VENDOR: Indeed, that is a wonderful record. Yours is no whit inferior to mine. Suppose we explain the composition of our ointments, and then try them against each other. What do you say?

SECOND VENDOR: Certainly. And what are the ingredients of your ointment? How is it made?

FIRST VENDOR: Ah, mine is very difficult to make. It has all sorts of strange things in it; for instance, the fish that traverses the ground; the turtle that flies through the sky; the clam that lives in a tree, and things of that sort.

SECOND VENDOR: Ah, it must be difficult to get such things. My ointment is made of very precious things too; for instance, white crows; the living liver of red dogs; three-legged frogs, and so forth.

FIRST VENDOR: Things like that are indeed difficult to come by. They aren't to be had at all now. So what do you do?

SECOND VENDOR: That's just it. You can't get those ingredients at all now. The ointment I have is what has been handed down from my ancestor, and used sparingly, a very little at a time, ever since.

FIRST VENDOR: So I supposed.

SECOND VENDOR: Now shall we make trial of our ointments?

FIRST VENDOR: All right. Pray proceed.

SECOND VENDOR: Let us smear some on the end of our noses and see which will pull best. Ready?

FIRST VENDOR: I'm all ready. I'll pull you right to Kamakura!

SECOND VENDOR: That's not likely. Ah, ah! Mine is pretty powerful too. I'll pull you all the way to the capital!

FIRST VENDOR: Oh, no! I shan't go to the capital. How now? Ha! How strong it is. Come on, to Kamakura! One pull won't do it!

SECOND VENDOR: No, that it won't. Mine is strong too. Now then! One pull to the capital! Ya-a!

FIRST VENDOR: No you don't! What's this?

SECOND VENDOR: I've pulled you over anyhow! I've won! I've won!

FIRST VENDOR: No, no! That wasn't fair! Another try! No you don't! I won't let you off!

RAKU-AMI

TRAVELER: Alas! The poor mendicant finds a dog at every gate! I am a man of the eastern provinces, and as I have never seen the Shrines of Ise, you now behold me on my way thither. Weary and travel-stained, I plod my way onwards, lacking even a change of raiment, and now I have come to Beppo in the far-famed Province of Ise.

PILGRIM-SONG: Rapidly he pushes on his journey, and soon he has come to the pine-grove of Beppo. And on a certain pine he sees the tablets and "tanzaku"* are hanging, and what look like many "shakuhachi."† Surely concerning these things there must be some tale, so he would ask the people of the place. Is no one here?

MAN OF THE PLACE: What would you ask of us who live round here?

TRAVELER: I see these tablets and "tanzaku" on this pine, and many "shakuhachi" hang upon it. There must be some story of these things, and 'tis of this I would inquire.

MAN OF THE PLACE: Ah, concerning that matter. In former days there was a flute-player called Raku-ami who played the "shakuhachi" until he blew himself to death, and the people about here, feeling sorry for him, buried him here, and planted this pine in memory of him. Perhaps your reverence will, of your charity, say a prayer for him in passing, even though your affinities have nothing in common. I perceive that you also play the "shakuhachi" for you carry one stuck in your girdle.

---

* Poem slips.
† A vertical flute.

TRAVELER: No, no. That is only to frighten away the dogs. Still, though I have no connection with him, I will not refuse him my prayers.

MAN OF THE PLACE: And if there is anything else you wish to know, please ask us.

TRAVELER: I will.

MAN OF THE PLACE: At your service.

TRAVELER: So here lies the remains of Raku-amida-butsu. In memory of his sad story I will take this "shakuhachi" that I have here and play a tune.

GHOST OF RAKU-AMI: How delightful the sound of the "shaku-hachi." He plays the tune called "Sochogiri."

TRAVELER: How strange! It is as though I saw a shadow haunt my dreams.

CHORUS: The tenor flute; the alto flute; the soprano flute; the double flute he hears! And who is he who stands enchanted by the liquid tones?

GHOST OF RAKU-AMI: I am that Raku-ami who of old time did blow myself to death upon this pipe. Your mellow notes have charmed me from the shades.

TRAVELER: A miracle! To hear Raku-amida-butsu of ancient fame thus speak to me is strange indeed!

GHOST OF RAKU-AMI: Wherefore do you think it strange? For in the book of the "shakuhachi" in the Temple of Ryoanji we read, that when the two extremities of the bamboo are cut and determined, between the eighteen inches of its length a whole world lies. And in one melody that breathes the spirit of impermanence there lies a power of communication that transcends the confines of the Empire.

TRAVELER: Indeed you speak truth. For it is by virtue of this flute that I hold intercourse with Raku-amida-butsu famed of old. In it is the knowledge of all ages.

GHOST OF BAKU-AMI: 'Tis true indeed. For by the flute I was well-known even in the eastern provinces.

TRAVELER: Indeed!

GHOST OF RAKU-AMI: How full of meaning; wondrous pleasing is this pipe! But I can play nought but discordant tones. Such have no power to sound beyond our borders, so I will lay my instrument aside, and do you play.

TRAVELER: We'll play in concert.

GHOST OF RAKU-AMI: No, no! I would not make your melody discordant.

CHORUS: So at his bidding he takes the tenor flute, and puts it to his lips and plays a tune: To-ra-a-ro-ra, ri-i, ri-i, to-ra-a-ro, ra-a-ro, fu-u.

GHOST OF RAKU-AMI: What cherished memories it recalls! But now I must return.

TRAVELER: Alas, how sad your fate! Pray tell me how it came about.

GHOST OF RAKU-AMI: Well, I will tell you. In former days I used to wander round with doleful countenance, playing my "shakuhachi" to chance travelers or in front of rest-houses or at people's doors, whether they would or no; and if I did not get a copper for my pains, I would get angry and would revile them, and then, crying out that my playing was execrable and not to be borne, they would take a carrying-pole and send me flying. And to this day among the shades I labor with pole and cord at my old flute, heating and treading and twisting and pulling to shape the bamboo aright. I pray thee aid me, priest. For until now my great attachment to this art has kept me bound to the circling wheel of birth and death. How hateful is my love for this old flute.

THE ACOLYTE'S WATER-DRAWING

INCUMBENT: I am the incumbent of this temple. Today I am expecting several of the donors who are coming to consult about something, and I must have plenty of water for tea, so I will call that acolyte to go and draw some at Shimizu. Hullo! Where are you?

ACOLYTE: Here I am!

INCUMBENT: Ah, that's right! There's just a small matter that I want you to do. I'm expecting my wardens in a short time, and I must have some water for their tea, so just go and get me some at Shimizu, will you?

ACOLYTE: I should be very glad to go I'm sure, but the fact is that I am suffering from an attack of that beriberi that I so often have, and am quite incapable of the exertion of drawing water, so please send Icha who lives by the gate here.

INCUMBENT: No, no! I don't want to have to send women. Besides it is getting dusk now, so I think you had better try and go.

ACOLYTE: Oh no, I really cannot. Please send Icha.

INCUMBENT: Well, well, it's no good my saying anything, I suppose. You'd better take yourself off, as you're no use.

ACOLYTE: Yes, sir. (*Aside*)–Ha, ha! Splendid! I've got off just as I meant to, and I daresay Icha won't mind much either.

INCUMBENT: H'm, this is very annoying! Still, there's nothing else to be done, so I must send Icha, I suppose. Hullo! Are you there?

ICHA: Yes, sir. Do you want me?

INCUMBENT: Er, there's just a little thing I want you to do. I'm expecting some guests in a minute or two, and I should be much obliged if you would go to Shimizu for me and draw some water for tea.

ICHA: Oh certainly, sir. That's no trouble at all. I'll go immediately.

INCUMBENT: Ah, I'm glad of that. I'll wait here. Here's the bucket, and please be back soon.

ICHA: Certainly, sir. I'll be back in a minute, so please don't be anxious.

INCUMBENT: Yes, yes. Please do.

ICHA: Dear me, what a bother! Coming like this all of a sudden and telling me to go down to Shimizu and get water! Troublesome old nuisance! It's that acolyte's business to draw the water. What is the meaning of his coming and asking me like this? Well, well, here we are. Ah, this water is always so clear and crystal. Just the thing for tea. Yes, he's right there.

ACOLYTE: Ah! I got him to send Icha for that water instead of me, and she must be already at Shimizu by this time. She and I have become very friendly lately on the quiet, so I have told her that I shall go there after her and we will have a little talk together at leisure. That will be nice. Now I shall be off to meet her. The old rector doesn't know anything about this, and he doesn't seem very pleased that I refused to budge. Well, here we are, and now where is Icha? Ah, there she is all alone, singing to herself as she draws the water. Hullo there! Icha! So here you are.

ICHA: Oh! You are here, are you? I heard that you declared that you couldn't go out because of your illness when the rector told you to draw the water, so what are you doing here?

ACOLYTE: What have I come for? Why you know we haven't had a really good chat for a long time, and as I have a lot to say to you

I thought it would be a good idea to meet you here, so that's why I suggested your being asked. It's all lies about my being ill; the fact is I wanted to see you.

ICHA: What a silly thing to do! Someone is sure to see you. And I didn't want the bother of having to come here either. You had better go back at once. I think it was very unreasonable of you!

ACOLYTE: Well, I never! But I want to talk to you, so I shan't go.

INCUMBENT: I sent that girl Icha to draw water, but she seems a long time about it. I wonder what she's doing. I'll go and see. Why, what's this? If it isn't that acolyte! Didn't you tell me you couldn't go because of your beriberi? What do you mean by it?

ICHA: Oh, you see he thought I was a long time, and so he came to see why it was.

INCUMBENT: Why, what next? Do you expect me to believe that? I'll turn you out! Don't you show your faces near me any more!

ICHA: Oh but, your reverence, really it wasn't his fault at all!

INCUMBENT: Now, Icha, you wench, don't try to get around me, you bad girl!

ICHA: What's that you call me? I won't stand that! I don't care even if you are the rector!

INCUMBENT: Why, what do you mean, you pair of loose good-for-nothings?

ACOLYTE: What you want is a good spanking! (*Beats him.*) Come, Icha, I'll give you a pickaback home. Poor thing!

INCUMBENT: Yai! Yai! What do you mean by treating your master in such a way? Your next rebirth will be a wretched one! I'll pay you out!

THE CUTTLE-FISH

PRIEST: "Without a little tea-money how can I get on my way? I am a priest from far-off Tsukushi, and as I have never seen the capital, I thought I would like to make a pilgrimage thither, begging bowl in hand. Perhaps you may think that the people of Tsukushi are liars, but in truth I am a real pilgrim, and thus I have arrived at the shore of Shimizu. No time have I lost, and this is the place that is called the shore of Shimizu.

GHOST: Ho, there, priest! I have somewhat to say to you!

PRIEST: And who are you? And what have you to say?

GHOST: I am the ghost of a cuttle-fish who died here in the spring! Pray for my soul most earnestly!
   (*And so saying he vanished away.*)

PRIEST: This is a most extraordinary thing! I think I will ask some of the people about here. Is anyone there?

MAN OF THE PLACE: And what is it you would ask of me?

PRIEST: It is but a random question, but was there not a cuttle-fish caught here in the spring of last year?

MAN OF THE PLACE: There was indeed. Last spring a very great cuttle-fish came to this beach, and the people about here much admired its size; and those who caught it, fearing some retribution might fall upon them, set up this memorial and said prayers for its soul. But why is it you ask?

PRIEST: For no special reason except that when I arrived at this place, why I know not, the ghost of this cuttle-fish that you have told me of, suddenly appeared to me, and, after asking me to pray for its soul, vanished away.

MAN OF THE PLACE: Then there is no doubt that it is the ghost of that cuttle-fish, and though you may have no connection with it, I beg you to say a prayer for its welfare in passing.

PRIEST: Well, so I will.

MAN OF THE PLACE: And please tell me if there is anything else you wish.

PRIEST: I will. Well, there are many kinds of Buddhist prayers for the dead, but I will say the Hannya Shin-kyo over the ghost of this cuttle-fish. Ano-ku-tako-sambyaku-san-sen-de-kote—this will I offer to the Buddha for the soul of this cuttle-fish. Nama-dako! Nama-dako!

GHOST: Ah, how can I thank you for this blessed mass!

PRIEST: How very strange! Here in broad daylight, though it seems to be a man, yet a man it is not! I pray you tell me who you are.

GHOST: I am the ghost of the cuttle-fish who spoke with you before, and I have come to thank you for your prayers.

PRIEST: If you are the ghost of that cuttle-fish, I beg you tell me how you met your end, and I will say more prayers for your soul.

GHOST: I lived for long by this shore, and went hither and thither to escape the net of the fishermen, but last spring they spread a large net in the offing, and as I was unable to escape from it I was hauled up on the beach. Pulled upon the chopping-board I was stretched out and the knife was drawn across my back, and my eyes grew dark and I could not breathe. Thus I was I pressed down face downwards and scalped, and when I rose again on all sides there were cuttle-fish stretched out to dry and bleaching in the rays of the sun, salted and with their legs cut off. But soon I escaped from this torment, and entered the blessed Garden of the Law, there to attain Enlightenment and become a Buddha. How thankful I am for this grace, and now I lift up my voice unceasingly in the holy invocation, "Namu Amida Butsu."

(*And with this invocation, "Nama-dako," he vanished away.*)

DONTARO

DONTARO: My home is in the capital, but I have been away in the country for a long time, and have just returned. I have one house in the upper town and another in the lower, so I am wondering which to go to. My real wife lives in the upper town, so perhaps I'd better go there. Well, here we are. Ho! Within there! I have come back. Open the gate!

WIFE: This fellow has been away in the country for three years without sending me a single line. I shan't open the door to him.

DONTARO: I quite understand; but as I have been very successful, please open the door.

WIFE: But as I heard nothing from you I have taken a quarter-staff champion to keep me company.

DONTARO: I don't allow any men to stop with you without my permission.

WIFE: Hi! Hi! There's a troublesome knave here! Bring your staff and break his back for him!

DONTARO: Yah! All right, I've got a nice little maiden in the lower town. I'll be off there. Ah, here we are. Hullo there! Dontaro has come back. Open the door!

GIRL: What? That troublesome fellow again? Dontaro Dono went away into the country three years ago, and I've heard nothing of him since. I shan't open.

DONTARO: Open quickly! I've made my fortune and come back to see you.

GIRL: I've taken a halberd champion for my companion. Do you want him to give you a drubbing?

DONTARO: I can't have that. You mustn't have any men companions!

GIRL: What do you mean? How dare you bother me? I'll set my halberdier on to you!

DONTARO: Namsambo!* Both of them have got a man, have they? Women are a good-for-nothing lot! I think I will go off to Mount Koya and shave my head and retire from the world to seek enlightenment.

WIFE: Last night Dontaro came back and knocked at my door to be let in, but I wasn't sure, so I gave him a good scolding and he said he would go off to a girl he had in the lower town, and I suppose that's where he is. I'll go after him. Ah, here we are. Within there!

GIRL: Who's there?

WIFE: I'm the wife of Dontaro Dono. Last night he came to my house and wanted me to open the door, but I wasn't sure of him and gave him a scolding. I suppose he has come here. Please let me see him.

GIRL: Oh, you are the lady from the upper town? Yes, he came here last night too, but I also scolded him and sent him off.

WIFE: Is it indeed so? I heard by the way that he had shaved his head and was going to Mount Koya, so let us both go together and stop him.

GIRL: Yes, certainly.

---

* By the three sacred things.

WIFE: The two of us together will be able to stop him whether he will or no.

GIRL: So; let us wait here.

DONTARO *(in priest's robes and tapping a gong)*: Ah, that I should have come to this! Well, well, Namu Amida Butsu! Namu Ami-i-da Butsu! Na-a-mu Amida Butsu!

GIRL: Now then, stop him!

WIFE: All right. I say, Dontaro Dono, what is all this about? Please come back again.

DONTARO: No thanks. You've got your quarterstaff champion there, and that's a bit too much for me. Namu Ami-i-da Butsu! Namu Ami-i-da Butsu! Chi-rin, Chi-rin.
   (Rings bell.)

GIRL: Oh, but you really must come back.

DONTARO: It is very improper for young girls to approach recluses.

WIFE: I earnestly beg you to come back.

DONTARO: Halberdiers are the most terrible fellows in the world to come across. Namu Ami-i-da!

WIFE: Let us both try to stop him together.

GIRL: As we have both agreed to come and meet you thus, please forbear and come back again.

WIFE: Yes, do. We both beg you together. Please come back, and we will do anything you like to make you happy.

DONTARO: In that case suppose we agree that I spend the first half of the month in the lower town, and the second half in the upper.

WIFE: But there should be a little distinction made between us. Please spend the first half of the month with me.

GIRL: Yes, let it be so then.

WIFE: Very well.

DONTARO: I won't go back like this. You must make a sedan-chair for me, and I will return in style with a band playing.

BOTH WOMEN: Band? What do you mean?

DONTARO: When I exclaim, "Whose carrying-chair is this?" you must both chant together, "This is Dontaro Dono's carrying-chair."

BOTH WOMEN: Very well.
 (*They link their hands and make a chair for him. He struts round with a satiric smile, tapping the gong and singing.*)

DONTARO: Whose carrying-chair is this?

BOTH WOMEN (*chant together*): This is Dontaro Dono's carrying-chair.
 (*He sits on their hands and is carried away, continuing to tap with his mallet on their heads*).

THE LIQUOR-PIPE

MASTER: I am a man of these parts, and today I must go out on business, but as soon as my back is turned these two idle knaves of mine start drinking and dancing and making an uproar, and it is not safe to leave them. So I have devised a plan after some reflection, and I will now summon them and give them their orders. Ho! Is Taro Kwaja there?

TARO: At your service, sir.

MASTER: How prompt you are! All I have to tell you is that I have to go out today, so see that you look after everything properly in my absence.

TARO: Indeed I will. Master need have no anxiety about anything at all.

MASTER: Aye, well. But for certain reasons that I have I wish you to stay in this room while I am away.

TARO: As you bid me, sir.

MASTER: And tell Jiro Kwaja to come here too. I have something to say to him.

TARO: I will, sir. Hi! Hi! Jiro Kwaja!

JIRO: What now? Am I called?

TARO: Yes; come at once!

JIRO: At your service, sir.

MASTER: Today I am going out, so I want you to look well after everything at home.

JIRO: Indeed I will. We both will see that everything is safe.

MASTER: No, no! Today—I have my reasons for it—I want you to stay in that inner room alone, and there keep watch.

JIRO: I don't quite understand. Were it not better if we both looked after things together?

MASTER: No, no! That won't do at all. Taro Kwaja will stay in the next room, and you in the inner one. So do your duty.

JIRO: Certainly, sir.

MASTER: Now then, I'll see you in your rooms before I go.

BOTH: We are just going, sir.

MASTER: Well, be off with you!

BOTH: Yes, sir.

MASTER: And see that you are vigilant. I shall be back soon.

BOTH: We shall look forward to your return.

MASTER: Now that's all settled, so I'll be off.

TARO: This is a bit too much. I never heard of such a thing. I can guess what he is after. He is afraid to leave us together when he is out, for fear we shall begin drinking and making merry. That's why he has separated us. What a fix!

JIRO: Dear me, I feel very lonely. Whenever master has gone out before he has always left us together. Whatever has he done this for? I wonder what Taro is doing.

TARO: I wonder what Jiro Kwaja is up to. Hi! Jiro! Jiro! Are you there?

JIRO: Is that you, Taro? How lonely it is here.

TARO: It is indeed. I thought we would have a drink together today if he went out, so I have got some "sake" here.

JIRO: How nice! I suppose you've already started on it.

TARO: No, I haven't. I don't care to drink alone. I should like you to have some too.

JIRO: That's too kind of you. Can't you think of some way for me to get it?

TARO: If you could make a hole in this wall I could pass you some over. Ah, that's lucky! There's a hole here. I suppose the rats have made it. Now you can drink. Use this bamboo as a pipe, and I'll pour the liquor through it.

JIRO: That's got it. Look here! You drink, and then pour some through to me.

TARO: Good! Here goes. Now here's some for you. There, got it?

JIRO: Ah! Here it comes. I've got it. Splendid. That's enough! Down it goes. Ah, it tastes particularly good this way. Shall I pass you this "sake" cup?

TARO: No, that's all right. Here comes some more. Ready?

JIRO: Well, I don't mind. Ha! Here it comes!

TARO: How it is? Is it good?

JIRO: Beyond expression. I've never drunk better. It takes my breath away. Ah, that's enough. Let's have a song, shall we?

TARO: All right; come on.

BOTH: "Za-an Za! The sighing of the pines along the shore! Za-an Za!"

JIRO: Let me send you some. Here's to you! (*Drinks.*) Now then!

TARO: Thanks. I'll take a cup with you. Ah! Now for another song!

BOTH: "With their trusty friends carousing; soldiers are a jovial crowd!"

TARO: Hurrah! Splendid! Now have another!

JIRO: No! No! Let me give you one more.

TARO: No, I have too much already.

JIRO: Oh, but you must.

TARO: Very well then. Now I have it. One more song.

BOTH:
   "When the cherry doth bloom in the spring,
   Kiyomizu is the place for me!
   In spring-time, in spring-time, when all the flowers do bloom!"

JIRO: Ah, glorious liquor! I drink to you.

TARO: And I to you. Have some more!

JIRO: Thanks. I prithee pour.

TARO: Here you are then.

JIRO: Ho! What a bumper. It's running over! And so am I!

TARO: Oh, drink it up! I think that's all there is.

JIRO: Oh, well, in that case. So, down it goes. How glorious I feel! I'm tipsy! I'm tipsy! Now I'll send it back to you. Ready?

TARO: What? Don't you want any more then?

JIRO: What d'you mean? We'll have one more for the very last.

TARO: All right then. For the very last. There's just one left. This'll be quite enough. In fact, just a little too much. Ah! How good. I'm a bit tipsy. Jiro Kwaja, here's to you!

JIRO: Here's luck!

TARO: Yes, I'm a bit tipsy. I think I'll have a nap.

JIRO: What's that? Nap? Weren't you told to keep watch over the house? What do you mean by it? Hi! Taro! Are you asleep already? (*No answer.*) I don't call that proper. Well, if Taro Kwaja is taking a nap, I feel sleepy too. I can't hold out any longer. Here goes.

MASTER: Taro Kwaja! Jiro Kwaja! I've come back. As I put them in separate rooms this time, they won't have been able to drink as before, and so have looked after everything properly, no doubt. Why, what's this? Here's a hole in the wall! And what's this going through it? Why! Why! What a pair of devils! They've stuck a pipe through and been drinking that way! Taro! Jiro! Where have you got to? Why, here's one sprawling on the floor. And there's that rogue Taro lying there dead drunk. What's to be done with them? Get up, you devils, get up!

JIRO: No, no; I don't think I'll have any more.

MASTER: Don't think you'll have any more! I think that's for me to say.

JIRO: Ah, yes; you told us to keep watch. Pray excuse us.

MASTER: What next? What do you mean by lying there like that, you drunken sots! Get up, will you!

TARO: Ah, I'm tipsy! Let's have another song. "Zan- za-aa—"

MASTER: Ya-aa, you worthless knave! Zan-za-a! What next? I'll give you something.

TARO: Pray excuse us. Sir, pray let us off. Ah, I'm so sorry. I'll never drink any more.

MASTER: You'll never drink any more? Is that likely? I won't let you off!

TARO: Oh, yes, do!

THE GARGOYLE

DAIMYO: I am a well-known personage. I have been a long while in the capital and have won my lawsuit, and now I am going back again to my province. Ho! Is my page there?

PAGE: At your service, my lord.

DAIMYO: I have been here a long time and have won my suit, so I am now going home again, but I have great faith in the deity of the Inaba Temple, for I think he has greatly favored me, so I propose to pay him a visit before I return. Do you come with me?

PAGE: Certainly, my lord.

DAIMYO: When I reach my province again I intend to build an Inaba Temple there too.

PAGE: That would be very nice, my lord.

DAIMYO: Well, here we are. Now let us pray.

PAGE: Certainly, my lord.

DAIMYO: Yes, I will build one just like this in my province, so look carefully at it.

PAGE: I will, my lord.

DAIMYO: They say it was built by Hida-no-Takumi, and indeed it is a very beautiful shrine.

PAGE: It is indeed a very fine shape.

DAIMYO: But what is that thing up there in the angle of the roof?

PAGE: That is what is called a gargoyle, my lord. It is a very fine one. But why does my lord weep?

DAIMYO: That gargoyle is exactly like my wife's face. That's why I weep.

PAGE: When I come to think of it it is indeed very like the mistress.

DAIMYO: Those saucer-eyes are just like hers.

PAGE: And the mouth and those great bumps on the head. The mistress's are just as big as that.

DAIMYO: Someone must have carried her off and stuck her up there!

PAGE: It is really very strange, my lord.

DAIMYO: Then we shall have a very merry journey back! How splendid! There's nothing to cry about now. I shall laugh all the way home!

PAGE: It is indeed a very blessed thing. How jolly we shall be!

DAIMYO: Now then, laugh! Laugh, I tell you!

TSU-EN

PRIEST: Alas! Alas! Without a little money for tea how hard is the journey! I am a man of the Bando district, and since I have never yet set eyes on Uji I have now made up my mind to go thither. "Though we abandon ourselves like chestnut shells swept away on a flood, yet we may somehow find safety." And I, too, giving myself up for lost and drifting along, have thus managed to arrive at the bridge-pillars of Uji, and so without more delay I will hasten to the village. But, what is this I see? At this tea-house they are making offerings of tea. Surely about this there must be some tale, so I think I will inquire of the people of the place. Is there anyone here who can explain?

COUNTRYMAN: And what is it that you may wish to know?

PRIEST: I am a man of the Bando district, and it is the first time I have ever been here. I see here that they offer tea at this tea-house, and no doubt there is some story concerning it, so I pray you tell me what it may be.

COUNTRYMAN: Ah, yes! You see there was once a tea-master named Tsu-en, who was so devoted to his art that he died while making tea, and the people of the place took compassion on him, and so on the anniversary of his death they make offerings of tea and say prayers for his soul. I trust that you also will not disdain to say a prayer for him in passing by.

PRIEST: Ah, I understand. I thank you for your explanation. I will go on and, as I pass, I will pray for him too.

COUNTRYMAN: And if there is anything of which I can inform you, I pray you tell me.

PRIEST: I will. Ah, here is the tea-house that he spoke of. Spreading this tattered garment on the old matting of the floor, I will await a meeting in my dreams.

GHOST: Calmly the tea-guests take their seats while I prepare their tea. Drawing the water from the Ujikawa—how good is the edible seaweed! —the tea-makers draw the pathetic evanescent hot water—spite the heat of the handle of the kettle—ah, how lovely is the boiling hot water!

PRIEST: What strange thing is this? What figure is this that appears dimly before my dozing eyes, garbed like a priest and with a dipper in his girdle?

GHOST: I am Tsu-en, that tea-master who in this place of old died of making tea!

PRIEST: And are you indeed the shade of that Tsu-en? I pray that you will tell me how you came to die, and I, on my part, will pray for your soul.

GHOST: Then I will tell you, and I beg your prayers. When the service for the spirits of the dead at the bridge of Uji was but half finished, a band of pilgrims, some three hundred of them, came along all unannounced to drink up all my tea. With their mouths opened wide, in they rushed, a mighty multitude, and I seized the ladle to make a great brew, stuffing in all sorts of rubbish that would neither float nor sink. And I gave orders to my underlings that they should remember that there is sandy ground where the waves roll back, that the weaker should take the ladles and the stronger should carry the water, and that those likely to be washed away should take the tea-whisks, and all together should put forth all their strength. Thus at the command of one man, though the field of operations was such a wide one, like a desperate band determined to hold out to the last with leveled weapons, they stood their ground and fiercely plied the tea-pot.

Then with a roar confused came on the thirsty host,
All else forgotten, only wild to drink,

In their mad haste smashing the bowls and pots—Then did Tsu-en, giving all up for lost, to the last mindful of his famous name, taking his seat upon the sand hard by the Byodo-in,* spread out his fan, and, stripping off his robe, made his last verse before he slew himself:

As the fire whelmed in ashes burns not up,

When there is no hot water we can make no tea. Pray for me, O priest! Trifling as it may seem, this meeting here must have been pre-ordained from a former life!

(*And thus making an end, he gradually fades away and vanishes under the shade of the grasses of the drifting sand.*)

---

* The temple where Minamoto Yorimasa committed suicide.

THE BUDDHA-MAKER

COUNTRYMAN: I am a man from a distant province, and as Buddhism is very popular there, we have built a gilded shrine six feet square; but we have not got any image to put in it, so I have come up to the capital to buy one. Well, here I am, but I don't know any Buddha-maker in this place, so I will call out for one. Ho! I would buy a Buddha! Who has Buddhas to sell?

BUDDHA-MAKER: You see before you a dishonest sort of fellow who finds it difficult to make a living under the present circumstances. So I must pretend to be something or other, and perhaps I may come across someone who will enable me to better my luck. Hullo! There is a countryman calling out that he wants to buy a Buddha. I must have speech with him. I say, you there, what are you shouting about?

COUNTRYMAN: Oh, I am a man from the country. I have come up to buy a Buddha, but I don't know any Buddha shop, so that's why I am crying out.

BUDDHA-MAKER: Then you're in luck.

COUNTRYMAN: Oh, how so?

BUDDHA-MAKER: Why you're lucky in meeting me, and luck isn't a thing that you can always find sticking to your elbow either.

COUNTRYMAN: How do you mean?

BUDDHA-MAKER: Because I happen to be a Buddha-maker.

COUNTRYMAN: Ah, that is fortunate. And may I ask what school you belong to?

BUDDHA-MAKER: As you know, there are the schools of Unkei, Tankei, and Annami, and it is to the school of Annami that I belong.

COUNTRYMAN: Ah, I have heard of it. And have you any Buddhas ready made?

BUDDHA-MAKER: No, but I can make anything you like to order.

COUNTRYMAN: Ah, that's very convenient. Now what kind of Buddha would be best?

BUDDHA-MAKER: Well, what kind of a shrine is it that you have?

COUNTRYMAN: It is six feet square.

BUDDHA-MAKER: Then a standing one would be best, wouldn't it?

COUNTRYMAN: Yes, perhaps it would.

BUDDHA-MAKER: Then what kind of figure shall I make for you?

COUNTRYMAN: What do you think would be most I suitable?

BUDDHA-MAKER: Well, shall I make you an Aizen?

COUNTRYMAN: What kind of a Buddha is that?

BUDDHA-MAKER: Something like this.

COUNTRYMAN: Oh, but a fierce-looking affair like that I would frighten the children. Please make me a more ordinary one.

BUDDHA-MAKER: Oh, I see. Well, what do you say to a Monju, the Lord of Wisdom, who will protect you in this world and in the world to come?

COUNTRYMAN: Yes, that is the very thing. And how much will it cost?

BUDDHA-MAKER: A thousand cash.

COUNTRYMAN: Well, I won't haggle about the price. When can you get it done?

BUDDHA-MAKER: I don't suppose I could finish it in less than ten years.

COUNTRYMAN: Oh, I couldn't wait so long as that.

BUDDHA-MAKER: In that case I can have it ready by tomorrow.

COUNTRYMAN: Dear me! Why, how can you manage that?

BUDDHA-MAKER: Ah, you may well be surprised, but it is like this. If I carve it all myself it will take a long time, but if you are in a hurry I can set all my apprentices to work on it at once, and one will carve the head, and another the hands, and another the folds of the robe, and so on, and I will stick all the different parts together with glue, so it will soon be done.

COUNTRYMAN: Ah, that will be the way. Then may I ask where you are living?

BUDDHA-MAKER: Where I live? Oh, that doesn't matter. Suppose I deliver it to you at the inner temple of the Inaba-do.

COUNTRYMAN: All right. I will be there. So farewell for the present.

BUDDHA-MAKER: Till to-morrow then.

COUNTRYMAN: Very well.

BUDDHA-MAKER: Well, here am I calmly taking orders to carve Buddhas when I have never so much as made a toothpick. What shall I do, I wonder? Ah, I have it. I will go and keep the appointment with a Buddha mask on my face, and then at the right moment I will take it off and see what happens.

COUNTRYMAN: Well, that Buddha ought to be ready by now. I will stroll along and get it.

BUDDHA-MAKER: Is that you, Mr Countryman?

COUNTRYMAN: It is. Is the Buddha ready?

BUDDHA-MAKER: Oh yes. Quite finished. Here it is wrapped up in straw matting. I will open it and show it you.

COUNTRYMAN: Thank you. H'm. Yes, it is not bad on the whole, but I don't quite like the way the hands are made. Can't you alter it a bit there, eh, Mr Buddha-maker?

BUDDHA-MAKER: Bo!

COUNTRYMAN: Yes, I don't care about the hands, so I shall be glad if you will alter them.

BUDDHA-MAKER: I can alter it anyhow you like before the glue has set. So, I will show you.

COUNTRYMAN: Yes. This part, Mr Buddha-maker.

BUDDHA-MAKER: Bo!

COUNTRYMAN: Please alter this part; he looks as though asking for something.

BUDDHA-MAKER: Certainly. How will it do now?

COUNTRYMAN: This part is not right, Mr Buddha-maker; and this too.

BUDDHA-MAKER: All right. Now then, how is it?

COUNTRYMAN: This part won't do. Why this rascally Buddha-maker has put on a mask and taken me in. Look here, Buddha-maker, this isn't right, so please alter it quickly.

BUDDHA-MAKER: All right. How does it look now?

COUNTRYMAN: Why it is you yourself, you rascal! I'll be after you, you—!

AKUTARO

AKUTARO *(entering like a drunken shaveling)*: Is uncle in?

UNCLE: Is that Akutaro come again?

AKUTARO: I've just come to see how you are.

UNCLE: I'm sorry to see you intoxicated like this. Why don't you give up this drinking?

AKUTARO: Much obliged for your good advice. I really will.

UNCLE: That's a fine resolution. Give up what you are addicted to.

AKUTARO: Well, I will start abstaining from tomorrow. And now let's have a cup to drink farewell to liquor.

UNCLE: All right, I won't grudge you a farewell drink.

AKUTARO *(drinks five or six cups, babbling on the while)*: Well, well, it's time for me to say good-bye.
   (Goes out and then falls down in a tipsy slumber.)

UNCLE: H'm, he's gone off drunk as usual. Well, I hope he's sleeping peacefully on the road. I'll go out and see. Yes, there he is right enough, blind to the world. I know what I'll do. I'll shave his head and make a priest of him. A fine hedge-priest he'll make. So, I'll write his name on him, "Namu-Amida-Butsu." Now everybody will know him.

AKUTARO *(wakes up and stares in amazement)* : Well, I never—! What's all this? Ah, I suppose the Lord Buddha must have served me out like this!
   (Enters priest.)

PRIEST: Namu Amida Butsu! Namu Ami-i-da Butsu! I Na-a-a-mu Amida Butsu!

AKUTARO: Dear me! He's soon found out my name! What are you calling out for? What d'you want?

PRIEST: Namu Ami-i-da Butsu! Namu Ami-i-da Butsu! Na-a-a-mu Amida Butsu!

AKUTARO: Yah! Yah! Hai! Hai!
  (*The priest goes on chanting and Akutaro answers him.*)

PRIEST: Why on earth do you go on answering like that when I repeat the Nembutsu?

AKUTARO: My name is Akutaro it is true, but while I was lying asleep drunk someone served me in this fashion and wrote this name on me, so I supposed it must be mine, and when I awoke and you came along calling it out I answered.

PRIEST: Well, you are an ignoramus! There is a Buddha called Amida in the Western Paradise, and if you call on his name when you die you will be reborn again there with him; and that's why I am making a pilgrimage through the whole Empire and calling on him everywhere.

AKUTARO: Ah, naturally; you have good reason. I, too, should like to become your disciple and make the pilgrimage with you. Won't you take me?

PRIEST: Certainly. I shall be very pleased. Come along.

AKUTARO: Right. And let's sing a song as we go. (*They sing.*)
Putting away the things of this world,
Fixing our minds on Amida alone,
Chanting the Nembutsu continually,
Thus we go on our pilgrimage.

KABUKI

REVOLVING STAGE

FRONT STAGE

UPPER GALLERY

LOWER GALLERY

BOX

BOXES

BOX

BOX

BOX

BOXES TO SEAT FOUR OR FIVE PERSONS.

FLOWER PATH

THE CHERRY SHOWER

BY TAKAYASU GEKKO

PERSONS OF THE DRAMA

HAIYA SHŌYU	*A WEALTHY LANDOWNER*
HAIYA SABUROBEI	*HIS SON*
HON-AMI KO-ĒTSU	*ARTIST, POTTER, POET AND CRITIC, TEA-MASTER AND ARBITER ELEGANTIARUM OF THE TIME*
KONOE OZAN	*COURT NOBLE AND REGENT OF THE EMPIRE. TEA-MASTER AND AESTHETE*
YOSHINO	*A "TAIYU" OR SINGING-GIRL OF THE FIRST RANK*
KANETSUGU	*A SWORDSMITH*
YŌNOSUKE	*A DISSIPATED YOUNG MAN*
YOĒMON	*A GATE-KEEPER*
GOHEI	*SERVANT OF HAIYA*
GENGO ⎫ NAIKI ⎬ KAMON ⎭	*SAMURAI, RETAINERS OF KONOE*
KOSAKU	*A PUPPET-MAN*
HATSUBANA ⎫ TAMANOI ⎬ YAENO ⎭	*SINGING-GIRLS*

SAMURAI, CITIZENS, SERVANTS, BLINDMEN, BUFFOONS, GIRL ATTENDANTS, ETC.

TIME	THE ERA KWAN-EI, 1624-4

ACT I

SCENE I

Before a Tea-house in the Rokujo quarter

On the left the entrance. A curtain hangs before it on which is a crest of a cherry blossom in a circle done in black on a white ground. A green curtain hangs along the front for a space of twelve feet. In front of this, red rugs are spread on the ground. On the right a lattice front. In the middle of the street there is a mortar placed, and on it a candlestick in which a long candle is burning. The curtain rises on Yōnosuke sitting before the house. He is a young man of about twenty-two or three, dressed in gay clothes with a hood thrown over his head. On the right is the blindman Toku-ichi in a light green crested haori and white hakama, playing the samisen. In front a lot of tea-house girls and buffoons are turning the mortar and dancing and singing:

The trout lurk in the shallows and the birds live in the tree;
And man lives in the shadow of your pity.
The trout lives in the Yoshino River but love dwells in my heart,
But if you don't come I will fling away my pillow;
I'll throw it away though it has done me no wrong!

YŌNOSUKE *(petulantly):* Oh! That's enough ... that's enough!

FIRST BUFFOON: Certainly, sir. And now each of us will show you a very special trick in turn.

YŌNOSUKE: I don't want to see anything of that sort. You hurry up and call Yoshino.

FIRST BUFFOON: But tonight you know—

YŌNOSUKE: Call her, I tell you!

SECOND BUFFOON: Ah, please don't be so impatient. You see she's so immensely popular lately; there's no Taiyu so much in demand. Why, the Lord Konoe and Master Haiya are rivals for her favor. They are both doing all they can to get her.

YŌNOSUKE: Then it's all the more important for me to see her. I'll burst in on the pair of them and carry her off myself now!

FIRST BUFFOON: What's the use of talking like that when one is a great Court noble higher than the clouds, and the other is master of untold wealth?

YŌNOSUKE: That won't stop me from having my say, anyhow. I may never have looked above the clouds perhaps, but the mountain of gold is higher than Mount Fuji, and for one who has had the favor of Takao of Edo and Risei of Osaka—yes, and even been escorted by them right up to the gate—why should Yoshino of Kyoto be so unapproachable? Even if a thing is dear it can be bought, and if it can be bought I will buy it.

SECOND BUFFOON: That might be so with others for all I know, but you won't get Yoshino. No, not for piles and piles of gold. Why, when she takes her seat everyone naturally straightens themselves up respectfully just as though she were the living Buddha of the Temple of Hongwanji. And so they have good reason to do, for she is perfect both in form and face, and accomplished besides in verse-making and tea-ceremony and incense-comparing and flower-arrangement. Her interests are wide and her taste is fine, and, above all, she has a tender heart.

YŌNOSUKE: If her nature is gentle she is the more to be desired. Now, as my mind is so taken up with her, couldn't you just manage for me to see her?

THIRD BUFFOON: Why, how do we know how much you think of her?

YŌNOSUKE: How indeed? Well, then, look here! How many times have I been here this year? Ninety-nine or a hundred or a thousand days or ten thousand. It's all the same. I'll come and come again until I do see her!

FIRST BUFFOON: Now there's a strong attachment if you like! But there's no long grass about here. We have spring weather even on a snowy eve, so you need have no fear of freezing to death! I pray you, therefore, to be patient, and perhaps your luck may turn. Meanwhile won't you call someone else instead tonight?

YŌNOSUKE: Where can I find anyone else in place of Yoshino? You must call her. Where is she today I wonder? I'll go and call her myself.
 (*Starts off.*)

FIRST BUFFOON (*stopping him*): Please wait a moment!

YŌNOSUKE: Oh, get away!
 (*Pushes him away and runs in with the buffoon after him.*)

TOKU-ICHI: What a very impatient gentleman that is!
 (*Exit.*) (*Rin, an upper servant in the house, comes out.*)

RIN (*to the girls*): Now then, you girls, what are you doing here? You are wanted in the guest-room!

SINGING-GIRLS: Hai! Hai!
 (*They run off. Enter Kanetsugu in his soiled working dress. He stares round at the girls.*)

RIN (*fixing her eyes on him*): What does this man want? Come here, please!

KANETSUGU: Yes, yes. There is someone I wish to inquire about.

FIRST GIRL: Oh, who's that?

KANETSUGU: It is the Taiyu Yoshino.

SECOND GIRL: What? The Taiyu Yoshino?

KANETSUGU: Yes. Where is she to be found?

THIRD GIRL: What do you want with her?

KANETSUGU: Er, well—

RIN: He looks like some not very clean artisan. The Taiyu can have no business with such people.

KANETSUGU: Perhaps the Taiyu has not, but I have a little—

FOURTH GIRL: Well, what business is it?

KANETSUGU *(with determination)*: I want to see her and speak with her.

ALL: Ha-ha-ha!

RIN: Ah, he comes from somewhere or other in the country, but he seems to have heard some talk about Yoshino since he mentions her by name. No wonder, when she is so much in demand that even the Lord Konoe with his mountains of money can't make an engagement with her months in advance. To think that a fellow like you can see her is rather good. Why you could hardly produce change for one gold piece if you were turned upside down and shaken. Taiyu indeed! We haven't got anyone here at all that you could afford, so there!

KANETSUGU *(producing a purse)*: Afford? Here are fifty pieces of gold.

RIN: Fifty, eh?

KANETSUGU: I suppose you think that isn't enough, but there's fifty-three days' hard work. Yes, fifty-three blades I forged, scarcely stopping even to sleep. There's sweat and tears mixed with that gold. Won't you let me see her for a moment, even on the other side of the lattice?

FIRST GIRL: Well, you are devoted! I suppose you must have caught a passing glimpse of her sometime or other, eh?

KANETSUGU: Yes, and ever since I saw her I have suffered thus. Merry with my New Year's liquor a friend brought me along just to steal a glance, and that was the beginning of this illusion. Many and many a time have I told myself that it was an impossible thing. The vision of the Taiyu gave me no rest. But if one has money, however lowly, he need not abandon hope, and so I have worked thus madly for a chance of meeting her. There is the proof of my devotion. If it is not enough, nothing remains but to make away with this worthless body of mine.

RIN: That's about it, unless you can make it into that of a great landowner or noble. This Taiyu isn't one you can meet for fifty or a hundred ryo.

KANETSUGU: How can it be done then?

RIN: Ah, in another and luckier rebirth perhaps.
    (*She turns to go in. Kanetsugu stands lost in a disappointed reverie. Enter a Kamuro* from within.*)

KAMURO: The Taiyu herself has heard what you said. She will be pleased to see you.

ALL: What?

KAMURO: She says she will take a cup of wine with you. So please come this way.
    (*Kanetsugu is too overjoyed to utter a word.*)

RIN: Take a cup of wine with him! That's too much. If she will do so much for a fellow like him, how about the many others who have tried in vain to get an interview, even when they have trusted to my assistance!

---

* A girl attendant.

FIRST GIRL: Still, it is nothing but the earnestness of his devotion that has touched her sympathy.

SECOND GIRL: Yes, it is only Yoshino who would do a thing like this.

KANETSUGU: Then may I go in?

KAMURO: Oh yes. Come this way please.

KANETSUGU: Ah, how cold it has become.
    (*Shivers.*)

ALL: Ha-ha-ha!
    (*Stage revolves.*)

SCENE II

Inner apartment of the house. On the left an alcove nine feet long in which hangs a set of three kakemono. Next to it is a chigai-dana six feet long. The sliding doors are decorated in the Momoyama style of painting on a silver ground. On the right is a single leaf screen. On the left sits Konoe Ozan. He is about thirty years old and is dressed in Dōfuku and Kugyo-bakama He is sitting on a cushion, and on the right Naiki and Kamon are in attendance. The girl O-Kan prostrates herself before them.*

O-KAN: We are honored by the presence of your lordship.

KAMON: Your ear a moment! Today we have a very diverting plan.

O-KAN (*leaning towards him*): And what may it deign to be?

KAMON (*whispering*): ... Eh?

---

* Dōfuku: an upper garment worn in private by Court nobles above the rank of Dainagon— superseded by the Haori—worn usually with a white hakama or "sashinuki." Kugyo: Court nobles above third rank—Dayin, Dairagon, Chunagon, Sangi.

O-KAN: How gracious of you! Why any Taiyu would be most delighted I am sure. I'll go and tell them.

(*Exit. Segawa enters with the crab goblet and Tsune carrying the "sake" vessel.*)

NAIKI (*looking at the goblet*): Ah, you always have beautiful things here.

KONOE: In her left hand she carries the crab, and in her right hand the cup for "sake." If a liquor ship had a dancing-floor one could spend a happy life there. How diverting is this idea of the Taiyu of making a goblet in the form of a crab that walks round to the guests and serves the liquor of its own accord without giving anyone any trouble. Really, it quite sums up the views of the ancient classics.

KAMON: It looks like Luchu workmanship.

NAIKI: Her sash is of striped Kwantung material. She always has something out of the ordinary.

KAMON: Ono-no-Komachi and Sei Shonagon and Tora Gozen together could not equal her elegance.

SEGAWA: Please take a cup.

(*She winds up the works of the crab and it runs across and stops in front of Konoe.*)

KONOE: Nay, but even if the crab does run by itself, if the Taiyu herself does not come I shall have no heart to drink.

SEGAWA: Yes, that is your lordship's dearest wish, is it not?

KONOE: Well, everyone awaits the blossoms with impatience.

(*Enter the Taiyu Yoshino. She is twenty-one years old and her hair is dressed in the Tate-Hyōgō style. She is attired, in an outer robe of black with a design of cherry blossom and moneybags in gold and white. Under this is a white kimono with poems dyed*) *into it girt with an obi of Kwantung-striped material. The two Kamuro Koben and Kichiya attend her.*)

YOSHINO: It is long since we had the honor.

KONOE: But that is hardly our fault, is it? Though we pass by the foot of the mountain every eve, the mist hides the heights from our eyes.

YOSHINO: Even though the mist may hide them, your heart itself may be bright enough.

KONOE: When the moon of the heart does not shine wherefore is it that the clouds obscure it?

YOSHINO: On a moon-clouded evening of spring there are still the cherry blossoms. And this is a world where it is not always moonlight.

KONOE: But now that we look on your face it is sunshine enough. An hour of its brilliance is worth a shower of gold.

NAIKI: Flower to flower. Let us show you our dainty surprise.

KONOE: Well, if you are all ready, go on.

KAMON: At your service, my lord. (*To Tsune*): Enter there!

TSUNE: Hai! (*Enters.*)
  (*Hatsubana, Mitsuchiyo, Tamanoi, and Yaeno enter with tubs of plum, peach, and camellia flowers.*)

KONOE: I thought I would perhaps give you a little pleasure today by bringing you the flowers of the Four Famous Places. A little reminiscence of your verse: "Even the rape flower of this quarter, it may be the cherry to me."

HATSUBANA: Now here is the plum blossom from Kitano that comes out first and perfumes the four quarters with its fragrance.

MITSUCHIYO: And then the peach blossom that follows it. For though the glories of the Peach Hill Citadel have long ago fallen to ruin, yet the trees that grew there shall bloom like my name for three thousand ages.

TAMANOI: In the ancient courts of the Camellia Temple never failing are the variegated flowers.

YAENO: The Mirror Flower that reflects your form. From the Bubbling Well Village we have brought it for you.

KAMON: Your own name shall represent the cherry. Therefore from our garden we omit the flower of flowers.

NAIKI: And for flowers like the rape we have no need.

KONOE: Well? Don't you think it is brighter now?
  (*Passes her the cup.*)

YOSHINO: How you have delighted me with this surprise.
  (*Accepts it.*)

KAMON: Come! You mustn't be sparing of the liquor tonight.

KONOE: I won't be sparing of it either. Pledge me then with your own hand from the crab.

SABUROBEI (*coming forward*): Pray, wait a moment. I think it is my turn with the cup.
  (*Haiya Saburobei, a young man of twenty-three, in a crested long garment and woven girdle from which hangs a gold-lacquered Inro, bids one of the jesters wheel in a car of cherry blossoms.*)

KAMON and NAIKI: Ha! What's this?

SABUROBEI: Though we have all the flowers, if the Yoshino cherry is not there, how can we call it a flower-garden? But you have a beauty all your own, and so I lay these other cherry blossoms before you that we may see them blush for themselves. Now which of these flowers pleases you best?

YOSHINO: Indeed, that's hard to say.

SABUROBEI: To bring flowers from all round the capital is no more than an ordinary extravagance, but these are mountain-cherries brought all the way from the very hills of Yoshino.

KAMON: What? From Yoshino in Yamato?

SABUROBEI: Say, then, Taiyu, in which of us two is feeling the most deep?

NAIKI: You can bring cherries from Yoshino with money. What sign is that of deep feeling?

SABUROBEI: Money is nothing where affection is concerned. D'you think flowers will blossom for rank?

KAMON: What's that?

SABUROBEI: Prince or noble or whoever you like; in this quarter there is no distinction. If you can't see how feeling is shown by money, here I am quite ready to explain it.

NAIKI *(starting up)*: How dare you speak so rudely.

KONOE *(checking him)*: Let him alone.

SABUROBEI: Well, fair one, to whom will you give the cup?

YOSHINO: Oh, what am I to say?

KONOE: Yes, the cup?

KO-ĒTSU *(from right)*: I think you had better give it to me.
(*Hon-ami Ko-ētsu is about sixty years old and is dressed in sober-colored costume. He comes forward, pushing aside the attendant O-Kan who tries to stop him.*)

O-KAN: But this is most unreasonable of you!

KO-ĒTSU: Ah, go away!

KONOE and SABUROBEI *(together, looking astonished)*: You! Why—

KO-ĒTSU: Oh, all I came for was just to have a look at this lady, since I have heard so much about her beauty. That is all.

O-KAN: Is not this gentleman strange in his mind?

KO-ĒTSU: Oh, not at all. Moreover, I am quite respectable and no rowdy. And you'll be pleased to hear that I am no deadhead either. Hearing that money would be required I brought out a purse with me. A thing I seldom do. (*Taking it out of his bosom and handing it to O-Kan.*) There, I suppose that will be enough for a view.

O-KAN: Oh, well, perhaps—

KO-ĒTSU *(walking straight up to Yoshino and looking at her face)*: Indeed! Yes, she is beautiful, isn't she?

YOSHINO *(handing the cup to him)*: I pray you do me the honor.

KONOE: That cup!

SABUROBEI: To that old gentleman?

YOSHINO: Yes, certainly.

KONOE: And why?

YOSHINO: Because I think he seems to be without rank or money or love. He looks at me without any bias in his mind and so he has a real discrimination. Is it not so?

KO-ĒTSU: A girl of intelligence too. This is the kind that men go mad about. (*Drinks.*) And what shall I do with this?

YOSHINO: Please give it back to me. How I should like to become your pupil and learn to make my mind clear and cloudless like yours.

KO-ĒTSU: If I return it to you, it will do you no good. That won't do at all, so I think I had better keep it.

O-KAN: This fellow is a pretty grabber. Why, this cup is one of the treasures of the quarter. Do you think we are going to let anyone go off with it?

KO-ĒTSU: The cup is not the only treasure I covet. I should like to go off with this precious Taiyu as well.

O-KAN: What?

SABUROBEI (*impatiently*): It is with me that the Taiyu, is going. (*To O-Kan*): Here are a thousand ryo. (*Puts his hand into the flower-basket and takes out a money chest.*) Give this to your master. There! Now I have bought her out. From this moment Yoshino I belongs to me. No one else has any right to interfere.

KONOE: What's that?

SABUROBEI: Well, lady, get ready! I won't let you stay here a moment longer. We will be off at once.

KO-ĒTSU: And where will you go?

SABUROBEI: To the country house first of all.

KO-ĒTSU: And is the country house your property then?

SABUROBEI: What do you mean?
(*Ko-ētsu draws a document from his bosom and gives it to him.*)

SABUROBEI (*opens and reads it*): What! Disinherited!
  (*Stares in amazement.*)

KO-ĒTSU: Well? Will you buy her out even now?

SABUROBEI: What is it all about? And you—How—?

KO-ĒTSU: Oh, as for me, I happened to call on your honored father and found him extremely agitated. On asking the reason he presently told me that his son did nothing but visit the pleasure-quarter at Rokujo: and not only that but dared there to rival the great Lord Konoe with whose house his family had been on terms of respectful intimacy for many generations, thus forgetting himself in an inexcusable manner, wherefore he had determined to disinherit him at once. Then I implored him to wait until I myself went to see exactly how matters stood, and got him to give me this letter of disinheritance to keep it or to hand it to you according as my judgment should agree with his or not. And so I come to find things stand thus. What an infatuation indeed! But perhaps an excusable one. And so I hand you the letter. Do you still persist in buying her out?

SABUROBEI: How can I cease to love her?

KO-ĒTSU: Then there is nothing to be done. You must be disinherited.

SABUROBEI: Well, as to that—

KAMON: You'd better give it up and go home and stop there–and do watchdog in front of the family moneybags.

SABUROBEI: About money I have no feeling left. But thus penniless how will this lady fare with me in the future?

YOSHINO: What is that you say? Was this not your dearest wish?

SABUROBEI: Well, and what then?

YOSHINO: Thus far the affection of both yourself and his lordship has had a metallic taste, but now there is nothing but your hearts alone, and I have become just a simple girl, no more. Love needs no ornament if deep and true, so now I will choose the life I prefer.

SINGING-GIRLS: And that is?

YOSHINO: Go straight away from here, though after that, who knows? O-Kan! That money: take it!

O-KAN: Yes, I understand.
    (*Takes money in.*)

YOSHINO (*taking off her long outer robe*): Let the house keep this as a memento of me. All the rest you can divide among you.

SINGING-GIRLS: Oh, thank you! How kind!

SEGAWA: And this crab cup?

YOSHINO (*to Ko-ētsu*): I present it to you as a thank-offering for today.

KO-ĒTSU: It is rather late to take it perhaps, but if I leave it there will be more covetousness.

KONOE: And, lady, let me give you this as a parting gift.
    (*Draws from his bosom a fine piece of paper with a poem written on it.*)

YOSHINO (*reads*):
    Ah, this wretched life,
    Brooding o'er its trackless maze,
    Lost in thought I stand.

From amid the mountains, too,
Sounds the deer's yearning cry.

KONOE: I should have written "From the mountain fastnesses" instead of "From amid the mountains," but that slip will make it the more of a masterpiece in future, no doubt: that and the far-famed paper on which it is written.

YOSHINO: Yes, indeed from henceforth I shall have much food for meditation, disturbed by nought but the cry of the deer borne to my couch in our solitary mountain hut. How can I thank you? Whatever may happen in this short life of mine I will never part with it.

KONOE: No need for thanks. If but one small corner of your heart is left for me I am content.

YOSHINO (*standing up*): Then, all my friends, well!

KONOE: Do you go so soon?

KO-ĒTSU: Ah, mountain-cherry briefly blossoming—

KONOE: Like valley-brook that falls and flows away—

YOSHINO: And whither then to go I wonder?

SABUROBEI: And brief indeed was my prosperity!
    (*Stage revolves.*)

SCENE III
Outside the Quarter
    On the left a gate. Beside it the Willow of Parting and the Fence of Farewell. A standing lamp. Outside a tea-house with a sedge-hat hanging up. Rice-fields behind. Within the gate appear the houses with their lighted lanterns. The gate-keeper Yoēmon walking tipsily comes out of the gate, supporting himself on a staff.

YOĒMON: Ah! I'm drunk! I'm drunk! (*Sits down on the seat in front of the tea-house.*) A drink of water, please!

TEA-HOUSE GIRL TO TOSE (*from within*): Ha-i-i. (*Comes out with tea-cup*)
   Ah, Master Yoēmon! You're merry tonight, aren't you?

YOĒMON: Ah, the gate-keeper of this place is no common janitor. It would never do for him to be sober. So I have just had a drop or two.

TOSE: Yes, so it seems. But d'you think you're quite fit for duty?

YOĒMON: Fit? I should think so! You see me take up my stand here and examine everyone who comes by.

TOSE: Oh, but that will be very annoying for them.

YOĒMON: I don't care in the least whether it annoys them or not, so there! Ah, here come all sorts of fellows!
   (*The blindman Tokuichi comes out through the gate.*)

YOĒMON: Halt!

TOKUICHI: Yes? Who is it?

YOĒMON: Who is it indeed? Don't you know who I am?

TOKUICHI: Ah, Master Yoēmon. And is there anything I can do for you?

YOĒMON: There is. I want you to sing "Mount Yoshino."'

TOKUICHI: "Mount Yoshino"? Why I sang it for you just a while ago.

YOĒMON: Perhaps you did. But I won't let you pass till you sing it.

TOKUICHI: What's that you are saying. Oh, excuse me, excuse me. (*Hurries back again.*)

YOĒMON: Ya! Stop! Stop! Funny! Blind men are always swift of foot!
(*The servant Densuke comes out tipsy.*)

YOĒMON: Stop there!

DENSUKE: What's that? Who says, "Stop"? Who dares to tell me to stop?

YOĒMON (*mimicking a Noh-player*): Ha, ha! Descended in the ninth generation from the original Yoēmon, Yoēmon the gate-keeper am I!
(*Stands on guard, striking an attitude with his staff.*)

DENSUKE: Ah, this fellow is trying to be funny, is he? All right. Then I'll take the part of Benkei for you. (*Parodying the speech in "Benkei in the Ship."*) "Here will sword-work naught avail! Grasping his slippers he rattles them between his palms.* On the east Takao Taiyu. On the west Yugiri Taiyu. In the middle Yoshino Taiyu he invokes. Casting their mantle around him, one conjuring and the other conjured, the evil spirit of the gate-keeper draws ever farther from him."
(*The two of them thus caricaturing "Benkei in the Ship," the young samurai Harunojo comes out of the gate accompanied by the singing-girl Hatsubana who is seeing him off*).

---

* The original passage of the Noh "Benkei in the Ship" runs thus:
Here will sword work naught avail
Grasping his rosary
Rattles the beads between his palms
On the East Gosanze
On the South Gudari Yasha
On the West Dai Itoku
On the North Kongo Yasha Mioō
In the Middle Diashe Fudo Mioō
He casts the bond around them
He conjuring, they conjured
The evil spirits
Draw ever further from them.
G. B. Sanson's translation. *Trans. As. Soc. Japan*, vol. xxxviii, p. 3.

YOĒMON: Ah, here are Yoshitsune and Shizuka! Ha! Yoshitsune! Thus strangely met! Upon the waves—

HARUNOJO: Heh! Rude fellow! (*Gives him a push.*)
(*Yoēmon and Densuke go in with quaint gestures.*)

HARUNOJO: H'm, all drunk right up to the gatekeeper. Yes, that's just about the style of this quarter.

TOSE (*bringing out a pair of swords*): These are right, aren't they?

HARUNOJO: Yes.
(*He puts them in his girdle.*)

HATSUBANA: And I shall expect you again tomorrow, eh?

HARUNOJO: I shan't need much pressing.

HATSUBANA: Then, Harunojo San, if it must be—

HARUNOJO: If it must be—

HATSUBANA: Farewell.
(*The two part and Tose goes in again. Kanetsugu comes out of the gate with folded arms.*)

KANETSUGU: Ah, so I have come to the Fence of Farewell. To find a place in one corner of her heart; to be received and pledged in the wine-cup, and then to have to go away and forget, was her kindness merciful or merciless, I wonder? Yes, even though it may be a unique favor, and though I now leave this place, how can I forget? Better perhaps before the ending of this happy day I make this body of mine inanimate as this Willow of Farewell.

TOSE (*coming out with hot water*): Please sit down and rest yourself.

KANETSUGU: No, no! It would not be right to spoil the fragrance of the glorious liquor she so graciously granted me.
  (*Puts down tea-cup.*)

TOSE: Spoil it? Why a little hot water brings back the taste again, doesn't it?

KANETSUGU: That cup shall be my last drink on earth.

TOSE: Don't say such an ill-omened thing!

KANETSUGU: Ill-omened? No! Most auspicious. This is the luckiest day of my life. But if I don't write a word of thanks, she won't even dream of thinking of me again.

TOSE: Ah, and who is she then?

KANETSUGU: That's all right. Please lend me an ink-stone.

TOSE: Certainly, sir. And here is some paper.

KANETSUGU: Then I'll write it in here, I think.
  (*Enters the tea-shop.*)

SONG:
  Think you it is snowing on the Mount of Yoshino?
  It is not the snow you see, it is the cherry petals.
  (*Enter Haiya Shōyu, father of Saburobei. His appearance is that of a citizen of some distinction.*)

SHŌYU (*standing and listening to the song*): H'm! Snow! Flowers! Cherry petals! All things that have got to fall. Yoshino! Wherever I go I hear this name sung. I'm sick of it.

SONG:
  For your sweet sake upon the snow-clad moor I'd lie,
  And nothing reck to take my death of cold.
  (*Shōyu comes up to the front of the tea-house. Kanetsugu comes*

out of it, dropping a letter as he does so. He passes Shōyu and exit. Shōyu looks suspiciously and stumbles over the letter.)

SHŌYU (*picking it up*): What's this? "To Yoshino." What? Yoshino again? (*Opens it hastily—reads*): "In regard to your very deep and most unexpected consideration in receiving me, and even deigning to pledge me in the wine-cup, I am overwhelmed by feelings of gladness and also of sorrow. The clouds of vain longing, alas! Will not clear away from my heart, and so now, while your image still lives before my eyes, I go to cast myself into the River Katsura. Do not, I pray you be angry with me at all, but only pity me, and so shall I go to my end with a joyful heart." Why, bless my soul, this man's going to die! What next? (*Throws the letter down.*) How awful! A woman who can lead people astray like that! Why they can't forget her! And if it comes to not being able to forget her, I wonder whether my son too may not perhaps be in danger of some tragedy like this?

SONG:
    Ah, to forget her, but is there one who can?
    Forever and forever the way of love goes on.
    (*Yōnosuke swaggers out of the gate.*)

SHŌYU: I say, can you tell me where it is that the Taiyu Yoshino lives?

YŌNOSUKE: What's that? Yoshino? Oh! Oh, yes, I'll show you. You come along with me.
    (*Takes the arm of Shōyu.*)

SHŌYU: Here, what are you doing?

YŌNOSUKE: Look here, I'm just going to buy her out.
    (*Pulls him along.*)

SHŌYU: What are you talking about?

YŌNOSUKE: Talking about? Why Yoshino, of course. Of what else should I talk?

SHŌYU: Yah! This fellow's crazy.

YŌNOSUKE: Yes, I'm crazy! I'm going to die too! But I'll kill that fellow first, you see!

SHŌYU: What?

YŌNOSUKE: I'll kill him I tell you. I'll wait for him to come out and cut him down with one blow!

SHŌYU: What madness! Why don't you go back home instead of talking like this. Your parents will be anxious about you.

YŌNOSUKE: I haven't got any parents.

SHŌYU: Oh, I'm very sorry to hear that.

YŌNOSUKE: As I have no parents I can't be disinherited!

SHŌYU: What's that?

YŌNOSUKE: Yoshino is more to me than parents or children or anything. Ah, how I should like to see her face just once again.
   (*Goes back again within the gate.*)

SHŌYU: Well! This one's mad. That one has gone to drown himself. And what of my son, I wonder?

SONG:
   When the thong of my tattered straw hat is broken I can't wear it again, but still I won't throw it away.
   (*Saburobei, his face hidden by a wattle hat, comes out of the gate with Yoshino. Shōyu passes by them.*)

SABUROBEI: I wonder–That looks like—

YOSHINO: What?

YŌNOSUKE *(coming straight up to them from within)*: Ah, Yoshino!
   *(Presses up to them. Shōyu stops him. Konoe comes out behind
   and gazes regretfully after them. Curtain.)*

ACT II

The solitary retreat at Sakura-machi
   *In front, a tokonoma six feet wide in which hangs the poem
written by Konoe. Beneath it is a flower arrangement of hazel
and winter-chrysanthemum. The walls have a dado of plain white
paper, and are stained in places with rain that has leaked in. In
the center of the room is a hearth cut in the floor with a tea-kettle
over it. On the right, a window. A small garden in front with a
water-basin and a few trees bounded by a rough bamboo fence
with a rustic gate. Outside, a road runs lengthwise with some
houses on the other side of it. A withered willow tree and the
Otowa River completes the scene. Saburobei is making pottery. O
Toku is folding the paper for fans. The puppet-man Kosaku appears and shows his puppets before the window.*

SONG:
   Alas, for Tsushio Maru and Anju Hime,*
   Turned out to work by Sansho Taiyu.
   They must go separate ways,
   The brother must go to the hills,
   The sister must stay on the shore.
   Farewell! Come back soon!
   They cry to each other.

SABUROBEI: O Toku! Go and give him something.

YOSHINO: All right.
   (Stands up and looks out.)

---

   * Tsushio Maru and Anju Hime, the children of an exiled noble, were sold to a landlord in Sado named Sansho Taiyu who treated them harshly and made them work at the
hardest tasks—Ancient local tradition of Sado which has become the subject of Jōruri
recitation.

KOSAKU *(looking at her)*: Oh! It's the Taiyu Yoshino, isn't it?

YOSHINO: Do you know me then?

KOSAKU: Well, I haven't exactly the honor of your acquaintance, but I have been called to the house you used to be in two or three times for performances. But what a change! (*Looking round.*) There's some difference between this place and where you were before, isn't there?

YOSHINO: Yes, and as they say, one's spirits change with one's surroundings. I feel quite at home and free from care here.

KOSAKU: Ah yes, you won't find much to bother you in a place like this. I'm pretty free from care too, going round with my puppets, and I hope to call on you again before long.

YOSHINO: Yes, please do.
   (*Takes a pin from her hair and gives it to him.*)

KOSAKU: Oh! What a beautiful pin! But I don't like to take a costly thing like this. You are too generous. A few halfpence would suit me much better, really.

YOSHINO: But I haven't got even a few halfpence, so please take this instead.

KOSAKU: What? Not got even a few halfpence! Oh! Ah well, that's lucky for me anyhow, so I will accept your kind offer. But this is a change indeed—after what you have been used to. Even worse than the fate of Anju Hime.
   (*Starts his puppets again.*)

SONG:
   On the beach the little princess
   Drops the salt-water pails she has no strength to carry.
   Longingly she looks to the hills for her brother,
   And he is too weak to cut the brushwood,

And slips and stumbles on the rocks and tree-roots.
She fears he will fall down into the valley—
Both weep and lament on hill and strand.
Ah! In this case the puppet-man feels the pathos of it more
than the audience. (*Exit looking very sorrowful.*)

SABUROBEI: Oh dear! What a bother it is to be known to all the world.

YOSHINO: Yes, and so it is a good thing that we came to such a quiet place among the hills, isn't it?

SABUROBEI: Perhaps so, but it is not a very good place for business. I mean to make a living somehow or other even by this poor clay daubing, but in this mountain hamlet we may have to dress in leaves and eat berries, for all I know.

YOSHINO: Well, the hermit Kanzan and the Mountain Lady living together would be a new subject for the painters.

SABUROBEI: Ha-ha-ha-ha!
    (*Enter Gohei, servant of the Haiya family.*)

GOHEI: Is anyone at home?

YOSHINO: Ah, Gohei San? Please come in.

GOHEI (*enters the room*): So you are hard at it, sir?

SABUROBEI: If your hands aren't busy here your mouth suffers.

GOHEI: Master seems quite hardened to this, er—low water, eh?

SABUROBEI: I may be hardened to it, but I haven't taken it at the flood yet. You get pretty well buffeted in the sea of life at times.

GOHEI: But haven't you any mind to come back to the safe refuge of the paternal bark?

SABUROBEI: I may not be without such an idea perhaps, but that little word disinheritance is somewhat of a bar, isn't it?

GOHEI: Ah, but that disinheritance isn't irrevocable. If master wished —

SABUROBEI: What d'you mean? If I wished?

GOHEI (*looking at Yoshino and hesitating*): Well, that's rather difficult to explain here.

YOSHINO: Oh, I'll go and get some tea, I think.
(*Exit.*)

SABUROBEI: How is it difficult to explain?

GOHEI: Well, it's er—that lady, you see.

SABUROBEI: And what about her?

GOHEI: Well, if master would give her up.

SABUROBEI: What?

GOHEI: Perhaps my clumsy way of speaking may offend the master, but whatever you say the Taiyu is the cause of all this trouble, and as long as she stays with you things must remain as they are, and however painful your circumstances may be I don't see how your father can alter his decision. Now I don't know what the master may think about it, but if she were to be sent away that would be, at any rate, a proof that you had repented, and then, if the family put their heads together in the matter of intercession, I have no doubt that everything would be all right.

SABUROBEI: Pooh, Gohei you were born in poverty and you've spent all your life up till now as a servant in our family. You've never spent any money, and so you don't know anything about the value of it. I should like to stick you in the place of Konoe for a few days.

GOHEI: Eh?

SABUROBEI: I may have spent a little money, but now I come to think it over it was the money that was amusing itself. All the flattery and adulation was merely for the money, but my real self was not there. It had flown away somewhere—up to the seventh heaven perhaps. But when the money had taken itself off and there was none left, then, in amazement, I came back to myself, and did so with a complete understanding of human nature and the real zest of life. True, in my father's house there is a lot of money, but while I was living there, even before I took to frequenting the gay quarter, I was quite without my soul, for I was just a well-behaved watch-dog of money-bags. Now I have to get along without a penny in my pocket, but in this rough hut I am master of my soul. I have a calm deep-rooted appreciation of things, and palace and thatched cottage are all the same to me. Ah, and never knew till now the proper taste of powder-tea!

GOHEI: But this is frivolous talk!

SABUROBEI: What d'you mean? Frivolous talk indeed! Here, let me offer you a cup, you unenlightened fellow.

GOHEI: No thanks. I have no need of it.

SABUROBEI *(producing two tea-bowls)*: Look here! This tea-bowl was brought back from Korea by the great General Kato Kiyomasa when he helped to conquer it in the sixteenth century, and by him presented to his lord the Taiko Hideyoshi. And it was highly approved by Sen-no-Rikyu the chief of all tea-masters. A thousand pieces of gold would not buy it. And this is one that I have made myself after studying it and so absorbing its rhythmic harmony of form that it has become a part of me. These two vessels are just like what I was in former days and now. When I was at home and in affluence I was like this Rikyu tea-bowl: a famous object enough to be kept in a box, but without any bottom, and quite useless either for tea or water. Now I am just a bowl of soft pottery of no intrinsic value, but complete and able to hold the zest of life.

GOHEI: Ah, but tea must taste better if it is drunk out of a cup worth a thousand pieces.

SABUROBEI: What do you mean? Taste better! You don't understand in the least!

GOHEI: I think it must be master who does not understand. Now, why not try and see things in the proper light?

SABUROBEI: What proper light? There!
   (*Strikes the Rikyu tea-bowl with his pipe so that it breaks in two.*)

GOHEI (*amazed at him*): Oh! What have you done? It's worth a thousand pieces!

SABUROBEI: Ha-ha-ha! Broke! Yes, that's just like me when I wasted all my substance in riotous living, Great man or precious pot, it's all the same; they'll break quickly enough. Just give them one whack!

GOHEI: Ah, what a pity! What a loss! What a waste of money!

SABUROBEI: Yes, there's no more money value in it now however well you may mend it, it will never be what it was before. But if you make a new one like this. There's elegance for you! And your tea will have as fine a taste as you could wish.

GOHEI: How will it have a good taste?

SABUROBEI: Oh, you dolt, you haven't the least glimmer of understanding! Here! Do have a cup for goodness sake.

GOHEI: Er—thank you very much, but that's all right. Next time I come perhaps—

SABUROBEI: Oh, people who don't like tea had better stay away from here!

GOHEI: Excuse me. I am very sorry to have troubled you. (*As he goes out of the gate*)
  Ah, what a pity that he should still remain so deluded.
  (*Exit with an air of dejection. Yoshino comes in again.*)

SABUROBEI: Well. Did you hear what he said? That's a fellow it's no good arguing with.

YOSHINO: Whatever happens you will still—?

SABUROBEI: How should I think of leaving you.

YOSHINO: But we've hardly enough to keep a wreath or two of smoke above the eaves, much less can we think of anything in the way of comforts.

SABUROBEI: Even if I starve it will be with Paradise within me.

YOSHINO: Ah, but that splendid home of yours!

SABUROBEI: Mere stones and tiles where no affection is.

YOSHINO: But this bare-plastered solitary hut—

SABUROBEI: It is a very happy wretchedness.

YOSHINO: You really mean it?

SABUROBEI: Why should I tell a lie to you?

YOSHINO: Ah!
  (*Bursts into tears*)

SABUROBEI: Ah, now I have come to savor the "patina" of life.
  (*Sound of a flute. Saburobei gets up and goes out taking the tea-bowl with him.*)

YOSHINO (*going to the gate and looking after him*): The moon in the west, and you going off toward the sunrise at early dawning. That was the way we used to part before. But now we are together all day long, and even this unaccustomed work is not very hard. So for your sake I'll face the trials of this fleeting world, for I can trust you never to leave me. Even though the snow beat through our broken fence. Still women will brood over things, and their minds are always full of thoughts of their former life. Ah well, now I will put on the kettle so that the sound of its boiling recalls the song of the wind in the pines.

(*Goes up stage and busies herself with the tea utensils. The stage makes a half turn. Enter two townsmen talking.*)

ICHISUKE (*peeping in at the gate*): Yes. She's in. Taiyu! Taiyu San!
(*Yoshino takes no notice but goes on putting in charcoal.*)

FUTAHACHI: Yoshino-han! Yoshino-han!
(*She still pays no attention but puts on the kettle.*)

ICHISUKE: Didn't you hear me call her Taiyu and yet she doesn't answer. Since she doesn't even look up when I address her so respectfully I suppose she must have become deaf. Perhaps this noisy river, for that's what Otowa-gawa means, you know, has made her deaf. Perhaps the people in this valley are all deaf.

FUTAHACHI: Ha-ha!
(*Enter Yōnosuke hastily, dressed as a mendicant priest beating on a gourd.*)

YŌNOSUKE (*standing outside the gate*): Namu Amida Butsu! Namu Amida Butsu! (Hail, Amida Buddha!)

ICHISUKE: Ya-ah! You can tap there as long as you like they're deaf there, so they can't hear you.

YŌNOSUKE: Indeed?

FUTAHACHI: Yes. Formerly the Taiyu Yoshino in all her glory, now she has gone to the dogs and is as deaf as a post!

YŌNOSUKE: What d'ye say? Yoshino? Is this the Taiyu's house then?

ICHISUKE: That it is, sure enough.

YŌNOSUKE: Oh, how lucky! What happiness.
　(*Tries to rush in.*)

ICHISUKE (*stopping him*): Here! What are you up to?

YŌNOSUKE: To see the Taiyu, of course!

FUTAHACHI: This is a devoted sort of fellow, isn't he?

YŌNOSUKE: Because of my devotion I put on this pilgrim garb, and thus in altered guise I wandered every where in search of her.

ICHISUKE: Well, you're a cleverer fellow than we, no doubt, but now she's another man's wife you see, so you must be careful what you do.

YŌNOSUKE: What of that? What do I care? I mean to see her at all costs and pour out on her to my heart's content all the hatred that has been accumulating all this time.

FUTAHACHI: What terrible resolution! But what is this hatred about?

YŌNOSUKE: What's it about? That's pretty obvious. Didn't I visit her time after time, so great was my attachment, and she would not deign even to let me see her once. And then to let herself be bought out and come and live in seclusion in a place like this. Isn't that enough to make anyone hate her?

ICHISUKE: Oh yes, but you were not the only one were you?

YŌNOSUKE: Does anyone else feel the hate that I do? You there, Taiyu! You may try to get rid of me, but I won't go!
(*Looks in.*)

FUTAHACHI: I don't like this. He's an uncanny fellow.

ICHISUKE: This crazy drumming pilgrim amuses me. Here! Let's see you dance. If you dance the Taiyu is sure to look at you.

YŌNOSUKE: Do you really think so?

FUTAHACHI: Oh yes, of course.

ICHISUKE: He's dancing. Just look!

FUTAHACHI: So he is. Well I never!

SONG:
When I listen to the Harmony of the Universe
In the mountain blast rings the sound of her harp.
When I contemplate the Unity of Phenomena
In the murmur of the streamlet I hear her voice.
While you still abide in this World of Impermanence
How can I think it but vanity and pain?
Though the Angel of Death arise before me
And bid me go forth straight to hell
So great is my desire to be with you
That I should scarcely heed his summons.
Over the eastern hills rises the smoke at sunset,
On the north peaks the dew falls morning and evening
Our days in this life may be long or short,
But all save love is a transient dream.
And as I sing even the Buddha assumes your shape.
Namu Amida! Namu Amida! Namu Amida!
(*Dances and taps his gourd.*)

BOTH THE OTHERS: Ha-ha-ha! How droll! Well, we must be off.
(*Start off.*)

YŌNOSUKE: Ah, won't you get the Taiyu to meet me?

ICHISUKE: The Taiyu can't see and can't hear. She has in fact become one of the Three Not-hearing Not-seeing and Not-speaking Monkeys, you see.

BOTH: Ha-ha-ha!
  (*Exit.*)

YŌNOSUKE: Oh, what liars they are! Hi! Stop, stop!
  (*Runs after them. The sound of rain. Enter Shōyu accompanied by a boy without an umbrella.*)

SHŌYU: It's a regular downpour! Run and get an umbrella somewhere!

BOY: Certainly, sir.
  (*Runs off.*)

SHŌYU: Well, I'll take shelter under those eaves over there. (*Goes over in front of the window. Smells the incense.*) Ah, that's choice. (*Listening.*) Yes, there's the sound of a kettle. H'm, this is an elegant sort of cottage.

YOSHINO (*looking out of the window*): Oh, you'll get wet there. Won't you come inside, please?

SHŌYU: Thank you very much.

YOSHINO: It doesn't look like stopping yet. Please make yourself at home here for a while. Please, this way.

SHŌYU (*entering and standing in the doorway*): Then please excuse me. I'm sorry I can't help troubling you

YOSHINO: But pray come in. Please don't stand on ceremony.

SHŌYU: Well, since you are so kind I will ask you to excuse my rudeness. I am indeed most impolite to intrude.

(*Enters the room and sits down, looking about him the while. A harp is heard in the distance. Yoshino makes tea and serves it.*)

SONG:
> The cherry blossoms are like falling snow,
> But whose tears are falling in the shower?
> This poor makeshift cottage is our fate.
> For this life is a dream even if we know it not.
> To shun this life entirely would be well,
> But even if we make the best of it,
> 'Tis but a sepia sketch of the sound of the wind in the pines.

SHŌYU (*sitting in front of the alcove and looking at the hearth*): Ah, that's a rare piece of writing on that scroll "From amid the mountains, too, sounds the deer's yearning cry." And this shower just gives the right effect of light dew. The sound of the bubbling of the water in the kettle made by a master recalls the breaking of the waves on the shore by some lonely temple. And the tea-bowl, it is by the great Ko-ētsu, is it not?

YOSHINO: Oh no. That is my husband's work.

SHŌYU: Ah, that makes it the more interesting. Just like the one splash of color of the maples in autumn when the sun sets on the deep green of the fir-clad hills, and everything is all calm and still. Yes, this tea-drinking has been very, very charming.

YOSHINO: I am embarrassed by your kind remarks. And will you not take another cup?

SHŌYU: Thank you, that is just enough. A most delightful entertainment when I came in thus unexpectedly. Excuse the rudeness of my remarking it, but you seem to have no help. (*Looking round the room.*) The master is not at home perhaps.

YOSHINO: No, he has gone out for a little while.

SHŌYU: And there are just the two of you?

YOSHINO: Yes, that is all.

SHŌYU *(picking up a verse written on a slip of paper)*: Eh, what's this?

Through the broken window comes the scent of the rain,

Sweeter by far than the rarest incense of China.

Ah, how exquisite! That's the very essence of taste! One who re-tires from the world merely for amusement, and lives in idleness to kill time, is a waster of good rice, a mere drone. If the love of solitude is not reinforced by strong character, the hermit's life is a living death. But here, how different. You have occupation and amusement also. A quiet, restful gray relieved by the brightness of a single flower. That's the proper contrast. That's the real he-donism. That's the very spirit of Teaism. Well, your husband is a fine fellow but I have an only son who likes liquor better than tea and knows more about wasting money in sprees than he does about the way of the aesthete. In fact he has played the fool to such an extent that at last I have had to disinherit him.

YOSHINO: Ah, and what did he do then?

SHŌYU: I know nothing more about him. He's disappeared and I don't know what he's doing.

YOSHINO: And why don't you forgive him?

SHŌYU: That I cannot do. What would be the good of him if he came home? I want a man in my house, not a fool who doesn't know how to live.

YOSHINO: But if he were to become enlightened?

SHŌYU: Well, even then there is another reason.

YOSHINO: And that reason is—

SHŌYU: That reason is—er—I'd rather not say what it is.

YOSHINO: And how long will things remain like that?

SHOYU: H'm. They'll have to be left like that I'm afraid.

YOSHINO: What, for the rest of his life?

SHŌYU: You may think me hard-hearted perhaps, but that is the way of the world. If a man isn't cultivated in his inner self he won't be any good either to himself or his family. 'Tisn't entirely that he wasn't taught, but he had everything he wanted, and so he grew selfish and wayward and fell an easy prey to women's attractions. Yes, I wonder what has become of him. I wonder whether he is still deluded or perhaps he now understands his folly. He may be mad or dead, for all I know. In the long autumn evenings, as the weather grows colder and colder, I lie awake and think of him, he may be wandering aimlessly about the city wretched and out-at-heels, or toiling painfully to keep body and soul together in some far-off province. Then when his strength and his hopes fail him there will be nothing to look forward to but a miserable old age. Ah, how many tears have I not shed in secret thinking of it (*Wipes his eyes.*) But I am ashamed of myself giving way to this selfish and querulous talk.

YOSHINO: Pray don't mention it. I quite sympathize with your feelings. It is very natural. Now please let me give you another cup (*putting in some more tea*)

SHŌYU: Thank you very much.
    (*Konoe's retainer Gengo enters hurriedly.*)

GENGO: Are you the master here?

SHŌYU: Oh no. I am but a chance-comer.

GENGO: Where is he then?

YOSHINO: He has just gone out for a while. Have you any business with him?

GENGO: I should think so! You'd better produce him at once. Hurry!

YOSHINO: Oh! What do you mean! What is it all about? I don't understand.

GENGO: Don't try and deceive me! It's about that Rikyu tea-bowl.

YOSHINO: Oh?

GENGO: Yes, you know very well! We ordered him to repair it carefully, and what does he do but make a copy of it and then deliberately break the original. I never heard of such an impudent rascal! Don't bandy words with me! Bring him here at once!

YOSHINO: Yes, it's true enough that he broke it.

GENGO: You admit it, do you? Why that only makes it worse! Such insolence is unpardonable! Think of it! A treasure among treasures like this that you couldn't buy for a thousand or ten thousand pieces of gold. Do you think its being broken is a thing that can be by any means overlooked? Do you suppose I dare go and tell my lord that it has been broken? Certainly I must expiate my carelessness in the matter by cutting open my belly, and that I think nothing of, but that is not enough. If I don't lay your husband's head before my lord first his anger will hardly be appeased. So bring him out without more ado!

YOSHINO: Yes, but he has not come back yet. Meanwhile let me give you a cup of tea.

GENGO: D'you think this is a time to be drinking tea? What on earth led him to break it, eh?

YOSHINO: That's a difficult question.

GENGO: You'd better tell the truth.

YOSHINO: It's not easy to say.

GENGO: Then you refuse to tell me?

YOSHINO: Why should I tell you lies?

GENGO: Then why was it?

YOSHINO: Well

GENGO: Well?

YOSHINO: Well

GENGO: Well, if you have nothing to say, prepare yourself!

YOSHINO (*nodding assent*): Very well, then, pray take me with you on the dark road.

GENGO: What's that?

YOSHINO: The mistake was mine.

GENGO: Yours?

YOSHINO: If a life must be given, take my head instead of my husband's, and so let atonement be made.

GENGO: H'm, that's a good resolution. Then sit up properly!
    (*Draws.*)

YOSHINO (*lifting up the tea-bowl*): Just a last sip.
    (*Drinks calmly. To Shōyu*)
    And after I am gone may I ask you to give my regards---

SHŌYU: Oh, please, wait a moment! I don't quite understand what it is all about, but, anyhow, surely there must be a way out of this without the necessity of giving a life in exchange for a broken Rikyu tea-bowl, however rare and precious? Can you not give some suitable explanation?

YOSHINO: I don't know exactly how it came about, but from what I heard I think it happened thus. The tea-bowl was so badly broken that if it were mended and a new bottom made of clay of a different period and quality, there would be no harmony in it any longer, so after saturating himself with its rhythm and form he made another in the same spirit, and thinking that the original was so damaged as to be useless, and might lend itself to deception, he smashed it to bits.

SHŌYU: Well done! Capital! That's just right! That shows the very spirit of the philosophy of tea. To drink in the feeling and rhythm of a famous tea-bowl and create another in the same inspiration, and then destroy the damaged original instead of cherishing the dead thing reverently, simply because it is the original, that is a thing worthy of one of the masters of the Zen philosophy, of one who understands that the only important thing in life is not to take it seriously, for all is illusion.
(*To Gengo*)
I don't know who your honored lord may be, but I think that if you make report to him of all this as it is the matter may be settled peaceably.

GENGO: The explanation seems to me rather obscure, but anyhow I will report it to my lord. And I will come back soon to tell you what his august opinion may be, so don't hide or run away.

YOSHINO: I am not likely to do any such cowardly thing.

GENGO: Right. Then I shall have the honor again before long, I think.
(*Exit.*)

YOSHINO: It is by your kind aid that the consequences are not serious so far. I am indeed grateful.

SHŌYU: Oh, that is nothing. But I am rather anxious as to what he will say when he returns, so if you will allow me I will come again to inquire. I trust you will conceal nothing from me.

YOSHINO: I shall indeed be pleased to see you.

SHŌYU: Ah, the weather has just cleared up. Well, I have never seen tea better served.
(*Goes out. The stage makes a half revolution and brings the window to the left side. There is a view of Mount Otowa. Ko-ētsu approaches.*)

KO-ĒTSU: Ah, Master Shōyu? And whither away!

SHŌYU: Ah, Master Hon-ami! Now I wonder who he may be.

KO-ĒTSU: And whom do you mean by he?

SHŌYU (*pointing to the window*): The master of this house. A rough cottage, it is true, but what taste. And a wife who understands life and the tea-ceremony too and who treats her husband like a lover. Bless my soul, I never admired anything so much!

KO-ĒTSU: Ha-ha-ha! And whom do you think?

SHŌYU: The natural son of some great noble, perhaps; there is such an air of dignity about everything.

KO-ĒTSU: Oh no; someone quite different.

SHŌYU: Well, it might be some Ronin. Some exiled gentleman of the military class, if one might judge by the air of determination she wore.

KO-ĒTSU: Wrong again.

SHŌYU: Such elegance and grace indeed! She looked just as if she were taken out of some old picture of Court life. Can she be some beautiful apparition or changeling, I wonder?

KO-ĒTSU: Ha-ha-ha! That's Yoshino.

SHŌYU: Eh? (*Looks incredulous.*)

KO-ĒTSU: Yes. The lady your son is so much in love with.

SHŌYU: Eh?
  (*Stands in astonishment.*)

KO-ĒTSU: Well, what d'you think of her? You don't dislike her do you?

SHŌYU: Well, I never expected such a thing!

KO-ĒTSU: You'd better revoke your sentence of disinheritance.

SHŌYU: Well, well! A lady of such dignity! And a life of such elegant simplicity! My son's ideas seem to have assumed some stability, but as to taking him back, there is still one thing—

KO-ĒTSU: What Konoe will think? Set your mind at ease there. I have just been to his mansion, and he showed me a certain tea-bowl and asked my opinion of it. When I examined it I saw that it was something out of the common. If Rikyu himself saw it he would be satisfied. So I told him it was a splendid piece of craftsmanship. Then he remarked that it was your son's work, and declared that his breaking the original and making a completely new one was most praise-worthy and showed the temper of a true artist. So you need not hesitate any longer.

SHŌYU: Well, I am obliged to you. Then I have nothing more to say.

KO-ĒTSU: Then you had better have another interview with her, I think. (*Stage moves back again as before.*) Yoshino Sama!
(*Goes in.*)

YOSHINO (*coming out*): Hai-i-i-i. Oh, it is you—

KO-ĒTSU: From now you are the real daughter of your husband's family.

YOSHINO: What? (*Looks surprised.*)
(*Enter Saburobei.*)

SABUROBEI (*seeing Shōyu*): Oh! Father!
(*Runs to him.*)

SHŌYU: Saburobei!

KO-ĒTSU: You're forgiven. Isn't that fine?

SABUROBEI: Is that really true? Thank you very much.

SHŌYU: Not at all.
(*To Yoshino*)
This is your doing.

KO-ĒTSU: Yoshino, like the cherry petals, has fallen to the ground, but may be said to have washed her robes quite white again in the surging billows of this world's troubles.

SABUROBEI: But in the home to which we now return she will find real peace of mind.

YOSHINO: My former life has been a sinful one, I fear.

SHŌYU: Ah well, the greater the contrast the greater the happiness. This life is nothing but a sudden shower of rain!
(*All smile happily. Curtain.*)

THE POTTER KAKIĒMON

BY ENOMOTO TORAHIKO
PERSONS OF THE DRAMA

ARITAYA GOHEI	*PORCELAIN-DEALER OF IMARI*
O IMA	*HIS WIFE*
HEISABURO	*HIS SON*
OSHIGE	*HIS DAUGHTER*
YOKURU	*HIS CLERK*
DENROKU	
TORASUKÉ	*SHOPMEN*
EIKICHI	
O MAKU	*A MAIDSERVANT*
MATSUTARO	*AN APPRENTICE*
NAKASATO HYŌDAIYU	*A SAMURAI, FORMERLY RETAINER OF THE LORD MATSUURA*
ASAKAYA	*HIS WIFE*
O CHIYO	*HIS DAUGHTER*
SAKAIDA KAKIĒMON	*MASTER POTTER*
O TSU	*HIS ELDER DAUGHTER*
O TANÉ	*HIS YOUNGER DAUGHTER*
KURISAKU	*HIS PUPIL*
ZENGORO	
RIEMON	*POTTERS*
BUNZO	
TIME	*MIDDLE OF THE SEVENTEENTH CENTURY.*

ACT I

The establishment of the wholesale porcelain-dealer, Aritaya Gohei, at Imari in Hizen. On the right of the stage is seen the front of a godown. Through its front and back doors, which are both open, is a distant view of the bright blue sea. To the left of the godown is a six-foot entrance with a shop-curtain hanging before it. Next to this is the raised and matted shop-front with shelves full of porcelain, and in the middle a desk with a lattice surround in Osaka style, while further round to the left are the sliding-doors of the entrance. On the mats are a brazier and cushions as usual. The shopman Denroku is sitting writing accounts in the shop while Eikichi and Torasuké are making up packages in front of the godown. The curtain rises to the sound of the singing and piping that accompany a Matsuri or Shinto festival.

EIKICHI: I say, Torasuké, do you hear the music? Everyone else is taking a holiday and we seem to be the only ones at work.

TORASUKÉ: I suppose you arranged to go to the Matsuri with one of the girls over the way, so that's why you keep on grumbling about it.

EIKICHI: Dear me, no, nothing so romantic. It's only because master never considers us, that I can't help a growl slipping out.

TORASUKÉ: Ah, well, better put up with it a little longer.

DENROKU: Eikichi! The *Daikoku Maru* is sailing tonight. Sorry to trouble you, but please go down and tell them that we still have some more packages left to go to Nagasaki.

EIKICHI: All right, I'll see to it.
   (*He shoulders a package and goes out through the godown. The servant O Maru comes out through the shop-curtain and is going across to the interior behind the shop, when Denroku stops her.*)

DENROKU: The guests don't seem in any hurry to go, do they?

O MARU: Indeed they don't. The master and mistress seem as though they can't do enough for them. I expect they won't go home till this evening.
   (*Vanishes into the house.*)

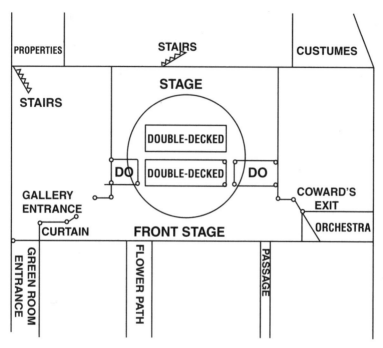

Plan of a Kabuki theater of the late eighteenth century. Revolving stage originated about 1760.

TORASUKÉ: And who may these very particular guests be then?

DENROKU: Oh, Nakasato Hyōdaiyu Sama, formerly a retainer of high rank in the service of the Lord Matsuura of Hirado. Accompanied by his wife and his daughter, so help me.

TORASUKÉ: Ah, then that long-sleeved young miss is to be the wife of the young master, I'll be bound.
    (*Enter the apprentice Matsutaro.*)

MATSUTARO: Jolly nice, isn't it? The young master to drink the marriage cup with that sweet plump little long-sleeved maiden! Makes you envious, doesn't it, Denroku San?

DENROKU: Yah! What are you babbling about now? Envious! What is it to me?

MATSUTARO: Well, then, you can take O Tsu San. Pleasant disposition and quite nice-looking. Would make a very good wife, I think. The only question is: Would she consent? That's what you can't be quite certain about.

DENROKU: Look here! Who put you up to all this saucy nonsense?

TORASUKÉ: Bah! You can't do anything with children these days. They say what they like. This young imp is forever trying to get the better of me too. But I say, Denroku San, it may be very nice for him to marry this young lady, but what about O Tsu San.

DENROKU: Yes, that's just it. It's awfully hard on her. You know the master must have intended to make her his son's wife or he wouldn't have got Kakiēmon to let her come and live here like that. But now he's got on in the world a bit, he naturally looks for something higher than an artisan's daughter.

MATSUTARO: That's a damned reason, isn't it? Take it all round, the guv'nor's an outrageous old man, isn't he? (*His voice rises involuntarily.*) Oh! Don't let it go any farther!
   (*Runs out holding his mouth with his hand. Just then O Ima is heard calling inside the house.*);

O IMA: O Tsu! O Tsu! Whatever is O Tsu doing?

TORASUKÉ: Ah, there's that noisy mistress shouting about the house again!

DENROKU: Well, that's nothing new. I say, lend us a hand.
   (*The two of them carry the package into the godown. Enter O Ima from the door on the left with her daughter O Shigé. She is a woman of some forty-five or six, and is dressed as such. Her manner is fidgety.*)

O IMA: O Tsu! O Tsu! Where can O Tsu have got to? And I so busy with my guests too.

SHIGE: I expect she's seeing to things in the kitchen. There's no need for you to call out like that, mother.

O IMA: What can she be doing? I can't think. O Tsu! O Tsu!
(Enter O Tsu from the curtained entrance. She is dressed in a striped kimono with an apron and her hair is done in Shimada style.)

O TSU: Yes, here is O Tsu.

O IMA: Well, that's something anyhow. But why can't you be a little sharper. Can't you see there's more to do on a Matsuri than on ordinary days. Ah, well, servants are all alike. And now go on into the house and wait on the guests.
(Hustles her off. Just then Heisaburo comes in from the house. He is dressed like a young merchant, and wears haori without hakama.)

HEISABURO : O Tsu is not a servant, mother.

O IMA: How absurd you are, Heisaburo. If O Tsu is not a servant in this house, what is she then, I should like to know?

HEISABURO: She is the honored daughter of Kakiēmon to whom this house is very much beholden, and she must be treated exactly the same as O Shigé.

O IMA: What do you mean? O Shigé is the daughter of the house. How can they be treated alike?

HEISABURO: Suppose she is. I think it's rather too bad of you, mother. You seem to forget to whom it is we are indebted for this fortune of ours.
(O Ima is at a loss for a reply. O Tsu comes forward.)

O TSU: Oh no, it was my fault. I was so stupid, and the mistress naturally got irritated with me. I don't at all mind going and waiting on the guests. Really I don't.
(Turns to go, but Heisaburo stops her.)

HEISABURO: Then let O Shigé go too and help her. She must not go alone.

O SHIGE: Yes, certainly I'll go. And that will be quite enough. O Tsu can go on with what she was doing.

O TSU: Oh, no. I'll go and wait. You stay here.

O SHIGE: No, no. Do go back to the kitchen, please.

O TSU: Very well. It's very kind of you.
    (*O Tsu goes back through the curtain and O Shigé enters the house. As she goes in Gohei comes out. He is an elderly tradesman dressed in haori without hakama.*)

GOHEI: What's this you're talking about? Did I hear you say that the Aritaya was under an obligation to Kakiēmon ?

HEISABURO: Yes. That's what I said.

GOHEI: Well, you're a fool. It was I who had the brains to think of taking the dishes he made to Nagasaki and selling them to the Hollanders, and so making his name known even in foreign countries. And then how about the fifteen years he spent trying to get the red designs of the Wan Li period of Ming? Kakiēmon could not get enough to eat then, and he might have starved to death if it had not been for my kindness in coming to his assistance.

O IMA: Yes, and we took his daughter in and looked after her as well. The least she can do is to work hard in the house for her living.

HEISABURO: That's rather too much, mother. When father took O Tsu into our family there was no question of her becoming a servant.

GOHEI: Oh, you know that, do you.

HEISABURO: Well, I couldn't help speaking out, especially as it is to your credit.

(*He looks defiantly at them, when Nakasato Hyōdaiyu comes into the shop from the house. He is in haori and hakama with two swords, dressed as becomes a samurai of some rank.*)

HYŌDAIYU: Oh, I'm afraid I have intruded on a private discussion of family affairs. Pray excuse me.

GOHEI: Not at all. We don't mind in the least. (*Turns toward the house.*) Here! Why doesn't someone bring the cushions?

HYŌDAIYU: Oh, please don't trouble. (*The maid brings in cushions and Hyōdaiyu sits down.*) You have been most hospitable to us today and we have enjoyed ourselves very much, especially my stupid wife and daughter.

GOHEI: We invited you for our shrine festival, but I'm afraid it is a poor sort of affair, and you must find it rather tiresome.

O IMA: But please make yourself quite at home and enjoy yourselves as much as you can.

GOHEI: Yes, I fear your honored wife and daughter must be rather bored. You and Heisaburo had better go in and keep them company.

O IMA: Indeed it is most inexcusable of me to neglect my guests so much.

HEISABURO: I have a little business in the shop, so I will follow you in a few minutes.

O IMA: Then please excuse me.
(*With a bow to Hyōdaiyu she goes in. Heisaburo goes to the shop.*)

HYŌDAIYU: Well, Gohei Dono, as I was telling you a while ago, my daughter Chiyo is by maternal descent the grandchild of Narimatsu Tōtōmi-no-kami, a warrior whose fame spread far and wide, and whose pedigree our family has in its keeping. And we are willing that she should become your daughter-in-law as you wish; and you understand, I think, the condition on which we consent.

GOHEI: The condition you allude to is, I think, er–a marriage allowance for your daughter and an annuity to be paid to yourself, is it not?

HYŌDAIYU: Indeed I blush with shame to mention such things, but please consider my straitened circumstances, I have had several proposals for my daughter's hand from good samurai families, but I have been compelled to refuse them because my poverty has made it impossible for me to give her the outfit that would be necessary for the wife of a retainer of a feudal lord. So I think it will be better if she enter a family wealthy enough to provide for her even though it be only that of a townsman. And even my wife has come to agree with me on this point.

GOHEI: Truly it is an alliance beyond my most sanguine hopes, and I consider myself indeed fortunate. Position, of course, I have none, but money, I am happy to say, I do not lack, so I shall esteem it an honor to be permitted to assist in the way you suggest.

HYŌDAIYU: I am extremely obliged to you. The pedigree I will hand over to you on the occasion of the wedding ceremony, but as I thought you might like to see it I have brought it with, me today, and here it is. Please deign to take a glance at it.
   (*He takes it out of its wrapper and shows it to Gohei.*)

GOHEI: Ah, what ancestors! A most ancient and noble family!

HYŌDAIYU: Truly Narimatsu Tōtōmi-no-kami was a loyal retainer of the Lord Nabeshima and did great services to his house; and as surely will the possessor of this pedigree be able to obtain admission to the rank of samurai.
   (*Enter Heisaburo from the left.*)

HEISABURO: Kakiēmon of Minami-kawara has just been into the shop.

GOHEI: To borrow some money as usual, I'll be bound.

HEISABURO: Yes. He said he wanted some in a hurry, so I gave him what I happened to have on me and he went off.

GOHEI: H'm. How much did you lend him?

HEISABURO: He asked me for ten ryo, but I thought that seemed hardly enough, so I made it fifteen.

GOHEI: Well, artists are proverbially hard up, and he's a good example. But you've just come in at the right time. Look here!

HEISABURO: What is it? Oh, a family tree.

GOHEI: Yes, that's it. It is O Chiyo's pedigree, rude though it is of me to speak of her in that unceremonious way, but her parents have done us the honor of acceding to our request that she may enter our house as your bride. A most illustrious match too for a townsman, isn't it now?

HEISABURO: A splendid match indeed. (*Handing back the pedigree.*) I don't think there's any need for me to examine it.

HYŌDAIYU: Well, we'll keep it until after the wedding.
    (*Puts it back into the breast of his kimono. Enter O Maru from the house.*)

O MARU: The lady is waiting for you, sir.

HYŌDAIYU: Dear me! I have been talking here and forgot all about her. Please excuse me, Gohei Dono.

GOHEI: Certainly. Please go in.
    (*O Maru escorts him into the house.*)

HEISABURO: Father, I 'm afraid I cannot consent to marry O Chiyo San.

GOHEI: Oh, indeed? You are still doting on O Tsu, I suppose. You are a spiritless sort of fellow.

HEISABURO: Yes, perhaps I am. So I ask you again, as I have done several times before, please let me marry O Tsu. It's no good, I can't fall in with this heartless plan of yours.

GOHEO: Oh, I see. You have a very fine sense of my heartlessness but none at all of your own unfilial conduct, it seems. You know very well that all my hopes for the future depend on your marrying Nakasato's daughter, and yet you insist on defying your father, do you?

HEISABURO: No doubt it is extremely unfilial of me to upset your plans in this way, but if you will let me have O Tsu I will do everything I can to be a good son to you. You will not regret it, I assure you.

GOHEI: Then I am to understand that you mean to disregard my wishes altogether?

HEISABURO: In this matter only I must beg you to excuse me.

GOHEI: Very well then. Do as you please. If you want to marry O Tsu, marry her. But understand, I disinherit you! Don't dare to cross my threshold again. And get out at once. I won't have you here. Get out of my sight at once, I say.

HEISABURO: If you tell me to go then I will go.

GOHEI: Yes, go with your beloved O Tsu. But when you both come to beggary don't repent when it is too late and say it would have been better for both of you, if you had done as your father told you! (*Heisaburo stands with bowed head. His father continues in a more gentle tone.*) Mind, I don't say this out of unkindness. It's for your own good. Now listen carefully to what your father is going to say. During these last twenty years my business has gone on increasing and I have been lucky enough to pile up a decent fortune, but whatever he has and wherever he goes a tradesman is still nothing but a tradesman. So I have been at some pains to try and better your position and get you admittance to the rank of samurai. Yes, and I have spent a lot of money over it too, but it was no good, because if you have no lineage or pedigree you can't do anything. Well, then, this unattached samurai Nakasato happened to come here to Imari to live, and his daughter is descended from Narimatsu Tōtōmi-no-kami, a most distinguished name indeed, and a family connected with the house of the Lord Nabeshima. And fortunately he has no money, and so I was able to arrange this match and the pedigree will be ours. Ah, it's a splendid match for you. But if you refuse to go on with it all our fine prospects go up in smoke. And as for O Tsu, whether you do as I wish or not, I intend to make myself responsible for her future and see her comfortably settled. Now look here, Heisaburo, it may be a bit unpleasant but won't you do as your father wishes?

(*Heisaburo is silent. Just then Eikichi comes in from, the right.*)

EIKICHI: I have just been to the *Daikoku Maru*. She is sailing immediately to take advantage of the tide.

GOHEI: Ah, the *Daikoku Maru* is bound for Nagasaki, isn't she? (*Considers a moment.*) Now, Heisaburo, what about your answer? Is it yes or no? I want you to decide now.

HEISABURO: I will do as you wish. And in return please do your best for O Tsu.

GOHEI: Certainly. I'll answer for that. I'm so glad you see it in the right light. (*Turns toward the shop.*) I say, Yōkuro!

YŌKURO: What is it, sir?

GOHEI: Send someone to the *Daikoku Maru* at once and tell them that there is a passenger for Nagasaki, so they are not to start till he comes.

YŌKURO: Very well, sir. But who is it who is going to Nagasaki?

GOHEI: I am sending my son to the shop there for a while.

HEISABURO: Oh, I am to go there, am I?

GOHEI: Yes, as you have made up your mind it is best for you both to be separated.

YŌKURO: Well then, young master, you had better get your things ready at once.
(*Yōkuro hurries Heisaburo into the house. O Ima who has been listening outside now comes in.*)

O IMA: I was in such a state of wondering how things would turn out. I'm so glad Heisaburo has done the right thing. It is such a load off my mind.

GOHEI: Ah, you see what a clever fellow I am. Ha-ha-ha!

O IMA: Well, we must get Heisaburo to meet O Chiyo Sama before he goes. I'll go in and tell him.
(*Goes in. Enter Yōkuro from the right.*)

GOHEI: Is Heisaburo ready?

YŌKURO: He's indoors packing his things. Shall I go with him and see him off?

GOHEI: Yes, please do.
(*Enter Hyōdaiyu from the left followed by his wife Asakaya dressed like a samurai's lady and his daughter O Chiyo in a long-sleeved kimono. After them come O Ima, O Shige, and O Maru.*)

HYŌDAIYU: So Heisaburo Dono is called away suddenly to Nagasaki. Well, I am sorry to hear it, for I had looked forward to having the pleasure of a talk with him.

ASAKAYA: And my daughter may perhaps be even more disappointed than my husband.

O CHIYO: And when will Heisaburo Sama be coming back again?

GOHEI: Oh, he will be home again in two or three months' time.

HYŌDAIYU: Anyhow, the wedding will be at the end of the year.

ASAKAYA: Does that please you, child?

O CHIYO: Oh yes.
    (*Heisaburo enters from the house in his traveling dress.*)

HEISABURO: Well, father and mother, I shan't have the pleasure of seeing you for some little time, I'm afraid. Hyōdaiyu Sama, madam, O Chiyo Sama, please excuse my rudeness in running away like this. (*Looks round.*) Sister, where is O Tsu? I don't see her.

O SHIGE: Oh yes, where is she? O Tsu San! O Tsu San!

GOHEI: Oh, that will do about O Tsu. The ship is just sailing. You had better hurry.
    (*Heisaburo gets up to go. O Tsu comes in from the curtained entrance weeping and trying to hide it.*)

O TSU (*with deep feeling*): Good-bye, Heisaburo Sama. Please take care of yourself.

HEISABURO: O Tsu San!
    (*Goes towards her. O Chiyo comes forward with an incense box in her hand.*)

O CHIYO: Please take this and think of it as though it were myself.

(*Heisaburo looks embarrassed as she offers it to him.*)

HYŌDAIYU: Don't you care for my daughter's parting gift?

GOHEI: Why don't you take it?

HEISABURO (*takes it, as he can hardly refuse*): Oh, thank you. I am very much obliged to you.

YŌKURO: Well, come along!
(*Goes off with Heisaburo to the right. The others watch them go. O Tsu turns aside and bursts into tears. Silence. Curtain.*)

ACT II

Kakiēmon's pottery at Arita. In the middle of the stage is a thatched building eight yards long. The right half of it is raised and matted as usual, with mats faced with Loochoo material, and has a curtained entrance in front. On the opposite wall is a cupboard a yard long, the upper part closed with two sliding doors and the lower fitted with shelves on which pottery is standing anyhow. The sidewall is of plaster, and on this too is a double row of shelves full of unglazed pots. Next to this, to the left, is an unfloored space on the ground-level showing a plaster wall in front. Here also are shelves, one above the other; on the top shelf is an old basket, and on the lower one a row of jars and tea-bowls and other pots not yet fired. The sidewall has a window of bamboo lattice. In a corner of this part is a potter's wheel, and beside it a pestle and mortar for pounding clay. Away to the right of this building in the background is seen a detached house. It has a door three feet wide, and beyond it a window with the shutter tightly closed. In front of it stands a persimmon-tree with ripe red fruit, and beneath it is a board on which several newly thrown plates and bowls stand drying. Outside all is a brushwood fence with a wicket-gate of plaited bamboo, and beyond the house there is

a view of a mountain path and woods bright with the tints of
autumn. It is three o'clock in the afternoon. Kurisaku is sitting in
front of the wheel doing nothing and staring at the clay in front
of him. O Tané has got up on to the mortar and is trying to fix a
large cloth wrapper attached to a bamboo so as to stretch between
the top shelf and the lintel of the room. The curtain rises to the
strains of a rustic song.

KURISAKU: O Tané San, don't do that, please. You are making it
dark now.

O TANÉ: Yes, but I can't have you keep on looking at me and saying things I don't want to hear, so I am putting this up so that you
can't see me. There, that'll do, I think. (*Goes to get down.*) Oh!
I shall fall! (*Squats down on top of the mortar. Kurisaku gets up*
and helps her down gently.) Yes, now it's arranged like that you
can't keep on peeping. The days are getting short, so we mustn't
waste any more time. So get on with your work.
    (*Gets up on to the matted part to the right and begins painting*
a piece of unglazed pottery with cobalt.)

KURISAKU: It's all very well to tell me to get on with my work, but if
I can't see your face I haven't got anything to inspire me to work.

O TANÉ: Oh, do stop that growling and go back there and get on
with your business.
    (*Leads Kurisaku behind the wrapper and then goes back to her*
place, takes up the vase and examines it. Kurisaku peeps through
a tear in the wrapper.)

KURISAKU: O Tané San! Just another word. And then we won't
talk any more.

O TANÉ: So you can't keep quiet then?

KURISAKU: I only spoke to get you to turn your face this way.

O TANÉ: Oh, there's a hole that you're looking through, is there? Really, you are a nuisance! Now, look here. If you speak another word to me till tonight I'll have nothing to say to you for a whole month. D'you understand that?

KURISAKU: Oh, that's awful. Well, if it can't be helped I must resign myself to looking at the wall.
  (*Starts the wheel. O Tané goes on painting the vase. Enter Aritaya Gohei dressed in haori over his kimono and long tight trousers with leather-soled sandals on his feet.*)

GOHEI: Hullo! Excuse me, may I come in?
  (*Gets up into the room.*)

O TANÉ: Oh, it's Master Aritaya. You are very welcome.

GOHEI: Is your father in?

O TANÉ: Oh yes. He's in his workroom.

GOHEI: H'm trying to get that red enamel as usual, I suppose. (*Laughs ironically.*) Well, he isn't likely to succeed. By the way, I want a message taken to Riēmon. Don't you think there is someone who can go with it?

O TANÉ: Yes. I'll send Kurisaku. Kurisaku!
  (*Kurisaku comes out from behind the wrapper.*)

KURISAKU (*to Gohei*): You are very welcome, sir.

GOHEI: My clerk Yōkuro is at Riēmon's. Kindly go and tell him that I am waiting here for him.

KURISAKU: Certainly, sir. (*Turns to Tané*): All right, O Tané San, I'll be off at once.
  (*Exit to the left.*)

O TANÉ: I'm afraid it is very untidy, but won't you please come in? (*She steps down and goes over and knocks at the door of the detached room.*) Father! Father! The master of the Aritaya has come! (*After knocking several times she comes back again.*) He will be here in a minute. Please take a seat. (*Brings a kneeling-cushion.*) I'll go and get some tea.

(*Goes in. The clerk Yōkuro comes in from the road on the left. He is in haori and tight trousers with his kimono tucked up.*)

YŌKURO: I'm afraid I have kept you waiting.

GOHEI: Oh, Yōkuro! And how did you get on with that business?

YŌKURO: Oh, splendidly. You will be pleased. I have managed to buy over all the potters in Arita, and they are all at Riēmon's house now, waiting for you to come and put your seal to the agreement.

GOHEI: Thanks. You've done well. But I say, Yōkuro, I am risking half my fortune on this venture, so we must consider carefully before we commit ourselves.

YŌKURO: Certainly, sir. But as I have already pointed out to you, the yearly output of the Arita potteries is considerably more than a hundred thousand, so we shall easily secure some tens of thousands profit. Not at all a bad transaction, and I don't see where the risk comes in.

GOHEI: There's none at present perhaps, but if this old chap here manages by any chance to succeed in turning out these dishes with the red decoration that he is forever working at, then the ordinary Arita ware won't be worth more than a few coppers a bale. That's where the risk lies in buying up all these potteries.

YŌKURO: Excuse me, master, but allow me to be so rude as to disagree with you. Is it likely that that simpleton Kakiēmon will find out how to get his red design? And if he does you can easily buy his secret from him for fifty ryo or so. You please leave all that to me and I'll manage it all right.

GOHEI: Ah yes, I expect you're not far wrong. Kakiēmon is always in want of money, so probably there won't be much difficulty.

YŌKURO: And may I ask, master, as a reward for these services of mine, that you consider setting me up in business of my own?
(*Watching his master's face narrowly.*)

GOHEI: Come now, Yōkuro, that's rather too much. You haven't much to complain about in being associated with a splendid concern like the Aritaya. No, no, you drop that foolish idea of a shop of your own and be content where you are.
(*Enter the apprentice Matsutaro from the left, singing.*)

MATSUTARO: Oh, are you here, master?

GOHEI: Well, what is it, Matsutaro? Have you some special business?

MATSUTARO: They're all waiting at Riēmon's house; and want you to come as soon as you can.

GOHEI: Oh, is that it? Ah, thanks for letting me know. Yes, you've done your errand very smartly indeed. I must give you something as an appreciation.
(*He takes out some coins from his purse, wraps them in paper, and gives them to him.*)

MATSUTARO: Thank you very much. Shall I come with you?

GOHEI: Oh no. I don't want anyone to come with me. I'll go alone. And now you can go and buy yourself something you like and then go on home.

MATSUTARO: So you will not need my services. Thank you again, master.

(*Runs off joyfully to the left. Yōkuro stands silent.*)

GOHEI: Well, as Matsutaro has come to call me I shall be off at once to meet the potters at Riēmon's place. You stay here and find out all you possibly can about Kakiēmon and his red decoration.

YŌKURO: Very well, sir. I'll get into his workshop and see just what he's up to.

GOHEI: Yes, that's just what I want.
(*Exit to left.*)

YŌKURO: It doesn't look as though he meant to set me up in business for myself, however long I wait, so if Kakiēmon does get his red color I must steal a march on the master and make some money that way.
(*O Tané comes in with teacups on a tray.*)

O TANÉ: Ah, Yōkuro San, you are very welcome. Has your master gone already?

YŌKURO: Yes, he has just this moment gone. So I will drink the tea.
(*Takes the cup and drinks. Just then Sakaida Kakiēmon opens the door of the workshop and comes out. He is an elderly man in working clothes and gazes about him abstractedly.*)

KAKIĒMON (*looking at the persimmon-tree*): When autumn comes then the persimmon too begins to redden. And what a splendid vivid red it is! Ah, there's a difference between the work of nature and man's handicraft.
(*Turns away in the other direction.*)

O TANÉ: Father! Yōkuro San has come.

KAKIĒMON: Yōkuro! Who is Yōkuro? (*Turns round with a blank look.*) Oh yes, the clerk of the shop. I didn't remember for the moment. Pray excuse me.
(*Sits down on the edge of the veranda of the house.*)

YŌKURO: Dear me! I suppose you must behave like this if you are going to do something remarkable.

O TANÉ: The master was here too until just a moment ago.

KAKIĒMON: Well, why didn't you call me then?

O TANÉ: Why, didn't you hear me? I banged at the door as hard as I could.

KAKIĒMON: I heard nothing.

O TANÉ: And that's why the neighbors have given you the nickname of Yumeēmon (the dreamer).

YŌKURO: By the way, Kakiēmon, how is that red enamel getting on?

KAKIĒMON: It's the one aim of my life to discover; that, but still it eludes me. When I shall get it I don't know.

YŌKURO: Is that detached room over there your workshop?

KAKIĒMON: Yes, that's where I keep all my secrets. My patterns and recipes and specimens of enamel.

YŌKURO: I say, won't you let me see them?
    (*Makes a move towards the right.*)

KAKIĒMON: I allow no one in my workroom.

YŌKURO: But I have some knowledge of these things, and if you let me into your secret I might be able to make some profitable suggestion.
    (*Pushing Kakiēmon aside he puts out his hand to open the door, but Kakiēmon thrusts him back with some violence and stands in front of the door to block the way.*)

KAKIĒMON *(sternly)*: My workroom is under the protection of the Deities. The only being allowed to enter is my daughter O Tsu. No one else must dare to cross the threshold.

YŌKURO *(getting up submissively)*: In that case there shall be no more talk of looking in. So please compose yourself again.

O TANÉ: I hope neither of you have hurt yourselves. My father is unfortunately very quick-tempered. I beg you will excuse him.

YŌKURO: Oh no, the fault was mine. It is I who must beg your pardon. (*Kakiēmon locks the door of the workroom and puts the key in his girdle.*) Kakiēmon San, if you do get this red decoration, who is the first person you will show it to?
  (*Kurisaku comes in from the left and stands listening outside the gate.*)

KAKIĒMON: That goes without saying. Naturally to Gohei San who has been my kind patron these twenty years and more.

YŌKURO: I know something better than that. You tell me about it as soon as you succeed and I will find someone else who will manage things so that you can make a lot more money out of it than if you trust it to Gohei.

KAKIĒMON: That's very kind of you, but doing the right thing seems more important to me than making money.

YŌKURO: Those ideas are a bit out of date nowadays. I think you'll find a little money-making more to the point than this talk about the right thing. Anyhow we'll talk about that again later on. I must be going now.

O TANÉ: Oh, must you go then?

YŌKURO: Yes, thanks. Kindly excuse my intrusion.
  (*Exit to the left.*)

KAKIĒMON: Ah, what a waste of my precious time. Well, I'll go up the hill and have a look at the kiln.
  (*Starts to go when Kurisaku enters.*)

KURISAKU: Please wait a moment, master. There is something I want to say to you.

KAKIĒMON: Oh, it can wait, whatever it is, till I have more time.
  (*Starts off.*)

KURISAKU: When the master has time! That'll never be in this life. It won't take a moment, so please listen to me.
  (*Kakiēmon reluctantly sits down. O Tané comes up to Kurisaku.*)

O TANÉ: Now please tell father just what you think.

KURISAKU: I'll speak my mind if I die for it. (*Squats down on the ground.*) Look here, master! You're content to go on working for Aritaya, toiling in your dirty clothes to make fine things for him year in and year out, and what's the result? You spend sleepless nights thinking out how to make those masterpieces of porcelain that you say will hand down your fame to posterity, and all it does is to put money into Aritaya's pocket and leave you perspiring and in debt. And everyone is loud in his praise, calling him the king of Imari and the paragon of merchants, and so on, and what do you think they call you, master? Why nothing but "that dreamer Kakiēmon" or "that silly old man."

KAKIĒMON: Well, whatever they say, let them say it.

KURISAKU: Ah, you may not care for yourself, master, but think how painful it is for O Tsu and O Tané. For their sake please do have a little ordinary human ambition.

KAKIĒMO: You've spoken well. You mean well, no doubt, and I don't blame you for saying what you have. But there's something you haven't thought of. In this wide world there are always any number of people who can make money, but for more than a hundred and twenty years no one else has set himself to think out a method of making dishes with red enamel decoration. You don't understand the mind of Kakiēmon: and I doubt whether O Tané does either. It is only O Tsu who really understands and sympathizes with me.

(*Goes out of the gate and starts off up the hill without looking back.*)

O TANÉ: Well done, Kurisaku. I *am* obliged to you.

KURISAKU: Ah, I'm all in a perspiration with trying my hardest to speak so as to please you.
   (*Wipes his forehead.*)

O TANÉ: Please me! Oh, I was murmuring "Bravo, Kurisaku," to myself all the time.

KURISAKU: Ah, there's nothing I like better than a smile from you, and I don't often get one. And if I don't take advantage of this opportunity to say what I want when you are in such a good humor I am not likely to get another in a hurry. It isn't easy for me to ask you, but...about yourself ....er....you know what I mean. Can't you give me a little hope, O Tané San?

O TANÉ (*with a suddenly altered expression*): Oh, no. Indeed it is very kind of you, but I must beg to decline.

KURISAKU: Do you dislike me so much then?

O TANÉ: No, I don't dislike you. But when you begin to talk like that you give me an unpleasant feeling, so don't do it again, please.

KURISAKU: I wonder, if you dislike me so much, that you wear that obi I bought for you every day.
   (*Pointing to the obi.*)

O TANÉ: Because I don't want to dirty the others I have, so I use this for everyday wear.

KURISAKU: Well, I never! And I so pleased thinking to myself that you wore it because you saw my meaning. The color of that obi is called kuri-ume. Now don't you understand?

O TANÉ: Oh! It's called kuri-ume, is it?

KURISAKU: How unfeeling of you not even to notice that. I got it so that when it enfolded your waist it would remind you of my name and how I would like to change places with it.

O TANÉ: Oh! If that's why you gave it I shall hate to wear it even a moment longer. (*Taking it off and flinging it down.*) There! You can take it. I don't want it.
   (*Takes another obi from the cupboard and puts it on. Kurisaku looks on bitterly.*)

KURISAKU: Yes, I see how you really feel now. I can't stay here any longer.

O TANÉ: Well, do as you please.
   (*Goes on painting the vase.*)

KURISAKU: I suppose it will be awkward for the master if I go, but I really can't stand it any longer. Last night when you were so unpleasant to me I made up my mind I would go, and so I went and packed up my things. (*Takes down the old basket from the shelf, crams in a shirt and pair of tabi* and throws it over his shoulder, catching up the obi in his other hand.*) There! I'm off. I won't live any longer! And when the master asks who was the cause of Kurisaku's end, mind you tell him it was you who killed him. Now I shall hang myself or go out of my mind. Good-bye, O Tané San!
   (*Walks away dispiritedly. O Tané gets up and goes to the gate and looks after his retreating figure. Then she goes back and resumes her work. Enter O Tsu with a bundle done up in a wrapper. She goes into the house.*)

---

* Japanese socks.

O TANÉ: Ah, elder sister, how are you?
  (*O Tsu sits down.*)

O TSU: I caught sight of Kurisaku just now. Have you been quarrelling with him again?

O TANÉ: Oh, that Kurisaku does nothing but hang around bothering the life out of me, so I really couldn't help giving him a scolding. That's all it was.

O TSU: Well, if Kurisaku doesn't please you, what sort of a man do you want?

O TANÉ: I don't want a blockhead like that. A nice-looking gentleman like Heisaburo Sama would suit me well enough. Yes, I should like to have a handsome fellow to live with as you have, but I suppose as I'm quite plain I shall have to put up with anything I can I get.

O TSU: That's where you make a mistake. Now, listen to me. Good looks and a fine appearance are just like a flower in full bloom that soon falls and comes to nothing. Kindness and honesty are what a woman needs most of all in a man; the rest does not matter. If an intelligent fellow like Kurisaku is so infatuated with you as to appear a fool or a simpleton you ought to be thankful for it. If he comes back again be kind to him and ask father's permission to marry him and live happily with him. Anyone ought to be satisfied with a good man like that.

O TANÉ (*looking surprised*): Well! Really, elder sister, what can have come over you today to give me a scolding like this? You have never done it before. What's the matter?

O TSU (*looks taken aback for a moment, but then goes on unconcernedly*): Oh, nothing at all. It's only because I am anxious about your future. You mustn't think I meant to scold you. On the contrary I have got something here that will please you—(*taking out of her bundle a gay long-sleeved kimono*). When I saw you last you said you would like a kimono with long sleeves, so here is mine. It is not a very good one, but please take it.

O TANÉ: Oh, elder sister, I didn't say that because I wanted yours. Please keep it.

O TSU: But I have got several others, so you needn't mind taking it.

O TANÉ: Oh, in that case, though it is too bad to deprive you of it, I should be delighted. (*Takes it and bows over it.*) Really, it is a beautiful one. I think it will just suit me, don't you?

O TSU: Just slip it on over the one you're wearing and see.

O TANÉ: Oh, yes, would you like me to?
   (*Puts it on. O Tsu brings a mirror for her to see herself.*)

O TSU: The bust of two sisters in a mirror. Tableau!

O TANÉ: Ah, yes, "even an ostler in fine clothes."
   (*With a very delighted air she takes off the kimono, folds it quickly, and bows low.*) Thank you very much, elder sister, for your kindness. But you did not come all this way only on purpose to give me this, did you?

O TSU: Oh, no. There's something I have to say to father.

O TANÉ: Unfortunately he has gone up the hill to look at the kiln, but I expect he'll be back soon. It will soon be time for supper, and I must go and buy his liquor. I suppose you aren't in any hurry to go back.

O TSU: I can't stay long. I shall go back as soon as I have seen father.

O TANÉ: Then I expect I shall not see you again today, but I shall come to your place and see you in a few days. (*Takes the kimono into the inner room and comes out again with a bottle in her hand.)* Good-bye, elder sister, don't hurry away.

(*Exit. O Tsu stands looking after her.*)

O TSU: You will never see me again.

(*Controlling her expression. Just then Kakiēmon comes down the hill with face wreathed in smiles and enters.*)

KAKIĒMON: Ah, O Tsu! Well, I'm glad to see you. And here's good news for you. You know so far practically all those red enamel pieces that I have fired have been failures, so I went up today and examined the kiln and I see now for the first time that it isn't built properly. I wonder why I didn't notice that before. Now with my secret of the glaze discovered success is at last within reach. Aren't you glad? Isn't that splendid, eh? Isn't that fine?

O TSU: Yes, that is splendid. I'm so glad. And how long do you think it will be?

KAKIĒMON: Well, it'll take a month or so to rebuild the kiln. Then we must allow another two to get the pieces ready and fire them I suppose. Say three months from now and overglaze enamelware quite equal to any of the Chinese work will be made in Japan. And by the end of this year I'll be able to buy you anything you want.

O TSU: I don't want anything at all, but please buy some nice clothes for O Tané San and Kurisaku.

KAKIĒMON: Of course I will. But before that we must see to your bridal outfit. You must have seven or eight chests and coffers and dresses of embroidery and an over-dress of figured crepe. But your wedding dress of pure white silk will suit you best of all.

O TSU: My wedding dress of pure white. Ah!

KAKIĒMON: Well, I hope to see it before long. Anyhow, by next spring we ought to have turned the corner and be quite well off.

O TSU: I must be getting back now, father.

KAKIĒMON: And I must be moving too. I'm sorry I haven't more time to stay and have a longer chat, but there is a lot of important work that can't wait; but come again in a few days' time.

O TSU: I don't think I shall be able to do that.

KAKIĒMON: Well then, anyhow, we shall expect you on the tenth of next month; that's the seventh anniversary of your mother's death. Come early in the morning.

O TSU: No, don't expect me then. I may be prevented from coming for all I know.

KAKIĒMON: What! You may not come on your mother's anniversary? Ah, I see; you are thinking it may be inconvenient for Master Gohei and his family. That'll be all right. I'll send O Tané to ask them to excuse you, so you need not be anxious about that. Well, I must be off to my workshop. Mind you are back before it gets dark.
   (*Steps down and goes off to the right, takes out the key and opens the door. There is a noise of pottery falling and breaking.*)

O TSU: Is anything broken?
   (*Steps down from the house. Kakiēmon goes into his workshop and comes out again with a broken tea-bowl in his hand.*)

KAKIĒMON: Just look here, O Tsu! Ah, how frail a thing is pottery!

O TSU: To speak of something less pleasant, as I came by I saw Niimura Hanbei San standing at his gate. Hasn't he grown old suddenly since he lost his daughter?

KAKIĒMON: Ah, it's a wonder he's alive at all. If it had been me I wouldn't have survived it.

O TSU: His daughter and I used to learn writing together. She was a sweet, gentle girl. But when she was deserted by her lover

I suppose there was nothing for it but to throw herself into the Arita River.

KAKIĒMON: It was a sad affair. But rather than live to be laughed at, and bring shame on her father, and so become guilty of unfilial conduct as well, to die in the way she did was far better.

O TSU: Then you think the way she died was a fine one?

KAKIĒMON: Can't say I do. People shouldn't go and throw themselves into the first river they come to, right under your nose like that. They ought to go to some place a respectable distance away to do it. But enough of that sort of thing. That girl was a namesake of yours, wasn't she?

O TSU: Yes, her name was O Tsu too.

KAKIĒMON: Even if it was. She was very different from my O Tsu.

O TSU: Still all the same, girls—

KAKIĒMON: Ought to take care they don't get broken. Ha-ha-ha! (*Laughs as he shuts the door of his workshop from the inside.*)

O TSU: O father, please forgive me! (*Leans against the persimmon-tree and weeps.*) Women are more frail than pottery, and I have been so unlucky as to get broken. I'll go to some remote place and die there so as not to bring any shame on you, so think of me as dead from today. (*Steps up into the room.*) Ah, this has all come about through my indiscretion. I seem to see my father's grief-stricken features when he knows I am alive no longer. I must write some explanation to him before I go, though I won't write everything…only that I can't stay at the Aritaya any longer.
There's a brush and ink-stone in here somewhere.
(*Goes in. Just then Kurisaku comes back with his basket and the obi in his hand. He looks in and then returns the basket to its place, puts the obi into a cupboard in the workroom, and then sits down*

again in front of the wheel to resume his work, but before doing so he gets up again and draws the wrapper closely in front of him so that he will not be seen, after which he gets on with his work. Then O Tsu comes out and lays the letter she has written on the God-shelf in the lower part, steps down from the house, and turns to the right.)

O TSU: Oh, father! Please forgive me for making this bad return for all your kindness.

(She makes a low obeisance and then hastens away up the road. Kurisaku comes out from behind the wrapper and runs over to the workshop and knocks vigorously on the door.)

KURISAKU: Master! Master!

(Kakiēmon opens the door and puts his head out.)

KAKIĒMON: If that's anyone come for money I owe, send them away.

(Goes to shut the door again.)

KURISAKU: Master! It isn't anyone for money. O Tsu has just gone off.

KAKIĒMON: Well, what of it? She's gone back to Imari. What are you making such a fuss about?

KURISAKU: If it was only her going back it would be all right, but she seemed strange somehow.

KAKIĒMON *(coming forward involuntarily)*: O Tsu seemed strange, you say?

KURISAKU: Just wait a moment, master. She seems to have put something on the God-shelf. *(Brings the note.)* It's a letter, master.

(Kakiēmon takes it and reads it, muttering the words to himself in a horror-stricken undertone.)

KAKIĒMON: I hadn't the least idea, right up to this moment, that she had any trouble. We must go after her.

KURISAKU: Right you are, master.

(*They start off. Gohei, who has come up and been standing behind the fence listening, now enters.*)

GOHEI: What's this I hear? O Tsu run away? Has she really?

KAKIĒMON: Oh, Gohei San. You are just the person I want to see. Please come in.

(*Both go into the house.*)

GOHEI: Is that a letter from O Tsu that you've got there? What does she say, I wonder?

(*Looks uneasy.*)

KAKIĒMON: She doesn't say very much; only that some misunderstanding has arisen between you and your family because of some fault of hers, and so she has gone away to a distant province where she will trouble nobody. The rest is only apologies for unfilial conduct. Now, what can it all be about, I wonder?

GOHEI (*looking relieved*): Well, as Imari is more than seven miles from here, I suppose you haven't heard anything about it, but the fact is that Heisaburo and O Tsu have been on pretty intimate terms for some time.

KAKIĒMON (*with an expression first of great astonishment and then of shame*): Oh, to think that O Tsu should do such a thing.

GOHEI: And so I have sent Heisaburo to my shop at Nagasaki, and so, it seems, O Tsu has run away from home.

KAKIĒMON: I must apologize again and again for my daughter's misconduct, but at the same time I have a request to make of you. Please do what you can to help O Tsu.

GOHEI: What do you mean by helping her?

KAKIĒMON: Why, this. Please let Heisaburo marry her. There is no other way. It isn't at all a proper thing for a parent to say, but that girl is far superior to any of her family and she wouldn't be such a very unsuitable match for your son.

GOHEI: I should very much like to oblige you if I could, but this, I am afraid, is quite beyond my power.

KAKIĒMON: Ah, you mean that it is Heisaburo who is unwilling. Then please let me go and see him and ask him myself.

GOHEI: I'm afraid that would be quite useless. The fact is that a marriage has been arranged for him in another quarter.

KAKIĒMON: Oh!

GOHEI: So you see it is impossible for them to marry. But there is something I can do. Let me offer you a hundred ryo as a consolation for O Tsu's disappointment.

KAKIĒMON: No! I don't sell my daughter! (*Takes money out of his purse.*) And here's the remainder of the money I borrowed from Heisaburo the other day! Take it! I should feel defiled if I kept it.
     (*Flings it down on the ground.*)

GOHEI: Well, if that is how you take it, there's nothing more to be said. I had better take my leave.
     (*Stands up to go out, Kakiēmon stops him.*)

KAKIĒMON: Wait a moment. There's nothing a parent will not do where his child is at stake. You see I put aside all my obstinacy and pride. If Heisaburo doesn't care for my daughter I don't wish him to take her for good, but if he would make her his wife just for a year, say, or even six months, and then divorce her. Won't you ask him to do that? Just that one little request. It would mean everything to O Tsu. And if you will I'll give you the whole of the rest of my life in return. The sweat of my brow and the strength of my hands...yes, I will work my fingers to the bone for you! If you have any pity or feeling at all, Gohei San, please do this for me. (*Bowing his head to the floor in supplication.*)

GOHEI: Whatever you say I'm afraid I must decline.

KAKIĒMON: It may not please you, but won't you let them marry as a kindness to my daughter and myself?

GOHEI: It's no good saying any more. It's no use, I tell you.

KAKIĒMON: Even after all I've said?

GOHEI: I'm sorry, but I must decline.

KAKIĒMON: Oh! (*Kurisaku comes back and comes into the room.*)

KURISAKU: There's no sign of O Tsu anywhere.

KAKIĒMON: Then you don't know where she's gone?

GOHEI: I'll look too and see if I can't find her. I may think of a likely spot. (*Goes out.*) And look here, Kakiēmon! If there is any way you can think of that I can help O Tsu, except this marriage of course, come and discuss it whenever you like. I promise you I'll do anything I can. Remember how long we've known each other and don't treat me like a stranger.
(*Exit.*)

KURISAKU: Well, I think I see it all now. After making a fortune of I don't know how many hundred thousand ryo for Aritaya, all he gets in return is the daughter he is so fond of made into damaged goods. I wonder what he thinks of that.

KAKIĒMON: Gohei is a creature without the least sense of gratitude or justice or decency! I'll have no more to do with him! And what's more, I'll ruin him! By my skill as a craftsman I'll take that fortune of his away from him!

(*Steps outside and stands staring fixedly in front of him. O Tané comes back with the liquor she has bought and stops surprised.*)

O TANÉ: Father! What is it?

KAKIĒMON: O Tsu has run away from home.

O TANÉ: Oh!
   (*Drops the bottle. Kakiēmon flings away the letter and, without looking round, strides over to his workroom and goes in. Kurisaku and O Tané read the letter. The stage gradually becomes dark. The leaves of the persimmon-tree keep on falling.*)

ACT III

Kakiēmon's kiln at Sarayama at Arita. A hill rises gently to the right, up which the range of kilns is built in a slanting direction. The boards of the roof over them have been taken away and only the pillars remain. Some pine faggots are burning in the kiln.

To the left the thatched roof of a house is seen. In front are the hills of Sarayama dotted here and there with the fires of potteries. Sparks are rising from the kiln behind on the right. Kakiēmon stands in front of the mouth of the kiln staring fixedly into the fire, partly illuminated by the red glare that comes from it. His clothes are soiled and he looks very tired. He appears much older than in the former act, and his hair is now quite white. The stage is dark, and there is a mist and the patter of rain. A bell strikes the hour. The curtain rises and the rain stops, and there is only the eerie sound of the autumn wind rustling the bare boughs.

KAKIĒMON: It's a good thing the rain has stopped, but the cold has made the fire dull, and now we shall have to keep it in another couple of hours or so. (*Turning round toward the left.*) O Tané!
   (*As he calls he throws more faggots into the fire and it flares up. As he does so a red glare suddenly appears in front to the right and the scene gradually grows bright. O Tané comes from the left and points to the light!*)

O TANÉ: Father, what's that light over there?

KAKIĒMON: The moon rising, I suppose.

O TANÉ: But you know there's no moon tonight.

KAKIĒMON: Oh well, a house on fire, most likely. A pretty useless sort of fire that is; we could do with some of it here.

O TANÉ: Yes, so we could. But what did you call me for?

KAKIĒMON: Hurry over to Gensuke and tell him to send up a hundred bundles of pine faggots at once. Tell him I'll pay him double for them when this kiln is finished. If you tell him the reason I expect he'll let us have them.

O TANÉ: Oh don't, father, you know it's no good. When I went there this morning and asked him, didn't he answer rather rudely that if I didn't bring the money he wouldn't let us have any more. He won't give us credit, and however many times I go he'll only say the same thing.

KAKIĒMON: Then go to Tōsuke. Tell him I don't care how much he charges.

O TANÉ: They're all the same. They all know we've got no money, so it's not the least use going.

KAKIĒMON: But you must tell them something or other. We must get faggots somehow. Don't you see how important it is to finish this kiln?

O TANÉ: Better give it up than worry yourself like this. You'll be worn out.

KAKIĒMON: What d'you mean? Never you forget for a moment that we've got to be avenged for O Tsu.

O TANÉ: Yes, indeed. Why, it's a hundred days today since she left us. I wonder where she can be.

KAKIĒMON: H'm, where can she be? Best think of her as dead. By the way I haven't seen Kurisaku for some time. Where is he?

O TANÉ: He's asleep in the house.

KAKIĒMON: What does he want to sleep for?

O TANÉ: He hasn't had any sleep for three days and three nights while he has been helping you and he's completely worn out.

KAKIĒMON: What's today?

O TANÉ: Today is the twentieth of the twelfth month. You haven't had any sleep for five days, since you started firing the kiln. If a strong young fellow like Kurisaku can't stand it, the next thing will be that you'll collapse, and what shall I do then?

KAKIĒMON: You needn't be afraid of that. I shall survive till this kiln is finished. And while you're talking the faggots are burning out. Do make haste and see about some more.

O TANÉ: Well, I can go and see, though it won't be any use.

KAKIĒMON: If you don't hurry it will be too late.
  (*O Tané runs off to the left. Kakiēmon throws in some more fag-gots and the fire flares up. The stage gets lighter as the flames grow higher. The clerk Yōkuro enters in haori and breeches and tucked-up kimono and leather-soled sandals and comes up to Kakiēmon.*)

YŌKURO: Kakiēmon San! Isn't the kiln finished yet ?
  (*As he speaks he looks round him on all sides.*)

KAKIĒMON: If I had the wood, you'd see it all done in a couple of hours. But look there.
  (*And he points to his few remaining bundles.*)

YŌKURO: Well, well, that's a pity. Let me lend you the money for some more.

KAKIĒMON: No, no! I won't touch a penny of Aritaya's money.

YŌKURO: I don't mean Aritaya's money. I mean my own. I'll lend it you. But business men don't lend money for nothing, of course. If you'll only give me the sole right of selling this red enamel-ware of yours, I'll lend you any amount; ten ryo or twenty, as much as you want. I rather thought you might be in a fix like this so I brought the agreement with me ready drawn up. (*Takes it from his breast.*) All you have to do is to put in the sum you need and write your name and put your seal to it. Why, the wood is almost finished. Won't you seal this and put new life into your kiln.

    (*Holds out the paper and money to him. Kakiēmon puts out his hand and then draws back again.*)

KAKIĒMON: It's very kind of you, but I'd rather not.

YŌKURO: Well, I think you're a fool. (*Stares toward the road.*) Hullo, that looks like my master coming along. Kakiēmon San, please don't say anything to him about what I was just suggesting to you, will you?

KAKIĒMON: I want nothing to say to Gohei.

    (*Stares into the fire. Yōkuro looks relieved and puts away the paper and the money. Enter Gohei wearing haori and kimono with hood over his head. He looks surprised to see Yōkuro.*)

GOHEI: Why, Yōkuro, what on earth are you doing here?

YŌKURO: Oh, I wondered how Kakiēmon's kiln was getting on, so I came to see.

GOHEI: Very solicitous of you, I'm sure. Especially on such a cold dark night. (*Sits down on a stone on the right.*) By the way, Kakiēmon, I hear you're pretty hard up. Now as you have worked for me all these years, and I must say I'm a bit indebted to you, I shouldn't like to think of your being beholden to anyone else, so I have come to see what I can do. Won't you be sensible and give up this stubbornness and let us resume our old relations?

KAKIĒMON: I don't want to see you yet. When it's time for that I'll come to you.

GOHEI: Don't be so obstinate. I know you're in want of money for wood at this very moment, for I have just seen your daughter trying to get Tōsuke to let her have some. If you'd only ask me instead of putting yourself to all that trouble I have only to say the word and you can have a thousand or two thousand bundles of pine faggots delivered here this instant. Look there! D'you see the fires of all those kilns? Well, they all belong to me. All the potteries in Arita. What d'you think you can do all by yourself against so many? Be sensible and consider your own interests and give in. I'll take all the ware you make and I'll pay you an income of a hundred ryo a year for life. What do you think, Yōkuro? That's not a bad offer, is it?

YŌKURO: A very handsome one indeed. Quite worthy of a great merchant like you. I'm sure Kakiēmon San will agree to it.

GOHEI: Well, Kakiēmon San, shall we consider that settled?
  (*Kakiēmon says nothing and does not even look round. Yōkuro looks from one to the other.*)

YŌKURO: Just a moment, master. (*Takes Gohei a little way down the Hana-michi.**) It's better to let him alone. His manner is very strange. You wait till next year when the spring weather affects him, and you'll see he'll go clean off his head.

GOHEI: What I'm troubled about is that red enamelware of his.

YŌKURO: Oh, that's all right. There's no need to worry about that. He'll never get it, however long he tries. It's only one of the dreams he's so famous for.

---

* Hana-michi.—The raised passage that goes across the auditorium from the back of the theatre to the front of the stage.

GOHEI: Well, I hope it is, for if this dream is realized. I shall lose I don't know how much. Hundreds of thousands, I expect.

YŌKURO: But fortune always favors you, master. There is no need for anxiety.

GOHEI: No, I suppose there isn't really. (*Looking at the fire in front.*) That looks like a fire somewhere. Surely it must be at Imari. That's about the direction.

YŌKURO: Rather nearer, I think.

GOHEI: Well, I don't like the look of it at all. I feel a bit apprehensive about it. Hurry back home as quickly as you can and make sure everything is safe there.

YŌKURO: And master...?

GOHEI: Don't bother about me. I've got something else to say to Kakiēmon, so I'll come on a little later.

YŌKURO: But don't you think it would be better if I waited for you?

GOHEI: There's no need, I tell you. I want you to get off immediately. (*Yōkuro starts reluctantly, while Gohei sits down to the right of Kakiēmon.*) I've something to tell you that may surprise you. O Tsu jumped out of a boat and drowned herself at Mojigaseki last month. It was on the twentieth, in the evening.

KAKIĒMON: Ah, so my daughter is dead then.
　　(*Staring in front of him unmoved.*)

GOHEI: Yes, but nobody knew anything about it till today when the boatmen who rowed her brought a mirror bag and showed it to me and told me about it, and I recognized it as O Tsu's. And so I knew for certain that it was she, and the bag I have taken and presented to our temple and ordered services to be said there for the repose of her soul.

KAKIĒMON: And Heisaburo ? What have you done about him?

GOHEI: Er... owing to circumstances over which we have no control, my son will be married into a certain samurai family very shortly.

KAKIĒMON: Be married, will he? H'm.
(*Looks mortified. Gohei eyes him closely.*)

GOHEI: Well! When I heard of O Tsu's death even I could not help shedding tears. But you...you don't weep.

KAKIĒMON: I have no tears. My eyes are dried up like my heart. Now I have work that must be done. And when that is finished I will weep for my daughter. And then too I will come and pay you a visit. But until then I want nothing more to say to you.
(*And he turns to the kiln and gazes into the fire.*)

GOHEI (*looking uneasy*): His determination is something uncanny! Even his daughter's death has no power to turn his mind from this purpose he pursues so relentlessly. And if he should succeed?
(*Enter O Tané from the left.*)

O TANÉ (*bowing to Gohei*): Good day, sir.

KAKIĒMON (*turning to O Tané*): Ah, O Tané. Well, how did you get on?

O TANÉ: Wherever I went it was the same. None of them would let me have a single bundle.

KAKIĒMON: H'm, no good, was it? (*Looks despondent.*)

GOHEI (*coming up to O Tané*): Come here a moment.
(*Leads her down stage to the left.*)
Look here, I have just asked Kakiēmon to make it up with me again because of our old friendship, and offered him a salary of a hundred ryo a year to work for me as before.

O TANÉ: It's no use, sir. I know father won't consent.

GOHEI: But if he doesn't there's nothing before both of you but starvation, so far as I can see. Still, however stiff-necked he may be, you can manage to talk him over. You're no fool. And when you've got him into a more reasonable state of mind so that he is likely to yield, I'll come round again. You can do it if you will, so please do your best. I shall rely on you.

(*Exit after a short pause. O Tané considers a moment and then goes to Kakiēmon.*)

O TANÉ: Father, if this kiln doesn't succeed, what are you going to do then?

KAKIĒMON: Start another. I shall go on, however many times I fail.

O TANÉ: But you know the saying that three spoilt kilns will ruin the richest, don't you. You may say you will go on, but this place and everything we have will be sold over our heads and we shan't know where to look for the next meal.

KAKIĒMON: Is it as bad as that?

O TANÉ: Indeed it is. If you will sell the spoilt pieces perhaps we can go on and make ends meet, but if you refuse, I don't see what we can do. Just look at this precious kiln of yours with all of the roof torn off and burnt. I don't wonder we are a laughing-stock to everybody. And as it looks as if there were no hope of getting this glaze, why don't you do as Gohei wants and be comfortable for the rest of your life?

KAKIĒMON (*with an expression of mingled sorrow and anger*): Do as Gohei wants? Sell my soul to my enemy?

Give up my revenge as well as my hope of success? What is this you're saying? Take money from the father of the man who made a plaything of my daughter and then left her to die, from the old devil who could have saved her and wouldn't lift a hand to do it? Do I hear aright? But you haven't heard yet. O Tsu has thrown herself into the sea and become food for fishes.

O TANÉ: Oh! Elder sister is dead then!
  (*Bursts into tears.*)

KAKIĒMON: Yes, O Tsu is dead. But Heisaburo is alive. And Gohei is alive. And Kakiēmon is alive too, and while he lives he does not give up hope of seeing the pair of them ruined. You may not have much spirit, but still you are my daughter, aren't you? I can't think how you can imagine that I should give in to such evil-doers. How different you are from your elder sister.

O TANÉ (*clinging to him*): Father! Please forgive me. It was only because I wanted to save you from hardship that I made such a bad suggestion. Yes, it's all my fault, and now I will try all I can to take my sister's place and help you in everything. You will forgive me, won't you?

KAKIĒMON: Say no more about it. You are indeed my daughter, aren't you? (*Draws her to him and looks into her face by the light of the fire.*) My two precious pieces of porcelain. Now that one is broken and lost I must take the greater care of the other, for treasures like these can never be replaced. (*They sit for a while in an affectionate attitude before the fire.*) But I mustn 't stay here any longer. I must go myself and see if I can't get some wood from those fellows. Call Kurisaku here, and look after the fire, both of you, so that it doesn't go out. While that is alive hope burns in me too, so be sure you keep it up.
  (*Exit to the left. O Tané turns to the house.*)

O TANÉ: Kurisaku! You're wanted! Wake up!

KURISAKU: O-o-o-i.

O TANÉ (*sitting by the fire and weeping*): Ah, that long-sleeved kimono my sister gave me, she meant it for a keepsake.

KURISAKU *(emerges rubbing his eyes)*: O Tané San, what are you crying about ?

O TANÉ: She is dead. My elder sister.

KURISAKU: Oh? O Tsu San! She's dead, is she? Namu Amida Butsu! Namu Amida Butsu!

O TANÉ: Stay here and look after the fire till father comes back, will you?
   (*Gets up to go when Kurisaku stops her.*)

KURISAKU: Stop here alone? It gives me the creeps! You stay too. Do stay, please, O Tané San. (*Both sit down by the fire.*) You treat me as though I were a centipede or a caterpillar, while I am fonder of you than your own parent. Well, even cats have their likes and dislikes, so it is natural that people should have too. But then people can like others if they try to, and even a fellow like myself may perhaps have something likeable in him somewhere. Don't you think you could find it out and try to care for me a bit? Since I am so fond of you, don't you think you could consider my feelings and speak more kindly to me?
   (*O Tané pokes the fire up as he speaks.*)

O TANÉ: The more I think about you the more I dislike the thought of you.

KURISAKU: Oh dear! I must have done evil things in a former life to have been born so unlucky.
   (*Folds his arms and sits thinking.*)

O TANÉ: Kurisaku San! Go and get some more wood!

KURISAKU: Oh, all right. (*Jumps up light-heartedly and throws all the wood that remains into the kiln.*) O Tané San. That is all the wood there is. There's no more.

O TANÉ *(looks blank when she hears this)*: I won't say that I like you. But I don't exactly dislike you.

KURISAKU: What's that?

O TANÉ: It isn't especially necessary for people to be in love with each other to marry, I suppose. So there may be no reason why we should not do so if you want to.

KURISAKU: O Tané San! Do you really mean it?

O TANÉ: I can't hold out much longer. You're so persistent.

KURISAKU: And you'll really be my wife?
   (Draws closer to her with an expression of great delight.)

O TANÉ: Yes, I will, but there is something I want you to do for me. Will you?

KURISAKU: Oh yes, of course. And I know what you want me to do. Get you plenty of nice clothes and let you do as you like. That's nothing. I'm quite ready to get up first in the morning and bring you your breakfast in bed if you want it.

O TANÉ: No, no. It's nothing for myself. It's about this enamel-ware of father's that he is always racking his brains about. Do you think he'll succeed in getting it?

KURISAKU: Ah, I wonder. I feel very anxious about it.

O TANÉ: Yes, so do I. But it isn't the least use trying to get him to stop, so you and I must do all we can to help him.

KURISAKU: Why yes. That goes without saying. Your father is my father too now.

O TANÉ: Well said. And if you mean it, I am ready to become your wife.

KURISAKU

How can I thank you enough? But that you should have changed so quickly when you disliked me so much before must be owing to O Tsu's influence. I think it is she who has brought us together.

O TANÉ: But we need not be in any hurry about marrying.

KURISAKU: Oh no, we need not be in any hurry, any particular hurry that is.

O TANÉ: And in return you will lend it to him, won't you?

KURISAKU: Lend him what? Lend who?

O TANÉ: Why lend father the money you have saved up on the quiet.
   (*Kurisaku looks dumbfounded.*)

KURISAKU: Why certainly I would if I had any. But I haven't a penny.

O TANÉ: What have you done with it? Have you spent it on something?

KURISAKU: The master told me to say nothing about it, and I would have said nothing, but if I don't tell you now you will misunderstand me, so this is what I did with it. I gave the master all the money I had saved to help him with his enamelware.

O TANÉ : Oh, so that is why you can't lend it? Because you have lent it to him already. Kurisaku San! I am indeed your wife after this.

KURISAKU: O Tané San! What can I say?
   (*They take each other's hands and stand silently. The fire has just gone out while they were talking. They do not notice it. Enter Kakiē-mon from the left, his arms folded. The two part as he comes in.*)

O TANÉ: Well, father, have you managed it?

KAKIĒMON: Wherever I went they refused. And the townspeople laughed at me and called me a madman. Why when I first came here and built my kiln at Minami-kawara there wasn't any Arita. It was a desolate forlorn spot. And now after I have taught them the way to make Nankin ware, see how flourishing it has become. And all this prosperity they owe to me. And they call me, Kakiēmon, a madman. Ah, it is a world without any sense of justice or gratitude. (*Seeing that the fire has gone out.*) What have you two been doing? Don't you know that if that fire goes out Kakiēmon's hopes and his very life are extinguished with it?

(*The two, looking surprised, go out to get some more wood.*)

KURISAKU: There are no more faggots.

KAKIĒMON: Bring that wood over there.

KURISAKU: All right.
(*He pulls down one of the pillars and throws that into the kiln, but it is damp and will not burn.*)

O TANÉ: That rain has wetted it through and it won't burn.

KAKIEMO: Just for want of a little fuel to keep it burning for an hour or two is all I have toiled for to come to nothing? My beloved daughter has drowned herself, and now the fire in my precious kiln has gone out. Is there no God or Buddha or Providence or anything?

(*With a look of despair, O Tané comes to him and supports him.*)

O TANÉ: Don't be downcast, father; keep up your spirits.
(*Just then Gohei hurries in from the front accompanied by the potters Riēmon, Zengoro, and Bunzo.*)

GOHEI: Now, Kakiēmon, how about your answer? I've brought these fellows with me because I thought you would probably want some faggots carried.

RIEMON: Look here! Look at the fire!

RIEMON and BUNZO *(together)*: It's out!
(*Kakiēmon pulls himself together.*)

KAKIĒMON: The fire in the kiln may be out indeed, but as long as there's any left in my body I won't take a single bundle of faggots from Gohei.

GOHEI: Still stiff-necked are you?

ZENGORO: I'll tell you what you are.

ZENGORO and BUNZO: You're mad!
(*They laugh derisively.*)

O TANÉ: Father! This kiln you took such pains over. It would be a stroke of good luck if by chance a piece or two did come out, wouldn't it?

KURISAKU: Yes, yes. Suppose it has. Let's open it and see.
(*Kurisaku and O Tané tear off the plastering and open the kiln and gaze dejectedly at the spoilt pieces of pottery as they take them out. Meanwhile the flames in front grow higher and higher until the sky seems to be alight. The shopman Denroku comes running up out of breath, with a towel round his head and one shoulder bare, carrying a lantern in his hand.*)

DENROKU: Master! There's a great fire!

GOHEI: What? At Imari? Is the shop burnt?

DENROKU: No, the shop is all right, but Nakasato's place is burnt out, and when I went to inquire they told me that the pedigree is burnt too.

GOHEI: The pedigree burnt? That pedigree…!
(*His face falls.*)

DENROKU: And another awful thing has happened. The young master jumped right into the middle of the fire.

GOHEI: Was he burnt to death?

DENROKU: Yes.

GOHEI: In that fire!
   (*Gazing in a dazed way at the flames that leap up in front.*)

O TANÉ: Father! Heisaburo San is dead too!

KAKIĒMON: H'm, O Tsu jumped into the sea and Heisaburo into the fire.
   (*Stands staring in front of him.*)

KURISAKU (*catching sight of a plate decorated in gold and colors in the kiln and bringing it to Kakiēmon*): Master! Look here!

KAKIĒMON (*taking it and looking at it*): Ah, that is it!

GOHEI: Ah!

KAKIĒMON: The color I've dreamed of these ten years! Now I've got it! (*Weeps tears of joy. Glares fiercely at Gohei as the latter comes up to him.*) Gohei San! This plate was wrought with the life of my daughter and all my boundless love and tears! It will shine through the ages as one of the treasures of our land, and with the secret of its glowing color I grasp your life too!

GOHEI: Kakiēmon San, I have wronged you very greatly.
   (*Sits down on the ground. Kakiēmon looks fixedly in front of him as though he saw O Tsu.*)

KAKIĒMON: O Tsu! I have avenged you!
   (*He hands the plate to O Tané and presses his hands to his face and weeps. O Tané and Kurisaku support him on each side. Gohei is bowed in an attitude of contrition. The flames leap higher and higher and the whole stage glows red. In the distance the sound of the hurried clang of the fire-bell is heard.*)

CURTAIN

THE VILLAGE OF DRUM-MAKERS

BY ENOMOTO TORAHIKO
PERSONS OF THE DRAMA

LORD AYAKŌJI	
SAMMI ARINOBU	*A COURT NOBLE*
SHIRAKAWA KEMMOTSU	*A HIGH MILITARY OFFICIAL OF THE COURT*
KOMPARU ROKU-NO-JŌ	*A COURT MUSICIAN*
ABO KAMBEI	*A DRUM-MAKER*
KURA-KO	*HIS DAUGHTER*
SUTEZŌ ⎱ SANNOSUKE ⎰	*HIS APPRENTICES*
O SAN	*A MAIDSERVANT*
JUICHIBEI	*VILLAGE HEADMAN*

IMPERIAL GUARDS, DRUM-MAKERS

SCENE I

The house of the drum-maker Kambei. It is of eight yards' frontage, divided into two rooms of equal size. The right hand one is matted and has a curtained entrance in front and on the wall are shelves on which stand newly made drum-bodies. The left-hand room is the workshop and has a boarded floor on a lower level. On the opposite wall is a cupboard containing boxes of tools and cherry wood for the drums. Over the entrance gate is a tablet with the inscription, "Abo Kambei, Court Drum-maker." Outside the house on the right is an old cherry-tree and a well and well-sweep. Beyond the gate to the left the distant scenery of Tabu-ga-mine with the River Kurahashi in the foreground.

TIME

About the middle of the third month. The house is situated on the outskirts of the village of Sakurai in the province of Yamato.

A number of young drum-makers, clad in striped kimono or in tight-fitting pantaloons, are assembled round the house, some standing and others sitting on the veranda. The curtain rises to the strains of a country folk-song.

ALL: Is the old master at home? Hullo! Kambei Dono! Kambei Dono!

KAMBEI *(from inside the house)*: I'm at home all right. What do you want?

(As he says this, Kambei appears at the curtained entrance. His hair is done in the style of an old man and he has the careless and unconventional manner of a master craftsman.)

What's all this about? Here have I just had my midday drop of drink, and feeling happier than usual after it too, so nice and tipsy that I'd clean forgotten all the troubles of life, and now you must come and disturb me with this unseemly row, like so many faggots spluttering. What d'ye mean by it, eh?

FIRST DRUM-MAKER: There! Now you've made the old master angry! Didn't I tell you not to shout so loudly?

SECOND DRUM-MAKER: What a liar you are! Why, you shouted louder than anyone. *(Turning to the others)*

Didn't he, you fellows?

FIRST DRUM-MAKER: You're the liar. My voice was as low as a temple gong.

SECOND DRUM-MAKER: Yah! A cracked temple bell you mean! A big one!

KAMBEI *(interrupting irritably)*: Stop that noisy jangling, do! Can't you say what you came for and have done?

FIRST DRUM-MAKER: Yes, of course, that's just what I say. It's like this, master: it's about that drum for the Court that we've all been working so hard for, all these weeks. It must be settled to-day whose work will be chosen. That's what we've come about.

SECOND DRUM-MAKER: Yes, and not only that. It must be settled who is to be chosen to marry the master's daughter too, eh?

THIRD DRUM-MAKER: And it's said the master and his daughter can't agree about it and keep on making objections and saying they won't have this one, and they don't like that one. That's not right. It ought to be decided properly, eh?

FOURTH DRUM-MAKER: Yes, we want to hear the master confirm the promise he has made that he will marry her to one of us, whatever happens.

FIFTH DRUM-MAKER: Yes, confirm it before everybody!

ALL: Promise you will, master!

KAMBEI: You needn't worry yourselves about that. I've never told you a lie yet. There's no need to tell you that this village of Sakurai is renowned for its drums. A thousand years ago a musician named Mimashi came to Japan from Kudara, what you call Korea nowadays, and by order of our Imperial Court taught the traditional music of China in these parts, and that was the beginning of the use of the drum called "tsuzumi" in our country. And ever since that time our ancestors have bent all their skill to making that drum as finely as it can be made, and so well have they wrought that drums made by our master craftsmen are regarded as unique treasures of our Imperial House. But times are not what they were, for the craftsmen of today think more of gain than of their work, and I fear that our immemorial skill may be departing and none be found equal to our forefathers. And this is a constant grief to me. And when a while ago the Lord Ayakōji Sammi Sama summoned me and bade me make a drum so that it might be comparable to the masterpieces of old, for he would have it for use in the Imperial Court, I could but tell him that I was now too old to do the work myself, but I would have the younger men do their best, and then he could choose from these if there should be one suitable. And he assented and told me to have them ready within a hundred days, and so to encourage you to put out your best efforts I promised that to the one who should produce a masterpiece I would give my daughter and make him heir to all my property. I'll give everything I have if it will revive our ancient renown. Why should I deceive you?

FIRST DRUM-MAKER: We don't doubt that, master. But as you've got two apprentices in your own house, Sutezō and Sannosuke, we thought you might want to make one of them the heir. That's all. That's what we were anxious about and what we came to ask you.

ALL: Yes, that's it, master.

KAMBEI: Well, and what then? Isn't the Lord Ayakōji himself deigning to judge the drums. And isn't he coming here to Sakurai especially for that purpose? Do you think he is likely to show favor to any special person? And as for me, d'ye think I am such a silly old dotard as to put my parental feelings before the interests of my family craft? What next, indeed?

THIRD DRUM-MAKER: Ah, you mightn't, master, but how about your only daughter Kura-ko? She may have her likes and dislikes, perhaps.

KAMBEI: Well, then, I'll turn her out. I'll show you all I'm not to be trifled with.

ALL: That's right, master.

KAMBEI: You can be sure of that.

FIRST DRUM-MAKER: We're all quite satisfied now you've told us this. Now let's go on to Lord Ayakōji's lodging.

SECOND DRUM-MAKER: Yes, we'll show him the work we've thrown all our souls into. And then we shall see who will be chosen.

THIRD DRUM-MAKER: Come along all of you then. And your apprentices, master?

KAMBEI: I'll see to them. We'll come on after you. Don't trouble about us.

FIRST DRUM-MAKER: All right, Kambei Dono, we'll meet you at His Lordship's lodgings.

ALL: Yes, we'll see you again there.
  (*The six of them move off to the left to the strains of a rustic melody. Enter Kura-ko from the house. She is in the gaily-patterned long-sleeved dress of a young girl.*)

KURA-KO: What, father, you'll give your daughter to any worthless fellow if only he is a master at drum-making?

KAMBEI: Worthless fellows can't be masters. That needs more than mere skill. That needs character.

KURA-KO: Still my late mother used to say that master craftsmen were a lazy lot on the whole. Spending all their time idling about and drinking and lying in bed in the morning, and so on; she often said she couldn't bear the sight of them about the house.

KAMBEI: Idling? They're not idling. They're thinking. I myself may not be all I ought, but here I am ready to give up my house and my daughter to anyone who will restore the ancient fame of our craft. And you see how they all admire my spirit.

KURA-KO: They may admire your spirit, father, but that doesn't do me any good. I want to marry the man I love.

KAMBEI: 'M! You want to marry Sannosuke, I suppose?

KURA-KO: Yes.

KAMBEI: Well, he's not a bad craftsman, naturally, as I've taught him, but he lacks something yet. I'm not sure there isn't a better one than he somewhere. And it's to find this unknown master that I offer my daughter and my house.

KURA-KO: Then you'll kill me. You'll kill my love. I mayn't be very much to look at, perhaps, but I have my feelings, and if you decide that a misshapen fellow like Sutezō is to be my husband.... Oh, what shall I do?

KAMBEI: And a very fine match too!

KURA-KO: Oh!

KAMBEI: Well, what's funny in that? He may have one leg shorter than the other, but what of that? His hands are wonderful. Put a chisel into them and he's like a son of God! And if he has a face like a monkey he has a fine spirit in him. However ugly the box may be, the value lies in the treasure that's in it. If you put a crock into the finest casket of gold lacquer it remains as worthless as ever. I doubt if there's a finer fellow in all this village than Sutezō.

KURA-KO: Oh yes, I admire him too. I've often said so. When you found him standing begging outside the gate in the snow eight years ago, playing on a broken drum, and brought him in and made him your apprentice and taught him so that he is now so good, I was the only one who was sorry for him and kind to him, when all the others despised him and called him beggar and foundling; but I certainly couldn't love him, and I should hate to be made to marry him.

KAMBEI: That's enough. That's enough. I won't hear any more of these self-willed excuses. Love or no love the duty of a daughter is to marry the man her parents choose, as you know well enough. And now with all this talking and fuss about you, the effect of all that fine liquor has clean gone. I must go in and drink it back again. (*Turns toward the inner room.*) Hi, there! Heat up some more "sake."

(*Exit. Enter Sannosuke from the opposite direction. He opens the outer gate and comes in carrying a black-lacquered drum-box. He is a fair complexioned, handsome young man.*)

SANNOSUKE: What is it, Kura-ko San? Has the old gentleman been talking roughly to you in his cups?

KURA-KO: Oh, I'm so glad you've come. I've tried hard to talk father round, but he's quite obstinate, and says he's determined to have no shilly-shallying but to marry me to the man who makes the best drum.

SANNOSUKE (*dejectedly*): Oh! Then all my hopes——

KURA-KO: All *my* hopes. How unkind that sounds. Why don't you say all *our* hopes?

SANNOSUKE: Yes, all our hopes, of course. I'm so sorry. They all depend on this drum here that I have brought for you to look at. (*Takes the drum out of the case.*) Look well at it. Ah, I've put my very soul into that cherrywood. Every stroke of the chisel wore away a bit of my life.
(*Hands it to Kura-ko.*)

KURA-KO: How finely wrought it is, without a flaw, this drum that holds the hearts of both of us.
(*Looks delighted with it.*)

SANNOSUKE: Still, I feel anxious.

KURA-KO: Why, do you think there's a better one anywhere, then?

SANNOSUKE: I don't think there are many as good, but there is one man I fear, and that is Sutezō.

KURA-KO: Oh, why?

SANNOSUKE: Last night I went to Tabu-ga-mine, and on the way back, when I came to the ford on the Kurahashigawa, there was Sutezō trying the drum he has made, under the late-blooming cherry-trees by the light of the cloudy moon, little thinking that anyone could hear it. And when quite suddenly the sound fell on my ear, echoing clear and full over the water in the still midnight, I was rooted to the spot and could do nothing but stand there weeping. Indeed he far surpasses any other craftsman, and how can I hope to rival him? I fear it is Sutezō who will be chosen to be your husband.

KURA-KO: Oh, don't be so downhearted. Even if Sutezō's drum is put first today, do you think I'll marry him? Besides he himself wouldn't dream of such a thing. All he wants is to make a reputation. That's all he thinks about.

SANNOSUKE: No, no, it isn't. You can see he's in love with you by the way he looks at you.

KURA-KO: That's only your jealousy. Why, if any of the young men speak a word to me you think they're in love. Don't worry about that. You know how kind I've always been to Sutezō. Well, if I say I don't want to marry him, do you think he will be so ungrateful as to press me?

SANNOSUKE: Quite likely. When people are in love they don't care a cucumber for duty or gratitude. You'll be pressed harder and harder till at last you'll have to give way and take him. And then you'll have a child and forget all about me, and it will end in my drowning myself or becoming a monk.

KURA-KO: Oh, you think I'm that kind of weakling, do you? I tell you if father won't let me marry you I won't marry anyone at all. I'll remain unmarried all my life, so there!

SANNOSUKE: You may think so now perhaps. But when you see Sutezō come back in triumph and hear everyone praising him and saying what a fine fellow he is, you'll be satisfied, even with a cripple like him. Even the hardest heart will melt at last.

KURA-KO (*gazing intently into his face and laying her hand on her heart*): Ah, Sannosuke, you don't understand. Your calm eyes cannot see the fierce passion that burns in this heart of mine. I swear by all the Deities that I will never change. Take me in your arms and hold me close to you once more.
   (*Clings to him.*)

CHILDREN'S VOICES BEHIND THE SCENE: Yah! Yah! Look at the cripple running away! Boo! Boo!
   (*The two separate quickly as Sutezō comes limping in at the gate, panting hard. He is a very ugly young man dressed in cotton clothes with straw sandals on his feet and a shock of long hair*).

SANNOSUKE: Hullo! What's the matter?

SUTEZŌ: Oh, it's only those little devils of children who have been teasing me again. What a curse it is to be born lame.
   (*Puts his hand to his forehead, from which a little blood is flowing.*)

KURA-KO: Are you hurt?

SANNOSUKE: How did you get that?

SUTEZŌ (*looking at his hand on which there is a stain of blood*): I slipped and fell on a stone as I was running away when those children chased me.

SANNOSUKE: The damned little devils! I'll go and catch them and give them something.
   (*Starts to go. Sutezō stops him.*)

SUTEZŌ: No, no, stop! I've forgiven them, so please don't trouble.

KURA-KO: Let me bathe your head for you. (*Draws water in a basin and wets her handkerchief in it and wipes the blood from his forehead. When she has done so, Sutezō stealthily picks it up. Sannosuke observes this and looks angry.*) It's stopped bleeding. Doesn't it hurt?

SUTEZŌ: Oh no, not at all. Thanks very much.
    (*Enter the servant O San from the house.*)

O SAN: Sannosuke San, the master is calling you. Please come in.

SANNOSUKE: Tell him I'm just coming.

O SAN: He'll be shouting at you if you don't hurry.
    (*Exit. Sannosuke stares at Sutezō*)

SANNOSUKE: Look here, Sutezō! In an hour or two our future will be decided. And then, whether we shall still be friends as we have been, or enemies, well, I wonder. Whether the showman will bring Buddha out of his box or the devil, that's the question!

SUTEZŌ: Oh, fellow apprentices are always snapping and snarling at each other, but rivals in the workshop are friends outside.

SANNOSUKE: I don't mean rivals in this business — (*tapping the drum-box*). I mean rivals in love!

SUTEZŌ: What?
    (*Looks surprised.*)

SANNOSUKE: Yes, whether it'll be the devil or Buddha depends on fate. But I fancy we shan't travel the same road in future. No, I don't think we shall go hand in hand any more.
    (*Goes in. Sutezō stares after him.*)

SUTEZŌ: I wonder what he means. I don't know in the least.

KURA-KO: Yes, we are coming to the parting of the ways. And now won't you show me the drum you've made. I hear it is a fine piece of work.

SUTEZŌ: Certainly. Here it is. (*Takes down a white wood drum-box from the shelf in the workshop, takes off the lid and brings out the body of a drum.*) Day and night I've thought and striven and toiled at this. And now at last I've worked out what I dreamed. No one has ever carved the body of a drum with such a sensitive chisel stroke before. In its four tones I've made reverberate all the sounds that are in earth and sky.

KURA-KO (*looking intently at the drum*): Even my father, famed craftsman as he is, can hardly handle a chisel like this. You'll win today.

SUTEZŌ: Won't that be splendid! Just fancy a lame fellow like me becoming perhaps the greatest man in Sakurai. Still it will be all owing to the kindness of the master and yourself.

KURA-KO (*in a low tone*): Yes, it will be very well for you to be the greatest man here...but how about the other?
    (*Bursts into tears. Sutezō looks perplexed.*)

SUTEZŌ: What has made you cry? Have I said anything to hurt you?

KURA-KO: No, no. Please let me alone.

SUTEZŌ: But it's strange to see you cry without any reason....Ah! I know. They're tears of joy. It must be because you are glad my drum is such a fine one. Ah, how sweet of you. I wish your tears were like the flood of the Kurahashi River so that all who speak ill of me might drink. Yes, everybody is against me and you are the only friend I have. Since I first came here eight years ago, if it had not been for you I should not have known what kindness meant. But as I was born lame like this, I was ashamed to say a word of what I felt for you. Oh, Kura-ko San, I have always loved you.

(*Kura-ko starts back in surprise at this.*) Yes, I don't wonder you look surprised that I should say such a thing. It must seem strange presumption for me to dare to think I should have won your love, when I am as ugly as I am as well as being lame. But if you are so pleased about me that you weep with joy...Surely tears cannot lie?

KURA-KO: Don't! Oh, please stop! It's all a mistake. It is not about you that I am crying...It's about someone else.

SUTEZŌ (*looking surprised in turn*): Oh! About someone else?

KURA-KO: Please don't be angry with me, Sutezō. There is someone I have loved for a long time, and he too has made a drum, but it is not to be compared with yours...and so I forgot myself and cried.

SUTEZŌ: Ah, that explains the riddle. Then please excuse me. I never dreamt that you and Sannosuke were in love with each other.
     (*Looks disappointed and dejected.*)

KURA-KO: Oh, don't look so downhearted, Sutezō. It is all my fault. You can't help doing the best work. You're such a fine craftsman there's none to equal you, and I shall be so pleased to see you make a great name and be honored. And how can I expect you to help me to marry Sannosuke. Ah, what shall I do?
     (*Gets up to go.*)

SUTEZŌ: And what will you do?

KURA-KO: Oh, I shall go into a nunnery.
     (*Puts her sleeve to her face and runs into the house crying.*)

SUTEZŌ: Well, I thought I was only lame, but I seem to have been blind as well. But now I see what I have to do, at any rate. I must give up all thoughts of her for myself and try and find a way for her to marry Sannosuke. That is the least I can do to repay all her kindness. (*Stands thinking. Catches sight of Sannosuke's drum-box.*) Ah, there's Sannosuke's drum-box. Now then, if I exchange my drum for his, he will be the one to win, and then Kura-ko will be able to marry him. (*Looks round to see if anyone is there. Then opens the black-lacquered box and takes out the drum from it, replacing it with his own.*) Well, I never imagined that I could sacrifice this masterpiece of all my labor to help anyone else.

(*Looks as if about to break down. Then pulls himself together and shuts the lid and puts Sannosuke's drum into his own box. Sounds of music of the Kagura of a shrine are heard in the distance. Enter Kambei from the house on the right. He is in ceremonial costume of crested haori and hakama and wears a short sword in his belt.*)

KAMBEI: Now then, it's time to start. Are you ready, Sutezō? Where has Sannosuke got to? Sannosuke! Sannosuke!
(*Enter Sannosuke from the house.*)

SANNOSUKE: Excuse my keeping you waiting, master.

KAMBEI: Have you got your drums all right?

SANNOSUKE: The one in the black-lacquered case is mine. Sutezō's is in the white wood one.

KAMBEI: Well, only one of all the drums can be chosen for the Imperial use, and I should like it to be the work of one of my apprentices if possible. (*Listening*). Ah, there's a Kagura at the village shrine. Some of the others are having prayers said for their success, it seems. We'd better put one up too on our way.

SANNOSUKE: Well, I'm off. Are you coming with me, Sutezō?

SUTEZŌ: My leg's bad, so I think I shan't go. You might take mine with you, if you don't mind.

SANNOSUKE: Oh, certainly. Hand it over then.

SUTEZŌ: Thanks very much. I've written my name on a piece of paper and stuck it on the box.
  (*Hands his case to Sannosuke.*)

KAMBEI: Hurry up and don't be late.

SANNOSUKE: Then excuse my going on first.
  (*Goes off with the two boxes.*)

KAMBEI: Why do you stay away on an important day like this?

SUTEZŌ: 'Tisn't seemly for a deformed fellow like me to appear before people of rank.

KAMBEI: Nonsense. What does it matter? You come along with me.

SUTEZŌ: But... with my deformity...

KAMBEI: What of it? It's a craftsman's skill that matters, not his looks.
  (*Stage revolves.*)

SCENE II

An apartment in the lodging of Lord Ayakōji. It is of eight yards frontage and has a veranda running round three sides of it. In front there is a tokonoma and a chigai-dana beside it with a cupboard under. The fusuma are painted with landscapes on a ground of gold-dust. It looks on to a garden with stepping-stones, trees and stone lanterns. On the left is the front gate. On a large cushion in the middle sits Lord Ayakōji Arinobu, Court noble of the Third Rank. He wears his hair in the Tea-whisk style, and is attired in the hakama and carries the fan used by nobles of the Court. On his left sits the Court Musician, Komparu Boku-no-jō, in haori and hakama, trying the drums. In front of him sits the military official, Shirakawa Kemmotsu, in black cap and robe of ceremony. An Imperial Guard sits by him, while on the veranda is the village headman, Juichibei, with his face to the ground. In the grounds outside to the left stand the six young drum-makers of the first act in an attitude of respect, holding their drums. The only sound is the tapping of the drums.

ARINOBU: That will do.
  (*Roku-no-jō puts the drum down.*)

ROKU-NO-JŌ: What does Your Excellency think of it?

ARINOBU: That you have played it very well, but the tone is not good. I fancy there is a flaw in the body somewhere. Take another look at it.

ROKU-NO-JŌ: Certainly, sir.
  (*Loosens the cords and inspects the body carefully.*)

SECOND DRUM-MAKER: There! Did you hear that? His Excellency doesn't seem to think much of the drum you're so proud of.

FIRST DRUM-MAKER: Well, if he doesn't, he doesn't, that's all. If it fails I shall smash it up. That's what I brought this hatchet for.

SECOND DRUM-MAKER: Quiet! His Excellency will hear you.
  (*Takes the hatchet from him. Roku-no-jō finishes his examination of the drum.*)

ROKU-NO-JŌ: It is as Your Excellency says. There is a very small flaw in the edge.

ARINOBU: Yes, I thought so. Hand it back again.

ROKU-NO-JŌ: Ha!
  (*With an inclination of his body. Hands it to the headman.*)

JUICHIBEI: This too will not be needed by His Excellency.

FIRST DRUM-MAKER: Oh, dear. Well, it can't be helped, I suppose. (*Takes his drum from the headman with a rueful look.*)

KEMMOTSU: Is that all? We must have submitted nearly a hundred drums for His Excellency's inspection.

JUICHIBEI: No, Your Honor. The two apprentices of Abo Kambei, Sannosuke and Sutezō, have still to come.

KEMMOTSU: Well, where are they? Let us see their work.

JUICHIBEI: Certainly, Your Honor. I'll send someone for them at once.
(*Goes to do so. A voice is heard from the left.*)

SANNOSUKE: There is no need. Here I am.

JUICHIBEI: Ah, there you are, Sannosuke. And where is Sutezō?

SANNOSUKE: I think he is not coming. I have brought the drum he is sending in with me. Please submit them to His Excellency.
(*Puts the two boxes on the veranda.*)

JUICHIBEI: Which is which, then?

SANNOSUKE: The black box is mine and the white Sutezō's, sir.
(*Points to them with his finger. Juichibei nods and then hands them up to the officials.*)

JUICHIBEI: These are the work of Kambei's apprentices, Your Honor.

ROKU-NO-JŌ (*taking the drum from the black box*): This is yours, Sannosuke, is it?

SANNOSUKE: It is, Your Honor.

ARINOBU: Try it.

ROKU-NO-JŌ: Ha!
  (*Bows. Fits on the head.*)

FIRST DRUM-MAKER: These are the last two. It lies between Sannosuke and Sutezō.

SECOND DRUM-MAKER: Ah! You know it's said that you and
Kura-ko are attached to each other, don't you? Well, they're whispering now that Kambei has given you some help with that drum
on the sly.

SANNOSUKE: What's that you say? What d'you mean? D'you think
anyone as straight as everyone knows the master is would do a
thing like that? And even if he offered to do so, I couldn't stand
it. It's doing a thing with your own hand that satisfies you. I don't
want to succeed even in love through other people's help. It's my
very best work, every bit of it, even if it isn't a masterpiece. Why
can't you wait and hear how it sounds before giving your opinion, anyway? If I get the credit of passing off the master's work as
mine I shan't have any reputation left. It's a big falsehood.

THIRD DRUM-MAKER: Well, if you say so, that's all right. We
don't believe it, so you needn't be so angry.

SANNOSUKE: Anyone would be if they were suspected of a thing
like that.

THIRD DRUM-MAKER: Oh, he wasn't serious about it. You can
say anything to a friend. So forgive him and don't say any more
about it.
  (*Placates Sannosuke. Meanwhile Roku-no-jō has prepared the
drum and strikes it. Arinobu listens.*)

ARINOBU: Ah! Now this is a drum. As I expected of a pupil of
Kambei. This is the finest we have heard so far. Now try the
other.

ROKU-NO-JŌ: Certainly, Your Excellency. (*Takes the drum out of the white box.*) This belongs to your fellow apprentice Sutezō, does it not?

SANNOSUKE: Yes, Your Honor.
  (*Roku-no-jō fits the head to it.*)

FOURTH DRUM-MAKER: Ah, he says Sannosuke's is the best so far.

FIFTH DRUM-MAKER: I expect his will be chosen. And he'll get Kura-ko as well. He's a lucky fellow.

SIXTH DRUM-MAKER: No, no. It isn't decided yet.
  (*Roku-no-jō strikes the drum. The tone is exceedingly fine.*)

ROKU-NO-JŌ: How is that, Your Excellency?

ARINOBU: Once more, please.

ROKU-NO-JŌ: Ha!
  (*Strikes it again. Arinobu looks delighted.*)

ARINOBU: Splendid! This is a masterpiece! I've never heard such a fine-toned drum before. Loosen the cords and let me look at it.

ROKU-NO-JŌ: Ha!
  (*Sannosuke looks very surprised. The other six look astonished also.*)

FIRST DRUM-MAKER: Did you hear that? Sutezō's is the best of all!

SECOND DRUM-MAKER: Ah, and the lovely Kura-ko's bridegroom...

THIRD DRUM-MAKER: Will be a cripple as ugly as the devil.

ALL: The cripple! The cripple!
  (*Meanwhile Roku-no-jō has handed the drum to Arinobu.*)

ARINOBU: The work in this is simply amazing. You would hardly think a man could do it. The greatest craftsmen of Nara have never done better. This is quite fit for the use of our Imperial Court.

SANNOSUKE: That drum is to be chosen for the Imperial use!

JUICHIBEI: It's a credit to the craftsman and a great honor to our village. We ought to be grateful to him indeed.
  (*Enter Kambei from the left with Sutezō.*) Ah, Kambei Dono, your son-in-law is to be Sutezō.

KAMBEI: What's that you say?

JUICHIBEI: Sutezō's drum has been chosen for use at Court.
  (*Sutezō starts in surprise.*)

KAMBEI: Sutezō's drum is the best, you say?

JUICHIBEI: His Excellency declares that even the work of the great masters of Nara is no better.

KAMBEI: Is Sutezō's work as good as that? Well!

SUTEZŌ: Master! I have a confession I must make. I did not make that drum. It is really the work of Sannosuke here.

SANNOSUKE: How? What do you mean?

SUTEZŌ: I wished you to win. And so I put my drum into your case.

SANNOSUKE: Oh!
  (*Looks more astonished.*)

SUTEZŌ: I was proud of my skill and I thought that my work was far better than yours. It was because I wanted to help you to marry the girl who loves you that I changed the two drums. I had no bad intention. It was only my unfortunate pride. I hope I may be forgiven since I really meant well.

JUICHIBEI: Then that drum is Sannosuke's.
   (*He and the six drum-makers look very astonished. Kura-ko runs in suddenly from the left*).

KURA-KO: Ah, Sannosuke, we are saved then! I can marry him after all, can't I, father?

KAMBEI: Why, what's this? How dare you say such a thing before His Excellency? Off with you at once!

SANNOSUKE: No, no. It is Sutezō that Kura-ko will have to marry after all.

KURA-KO: What do you mean? As your drum has been declared the best, I am to be given to you as my father promised. Your wife in the sight of all the world.

SANNOSUKE: No. That drum is not mine. It is Sutezō's I tell you.

KURA-KO: But how can that be?

SANNOSUKE Ah, I'm ashamed to say what an evil thing I did. As I came along here I could think of nothing but how much I wanted you Kura-ko, and when I came to the Kurahashi River with the two boxes in my hand, a disgraceful thought came into my mind and I slipped into the hut by the ferry and there, in the half darkness, I hurriedly changed the drums, and so I handed them to His Excellency. And all I did by this wretched fraud was to punish myself, for so I reversed the kindness that Sutezō meant to do me and put the drums just as they were in the first place. But Sutezō of course knew nothing of this and thought the one in the white box was mine, and so he has confessed to his own most innocent and kind deceit and filled me with the greater shame that I understand how fine his nature is. Ah, my eyes were blinded by love, and I thought to blind those of others too. I am a thief who tried to steal another man's skill. It is my own hand that has brought my love to nothing. Sutezō tried to save Kura-ko but my folly has ruined it all. It's all my fault. I'm the guilty one. Here, Sutezō, you can do what you like to me!

(*Throws himself down in front of Sutezō. Kambei, who has said nothing thus far, now breaks in.*)

KAMBEI As to what you deserve I think that's for me to say.

(*Turning to Arinobu*)

I am indeed ashamed at the disgraceful conduct of my apprentices. I don't know how to apologize to Your Excellency.

ARINOBU It's not so very bad. What Sannosuke did he did for love. It's more pathetic than evil. So don't blame him too much.

KAMBEI Your Excellency is too considerate altogether. I can't help feeling my responsibility for their behavior. Still it seems that this fine drum is Sutezō's work, and we must all be very thankful that it is considered worthy to be chosen for the Imperial Court.

ARINOBU Indeed I shall have the honor of presenting it there.

FIRST DRUM-MAKER Now, Kambei Dono, we shall expect to see you assert your authority as a parent, whatever Kura-ko may say, and give her to Sutezō as well as making him heir to your property as you promised.

SECOND DRUM-MAKER Yes, you promised us faithfully you would just now, and you won't go back on that.

THIRD DRUM-MAKER So we shall come round this evening to the celebration.

(*Kura-ko bridles up at this.*)

KURA-KO: Father, I don't want to marry Sutezō. Please let me go into a nunnery.

KAMBEI: What, more of that obstinacy? You're very fortunate. You ought to be proud to become the wife of a man like Sutezō, drum-maker to the Imperial Court.

KURA-KO: I don't care for famous craftsmen. I want the man I love. You think of nothing but drums, father, but a woman thinks only of her lover. Ah, how I wish my mother was still alive. She wouldn't have treated me in this way.

KAMBEI: Eh, you shut up! You've always got too much to say by half. What do you mean by always quoting your mother as an excuse for your unfilial ways? You think it was only your mother who is dead who was kind to you and that your father doesn't know what affection means, do you? I tell you it is parental kindness that makes me wish to see you married to a fine craftsman so that people may treat you with consideration and respect. If I do tell you to give up your lover, that won't kill you. Yes, my words may seem harsh, no doubt, but you must know that behind them there lurk tears that should be like balm, for they show how deeply a parent has his child's real welfare at heart. So now say you will give up Sannosuke and marry Sutezō. Here in the presence of His Excellency and all the village. It'll make an impression on them all, I can tell you. They'll say how they admire your spirit, the kind of spirit they would expect Kambei's daughter to show. Come now. (*But Kura-ko goes on crying and does not answer.*) Why don't you answer when I tell you all this. Do you refuse? Would you disobey me, you unfilial hussy? Ah, yes, I'll show you!
   (*Picks up the hatchet that is lying by and steps forward. Sutezō also steps forward toward him.*)

SUTEZŌ: Master! Wait a minute. I've a better use for that hatchet.
   (*Takes it from his hand, steps quickly up to the raised veranda, and with a blow splits his own drum in half. Kambei springs forward in astonishment.*)

KAMBEI: What have you done? (*Thrusts him back so that he falls. As he goes to get up he stands over him glaring.*) Are you mad then?

SUTEZŌ: Oh no, not in the least. But my drum is ill-omened. Can't you see that? It is a portent of evil. How can a thing like that be of any value? It isn't seemly that it should be used at Court. (*To the officials*): But please take this drum that Sannosuke has made back with you to the capital. It is really a fine one, and I should be so extremely grateful if you would.

ARINOBU: Ah, I see. Sutezō is a craftsman with a noble mind as well as a sensitive hand. Gladly I will present Sannosuke's drum to the Court.

SANNOSUKE: But that evil thing I did.

KURA-KO: His Excellency does not blame you.

ARINOBU: So the drum is chosen and all is well ended.

KAMBEI: Ah, but that precious masterpiece —

SUTEZŌ: Well, and what of it? If the drum is split in halves, these two have been brought together.

CURTAIN

RAIZAN

BY ENOMOTO TORAHIKO
PERSONS OF THE DRAMA

KONISHI RAIZAN	*A RETIRED DRUGGIST*
KONISHI SEIBEI	*HIS NEPHEW*
CHUĒMON	*HIS CLERK*
YAKICHI	
KUHEI	
KEISHICHI	*HIS FIVE NEIGHBORS*
CHŌSUKE	
SAKUZŌ	
TOKOI IYO-NO –KAMI	*LORD WARDEN OF OSAKA CASTLE*
ARIMURA ICHIGAKU	*A SAMURAI OF SATSUMA*
KO-FUJI	*A GEISHA*
O MACHI	*A WAITRESS*
O MATSU	*A NURSE-MAID*
TOMPACHI	*A JESTER*

TWO PALANQUIN-BEARERS

The villa of Konishi Raizan at Imamiya near Osaka. It is a tastefully built thatched cottage of twenty-four feet frontage, and stands in the center of the stage. It has a bamboo veranda on three sides, and under the eaves a wooden tablet with the three characters Jū-man-do written on it in white. To the right there is a tokonoma with a plain plastered wall next to it, while to the left are two sliding doors. The picture is by Ko-rin. To the right of the main building is a small, detached room nine feet square connected by a veranda, the shōji of which are shut. This also is thatched. Outside is the usual fence and rustic gate with a small garden inside, with stepping-stones and a stone lantern or two. The seven herbs of autumn are in flower. Beyond is an autumn view of the village of Imamiya. Within the room are arranged a writing-table with inkstone, brush and paper and some tea utensils. In a conspicuous place is a female doll made of pottery. It is two o'clock in the afternoon. The curtain rises to an antique melody. The waitress O Machi and the jester Tompachi come strolling in from the left.

TOMPACHI: O Machi San! Where's this villa of the Shimaya we've got to go to? Master Arimura has hurried on in front with Ko-fuji in a kago and left word that we are to come on there after him. I wonder where it can be.

O MACHI: I've never been this way before, so it's no good asking me.

TOMPACHI: Well, here's a pretty go! I thought you knew all about it, and so I didn't ask before I started. I'd better see if they know here. (*Approaches the garden gate.*) Hi! I say! The villa of the Shimaya tea-house must be somewhere near here. Can you tell me which is the road to it?
(*As he opens the gate Chuēmon comes out of the house. He is dressed in the style of a merchant's clerk.*)

CHUĒMON: The master is out just now, and I don't belong to these parts. I've only just come here, so I'm afraid I can't tell you.

O MACHI: There! D'you hear that? This gentleman doesn't know either. What are you going to do now, Tompachi San?

TOMPACHI: Well, I suppose there's nothing for it but to knock at each door we come to and ask.
(*They make to move on when the nursemaid O Matsu enters singing a lullaby.*)

O MATSU: Lullaby, lullaby, lullaby, baby! Where has your nursemaid gone?

TOMPACHI: Ah! Hullo! I say, little nursemaid, d'you know the way to the villa of the Shimaya tea-house?

O MATSU: Oh yes, I know. It's just behind here,

O MACHI: And which is the best way to get there?

TOMPACHI: Yes, show us the way, there's a good girl,

O MATSU: That's easy enough, but I don't care to do it for nothing.

TOMPACHI: Oh, what a greedy little nurse-girl!

O MACHI: Here, wait a moment. Here's something for you. (*Gives her a coin.*)

O MATSU: Oh! Is this for me, auntie?

O MACHI: Yes, that's to buy something for yourself,

O MATSU: Very many thanks. Now, what shall I buy? Bean-jam buns or rice-jelly? That's the question. (*Goes off to the left with the pair chanting this as a kind of refrain.*)

CHUĒMON: Seeing these people of the gay quarter naturally makes me think of the young master and his troubles. He gets more and more dissipated. When the master comes back I must certainly ask him to see if he cannot remonstrate with him or do something.
  (*As he waits Raizan appears coming up the road with his five neighbors, Heishichi, Chōsuke, Sakuzō, Kuhei, and Yakichi. He is dressed in the black "jittoku" or coat worn by professional and retired gentlemen, and his head is shaven like that of a Buddhist priest. He has manacles on his wrist. The others are in hakama and haori.*)

KUHEI: Well, Raizan Dono, we will say good-bye here.

RAIZAN: Oh, won't you come in and have a cup of tea before you go home?

HEISHICHI: No thanks, we won't trouble you now.

CHŌSUKE: Yes, I am afraid you have trouble enough with this affair, but you know the saying, "You can't beat a crying child and the local official."

SAKUZŌ: True enough. However much right you may have on your side it's not much good where the magistrate thinks otherwise. It is better to be resigned to it.

YAKICHI: And I suppose we may look for more of this treatment, so we had better be careful how we make our verses in future.

RAIZAN: This is a magistrate without any taste. His judgment is enough to surprise anyone.

KUHEI: Now that's not the way to take it. The safest thing is to say nothing, and see nothing, and hear nothing like the three monkeys.

HEISHICHI: Well, farewell, Raizan Dono.

RAIZAN: Much obliged to you all.

KUHEI: We'll be going then.
    (*Exit to the left. Raizan opens the gate and goes in. The stage makes a half turn.*)

RAIZAN: So unexpected misfortune does not spare an old recluse like me, who does nothing more than croon to the flowers and recite to the moon. But it might be a good deal worse. The only drawback is that I can't do my own cooking.
    (*Chuēmon comes in.*)

CHUĒMON: So you are back again, master? But what is the meaning of those manacles?

RAIZAN: These manacles are the price I have had to pay for making a poem.

CHUĒMON: What's that?

RAIZAN: I was summoned to the watch-house today, and when I reported myself an official appeared and said, "Here you are, Raizan. You're sentenced to seventy-five days manacles for having insulted the Bugyo."* I can tell you I nearly jumped out of my skin. It was as if cold water had been poured into my ear when I was asleep! And when I recovered myself so far as to ask what the insult might be, they reminded me of the verse I had made which runs, you remember:

"And so I have got through the year
Without even knowing the name of the Bugyo."

It seems to have caught people's fancy and got repeated until it came to the ear of the Bugyo himself. He flew into a great rage, declaring that for anyone living within the jurisdiction of Osaka to say that he didn't know the name of the Bugyo implied an insult to a high official that was not to be overlooked. I protested that I had never dreamed of such a thing, but that it was merely my way of suggesting innocently enough the feeling of living a life quite remote from the world. But they wouldn't have it, and I got the manacles as you see.

CHUĒMON: What a terrible affliction. The Bugyo is certainly quite devoid of taste. However we must find a way to obtain the good offices of His Excellency the Lord Warden and get a pardon from him. We'll get you off if it can be done however much money it may cost.

RAIZAN: Oh, don't you bother yourself about that. I've forsaken the world altogether, and my life is of no more importance than a bit of wood or stone. It certainly isn't worth while throwing away good money and bothering people for a trifle like this. So let things be as they are. It's no consequence.

CHUĒMON: How can I do such a thing? You who are the mainstay of the house of Konishi! And this fleeting world of trouble that you have cast off, I am afraid circumstances have arisen that make it necessary for me to entreat you to come back to it again.

---

* Magistrate

RAIZAN: My good Chuēmon, you really look very worried. And what are these circumstances you speak of then?

CHUĒMON: Well, master, the circumstances are these. Ever since you handed over the succession and property of the family to your nephew, the young master, and retired to this villa at Imamiya, I have done all I could with my small ability to keep the business as prosperous as ever. But some time ago the young master began to frequent the pleasure quarters. Well, young men will amuse themselves, of course, and if it had been what you might call just ordinary dissipation I should not have thought it worth while mentioning, but lately he has become more and more addicted to it, and now, to crown all, he intends to buy out a certain singing-girl named Ko-fuji and bring her home as his wife. That is bad enough, but when I made inquiries about her family, as I did at once, I found that though her mother was known, nothing at all could be ascertained as to who her father was or where he came from. Now however much the young master may be attached to her, I said, to bring home a foundling bride would be a great blemish on the house of Konishi, but he won't listen to my objections, and so I thought there was nothing to be done but to come and ask you to use your authority to make him give her up.

RAIZAN (*shaking his head*): I suppose I was the one who built up the fortune of the house of Konishi more or less, but seeing that I have handed it over to my nephew Seibei he must look after it himself and sink or swim as best he pleases. And whether he takes a singing-girl or a strumpet into the family, if he likes her, that's his affair. I, Raizan, have no more connection with this fleeting world and care for none of these things.

CHUĒMON: Yes, I suppose in the master's present way of thinking it is natural that he should not care what becomes of the property, but Konishi's is a house with a reputation. It stands among the very first druggists in the city. And though it is perhaps over-bold of, me to say such a thing, does not the master think it is his duty that he owes to his ancestors to see that people do not point the finger of scorn at it?

RAIZAN: If one is not of the world, how can one have any duty to the world?

CHUĒMON: Then I understand that you don't care what happens?

RAIZAN: I think you had better let things take their course.

CHUĒMON: Well, this is a pretty state of affairs!
   (*Folds his arms and sits silent with a gloomy expression. Meanwhile Tōki Iyo-no-kāmi, dressed in haori and hakama in the style of a Daimyo incognito, has come up to the gate and been standing there listening for a few minutes, and now enters.*)

IYO-NO-KĀMI: Ah, Raizan Dono! Excuse my want of ceremony.

RAIZAN: Oh, it's Uko Dono, is it? Very pleased to see you.
   (*Iyo-no-kāmi comes up and sits down by Raizan.*)

IYO-NO-KĀMI: I have just heard of the sudden misfortune that has happened to you. Really I am astonished at the stupidity of the Bugyo.

RAIZAN: Oh, don't mention it. I suppose a poet ought to think it a great honor to be persecuted for poetry's sake.

IYO-NO-KĀMI: Yes, you need that spirit of magnanimity to savor the real elegance of life. Still, it is possible to be too detached, for if one plunges too deeply into this world of elegance and taste there may be a danger of becoming indifferent to one's family and humanity.

RAIZAN: It looks as if Uko Dono must have overheard our conversation.

IYO-NO-KĀMI: Yes, as I came along by the fence outside I could not well help overhearing what you said. I admire your clerk's spirit and devotion.

RAIZAN: Then you were alluding to that in what you said just now?

IYO-NO-KĀMI: Ah, Raizan, you may put the world away from you, but you can't get rid of the fetters of duty.

RAIZAN: What do you mean?

ITO-NO-KAMI: Look at those manacles on your hands. Don't they show that you can't cut yourself free from the world, however much you try? You may say you are a man of letters who has retired from society, but still you are under the jurisdiction of the Bugyo and have to obey his orders. And just in the same way you are still liable to the claims of duty. Or would you venture to break those manacles and throw them away?

RAIZAN: Well, hardly, I think.

IYO-NO-KĀMI: Yes, even such a steadfast spirit as Raizan can hardly do that. And neither while one is alive can he get free from his duty to others. If you are not moved by this clerk's loyalty to his master's house, to go back and experience once more the trials of this fleeting world, I don't think you can qualify as a real man of taste.
(Raizan is silent, but Chuēmon comes forward.)

CHUĒMON: Please accept my very humble thanks for supporting my appeal to my master. My name is Chuēmon, a mere servant of the Konishi family. May I have the honor of knowing who you are?

IYO-NO-KĀMI: My name is Uko, and I come to this villa once or twice a month to enjoy the simple life of elegance with its master. Out of affection for him I have given this advice. Please don't take it badly, Raizan Dono.

RAIZAN *(perceiving his fault)*: No, no. On the contrary you have showed me where I was wrong.

CHUĒMON: In that case, the master will do as I ask?

RAIZAN: Until Seibei awakes from his dream of illusion, I will become once more Konishi Shirobei and again behold this world of unreality.

CHUĒMON: I am more than grateful. But indeed it is due to the kindness of Uko Sama, and to him also I cannot sufficiently express my thanks.

IYO-NO-KĀMI: There is no need to thank me. But I think these manacles on Raizan's wrists will inconvenience him, so I will relieve him of them.
   (*Draws near to Raizan.*)

RAIZAN: But that can't be. You know that no one can take these off without permission from the Bugyo.

IYO-NO-KĀMI: But I have already asked and obtained the permission of the Bugyo.

RAIZAN: Oh, that's very kind of you. Then it will be all right.

IYO-NO-KĀMI: Yes, we need not bother any more about that.
   (*Takes off the manacles and puts them aside.*)

RAIZAN: It is solely owing to your kindness that I am saved from this durance and can look on creation a free man again.

CHUĒMON: Yes, indeed, I must again thank you, for I feel yet more deeply indebted to you. But, sir, judging from the crest you wear on your haori and by the way you spoke just now, I can't help thinking we must be addressing His Excellency the Lord Warden of Osaka.

IYO-NO-KĀMI: Ah, ha! You're a pretty sharp fellow, Master Clerk. My friend Raizan only knows me by my nom-de-plume "Uko," sure enough, but as you say, I am Tōki Iyo-no-kāmi, the Lord Warden. (*Raizan and Chuēmon both sit in silent amazement.*) But that's just the charm of the aesthetic life, that noble and commoner can enjoy each other's company in it quite freely without any hedge of ceremony.

RAIZAN: Well, well! How graceful that is. But after all it is only what I should have expected of you, Uko. (*Turns to Chuēmon*): And will you hurry home and bring Seibei back with you as soon as you can. I'll give him a straight talk about his affairs.

CHUĒMON: I expect the young master is at Shima-no-uchi as usual, so it won't take long for him to get here. (*Turning to Iyo with a bow*): Excuse me, Your Excellency.

IYO-NO-KĀMI: No ceremony, please. I'm not the Lord Warden here, you know.

CHUĒMON: Ah, pray excuse my thoughtlessness, Master Uko. I must be off immediately, but please do not hurry away.
(*Exits in haste.*)

IYO-NO-KĀMI: Well, the house of Konishi is fortunate in such a worthy manager as Chuēmon. But I must be going too, for it's twilight already.

RAIZAN: Oh, there's no hurry. Won't you wait at least till I get you a cup of tea?

IYO-NO-KĀMI: That's very kind, but I think I must be off. (*Steps down from the room. There is a sound of the chirping of insects.*) Ah, what a charming sound!

RAIZAN (*after a moment's thought*): Imamiya shrills with insects' voices, but can't hear them.

IYO-NO-KĀMI: That's a good one. Yes, things are like that.
(*Just then several retainers come up carrying the hasami-bako and other insignia of a Daimyo. They approach from the Hana-michi.*)

RETAINER: At your service, my lord.

IYO-NO-KĀMI: Ah, obliged.

(*Retainers draw in their breath as they crouch down. Iyo-no-kāmi goes to the beginning of the Hana-michi.*)

IYO-NO-KĀMI (*repeats*): Imamiya shrills with insects' voices

RAIZAN: But can't hear them.

(*Both look at each other and laugh. Iyo-no-kāmi goes off laughing after the retainers. Raizan stands thoughtful.*)

RAIZAN: Ah, well, I suppose Raizan will have to become an ordinary man again even though he has forsaken this fleeting world!

(*Draws his writing-table toward him. Enter Ko-fuji barefooted and in haste. She is dressed as a geisha and she opens the wicket and runs in.*)

KO-FUJI: Please hide me for a while somewhere, if you will be so kind.

(*Looks anxiously behind her.*)

RAIZAN: H'm! You seem to have come from the pleasure quarter. How is it you have run away?

KO-FUJI: I had to go to the Shimaya tea-house with a guest and he tried to lay hands on me, and I wouldn't have it and so I ran away. And I'm afraid he is following me, so won't you please let me hide somewhere. Do, please, kind sir, and I shall be so grateful to you.

RAIZAN: Well, I'm sorry for you if that's the reason. Come in then and I'll see what I can do. There's a cloth over there, please wipe your feet and then come this way.

(*The stage makes a half turn. Ko-fuji wipes her feet and follows Raizan into the detached room on the right. From the right enter Arimura Ichigāku dressed in the style of a Satsuma samurai in hakama and wearing two swords. He appears to have followed Ko-fuji. After standing outside a moment considering, he comes in at the gate.*)

ARIMURA: Hullo! Hullo! Inside there! I want to know if a girl hasn't just run away and hidden in this house. Answer me, please!

RAIZAN (*appearing in front of the house with a lantern in his hand*): Girl? Why no. Not even a she-cat has come along this way so far as I know. I think you had better go and ask elsewhere.

ARIMURA: But this confounded girl certainly ran in this direction. There is no other place she could have found to hide in but this cottage, so please allow me to come in and see for myself.
   (*Goes to enter the house.*)

RAIZAN: I can't have that. This cottage may be little more than a tinder-box perhaps, but it is still the residence of Konishi Raizan. Cross the threshold at your peril.

ARIMURA: Bah! You silly blow-away-at-a-breath old man! I shall come in anyhow, so you needn't try to stop me.

RAIZAN: Don't you put one foot inside here, you woman-besotted samurai!

ARIMURA: None of your impertinence! (*Pushes past Raizan, who tries to stop him, but gets flung aside and kicked out of the way in doing so. The shōji of the detached room open and Ko-fuji runs out.*) Ha! There's Ko-fuji. You see you can't get away, so you had better resign yourself to be mine. Eh?

KO-FUJI: No, I won't. I have no intention of yielding to you. I only came out because I couldn't see you kick and hurt this kind old man. You ought to be ashamed of yourself. Hit me instead as much as you please. You can kill me if you like, but I won't do your will.
   (*Thrusts herself toward him.*)

ARIMURA: They say the greater the love the greater the hate. So it seems in your case. Now I'll thrust this sword of mine through that breast that is colder than its icy blade.

KO-FUJI: Do you want to kill me then?

ARIMURA: Why not? That's the way in my province, if the girl will not yield, to finish the matter with a single blow.

KO-FUJI: But I don't want to be killed by you. There is someone else I love.

ARIMURA: You wench! I'll slash your face in half!
  (*Draws his long sword. Ko-fuji jumps down on to the ground and Raizan interposes his body between her and the blade.*)

RAIZAN: Pray, wait a moment! Don't be so sudden! Is it to kill a woman that you wear that blade that you samurai hand down from generation to generation and treasure as your soul?

ARIMURA: What's that?

RAIZAN: It is the way of samurai to be violent and headstrong, and it is natural that Your Honor should want to cut down a troublesome wench like this, but please be so good as to think over it a moment. If you cut down a woman you will have to expiate it by cutting yourself open afterwards, and your parents will be made to look ridiculous over it, while to crown all the affair will be a blot on the memorial tablets of your ancestral shrine. And is there any woman who is worth such a price? What are women? They are just like this doll here, painted up on the surface to look pretty and nothing but clay underneath. The man who is infatuated enough to throw away his precious life for a thing like that must be a big fool. I have good reason to be convinced that women are a cold-blooded lot of painted dolls, but that's another story, and the fault wasn't on my side anyhow. But Your Honor is young and no doubt has a father and mother at home, and if it is only the scruple of a samurai that if he draws he must not return his blade to the scabbard bloodlessly, well, cut this doll in half and let the other go. Now isn't that a way out, Sir Samurai?
  (*During this speech Arimura becomes meditative, and at the end drops his head and sits down.*)

ARIMURA: Yes. You're quite right. I'll take your advice and leave the girl alone.

RAIZAN: Then you pardon her?

ARIMURA: You're lucky, girl, to escape with your life. You were within a hair of being in halves just now.
(*Exit humming an air.*)

KO-FUJI: I have no words to thank you. It is only by your kindness I escaped this danger.

RAIZAN: Yes, I was a bit anxious about you at one time. But that's just like a Satsuma samurai. Frank and outspoken to a fault. And now about yourself. Where do you belong to?

KO-FUJI: I come from the Shimaya, and my name is Ko-fuji.

RAIZAN: Oh! So you are Ko-fuji, are you?
(*Looks thoughtful and lights the andon.* Enter Konishi Seibei, who comes along the road in a palanquin with Chuēmon, dressed in the style of a well-to-do young tradesman.*)

CHUĒMON: Put us down here!

SEIBEI: Oh, is this Imamiya? Why we're here in a moment. It seems nearer than usual.
(*Gets out of the palanquin. Chuēmon gives the bearers a tip.*)

CHUĒMON: Thanks for your trouble.

FIRST BEARER: Don't mention it. Thank you very much, sir. The sky looks as if it was going to rain soon.

SECOND BEARER: Yes. We'd better get back before it comes on.
(*They turn back with the empty palanquin.*)

---

* Cylindrical paper-lantern.

SEIBEI: H'm, and my feelings are like the sky.

CHUĒMON: Oh no. On the contrary everything is going to clear up. (*Opens the gate and enters.*) I have brought the young master.

RAIZAN: Ha! You've come at the right time. This way, please. (*Seibei comes in and catches sight of Ko-fuji.*)

SEIBEI: Why! There's Ko-fuji!

KO-FUJI: Yes, sir. (*They run toward each other, but Raizan interposes himself between them.*)

RAIZAN: No. no. You had better keep away from each other. So it will be easier to resign yourselves to separate as I am afraid you cannot marry each other. When young people are in love with each other it is hard for them to part at the time, but ... well, after all, it's for their own good in the end. Now, Seibei, what have you to say?

SEIBEI: It is very painful to me to go against your wishes, uncle, after you have been so patient and not reproved me once all these years, but I have promised Ko-fuji faithfully that I would make her my wife, and if I break my word I shall feel not a man at all.

CHUĒMON: Just so. Very naturally, sir, but all the same if you take a girl for your wife whose father is quite unknown, then the family will not be able to hold up its face to the world at all. And after all if you can't keep to this contract, no doubt a certain sum of money will settle it. Please consider that a blot on the family name cannot be wiped out.

SEIBEI: However much I consider, my mind is made up. Anyhow ... If I can't have Ko-fuji for my wife.... Look here! I'll get right out of the Konishi family altogether! Then I can please myself. Chuēmon! You will arrange for my uncle to disinherit me at once.

CHUĒMON: Do you mean that you are asking to be disinherited?

SEIBEI: Yes. That's the easiest way out of it, I fancy. Well, come along, Ko-fuji.

(*He takes her hand. Raizan stands staring at them.*)

RAIZAN: Seibei! Wait a moment! If you cut yourself from the family and go off with this girl how do you propose to live from now on? It pains me beyond words to hear you ask to be disinherited in that calm unfeeling way. Have you no heart at all? Even though you may have some slight knowledge of the trade of a druggist, you have never known what it is to have to get your own living by yourself, and it makes me weep to think of you thrown on an unsympathetic world with your inexperience.

There is no need to remind you that I am your father's younger brother, and when he died, leaving you only a baby, the family responsibilities fell on me. And as your mother was already dead I felt sorry for you left without any parents at all, and though I had enough to do with the business I found time to bring you up myself without leaving you to outsiders, and a young child is no small tie either. But I did not grudge it, and without waiting till you were full twenty-five I handed over the property to you and retired, looking forward to spending my remaining years of leisure in peace and quietness. But you were not long before you gave yourself up to dissipation, and every now and then unpleasant rumors about you would come to my ears. Still I thought it better to let things go as they would and I didn't interfere, and you need not think that my coming back like this to reprove you and take charge of things again at Chuēmon's special request, after I had sworn that I would have nothing more to do with this silly world, is because I begrudge the money you are wasting in the least, because it isn't. It is simply my deep anxiety to prevent you becoming a laughing-stock to people. However many times you may tell me to disinherit you I won't do it. I know well enough that people laugh and say what a fool Raizan is not to turn out that profligate spendthrift Seibei neck and crop, but I don't care. So if you have the least feeling for me and any understanding of my affection for you, you will put aside your attachment for Ko-fuji and marry a girl of a respectable family. Do you let the tears of a singing-girl move you and yet pay no heed to the feelings of your uncle and this honest Chuēmon who are really

devoted to you? Haven't you any natural affection at all?
   (*He breaks down. Ko-fuji gazes at him.*)

KO-FUJI: Oh, sir, that is too much. Do not the tears of singing-girls and of respectable people come from the same place? Doesn't the same kind of pain produce both? How can you make such a distinction? But even though I am such a person, and though I do not know the name of my father, yet I can resign myself to have nothing more to do with the young master, and from today I give him up to you completely.

SEIBEI: Then you didn't tell the truth when you swore to love me?

KO-FUJI: Oh yes, I did. And from now on the remembrance of our love is all I shall have to live for.

SEIBEI: Thank you for those words. That's a fine idea indeed. I was fully determined to take you and stick to you whatever might happen and so live, and if the worst came to the worst so die. But you can't depend on anything in this life, not even on promises to meet in the next. And so we must both lead our separate lives, but, anyhow, we can rejoice in the scent that remains though the flower of love itself be denied us.

KO-FUJI: Then you too are resigned?

SEIBEI: I have sworn I will never see you again. Ah! We who promised never to part, now we shall be eternally separated.

KO-FUJI: But let us be together at least in our dreams.
   (*Falls down weeping.*)

RAIZAN: So you consent?

KO-FUJI: Ah, yes. Indeed I do.

RAIZAN: That's splendid of you. You have made a really wise choice. I am under a deep obligation to you.

CHUĒMON: We must be proud of the young master's strength of mind, and as for Ko-fuji words fails me. This is all I can do.

(*Turns to her and puts his hands together as though in worship.*)

RAIZAN: Now we have come to this conclusion, it is better that you should not be together any longer. Seibei, will you go into the house with Chuēmon, while Ko-fuji goes back to the Shimaya. I will see her on her way there myself.

CHUĒMON: No, no, let me do that.

RAIZAN: Allow me to see her as far as the post-house. I have something I want to say to her.

CHUĒMON: Very well, sir, then please excuse me. Now, young master, please come in with me.

(*Seibei gets up to go into the house.*)

SEIBEI: Ah, Ko-fuji, let me look at you once more!

KO-FUJI: Oh yes, indeed.

(*The two stand gazing into each other's faces with a rapt expression. There is a sound of rain.*)

CHUĒMON: It's hard to part, I know, but please before the rain gets worse.

RAIZAN: Shall we start now, Ko-fuji San? (*Gets an umbrella from the house and goes out with Ko-fuji to the gate. The rain grows heavier.*) Oh, this is a terrible downpour. We had better wait a little. (*They both go back to the house.*) Well, I suppose you feel pretty angry with me for a silly old bald-head talking a lot of nonsense, but I too was young once. And in those days I too went to amuse myself in the gay quarter. I remember very well how a friend first took me there on our way back from Noh practice. And so I got into the habit, and I ended by falling in love with a girl there and we were quite devoted to each other. But she was fickle and threw me over, so I threw all my energies into the business and built up quite a substantial fortune. So when I think it over now it was a good thing we parted. Still I was over twenty then; much older than you are, but you seem wise beyond your years. Anyhow I want to do something for you as a little compensation for all this disappointment, so won't you tell me if there is anything you would particularly like?

KO-FUJI: There isn't anything at all, thank you. And as for parting from the young master, it seems nothing when I think of what my mother must have suffered.

RAIZAN: Why, had your mother also the same kind of trouble?

KO-FUJI: She had indeed. My mother was a geisha like myself, and she and my father had pledged themselves to marry, but duty forced them to feign a coldness that they did not feel, and though in their hearts they still loved each other, outwardly they pretended to care nothing, and so parted as in duty bound. And afterwards I was born, and so my unhappy mother had one misfortune added to another. And isn't that just like my lot? To be parted from the young master because of his duty to the family and to live in solitude in the future with tears of regret for my only consolation. Is there anything more cruel than duty?
  (*While she speaks Raizan is deep in thoughts of the past.*)

RAIZAN: But this mother of yours. To which tea-house was she attached?

KO-FUJI: To the Naniwaya at Sonezaki. Her name was Ko-ume.
  (*At this an expression of amazement passes over the face of Raizan.*)

RAIZAN: Then you are Ko-ume's daughter, are you?

KO-FUJI: You speak as though you knew my mother.

RAIZAN: Ah, when I was young I often met her.

KO-FUJI: Then perhaps you may know my father too?

RAIZAN: Oh yes, indeed I do. There is no day I do not meet him.

KO-FUJI: And is he well, I wonder. Ah, but he knows nothing of my being born. He has never even dreamed of such a thing. And you must never tell him. No, no one must ever tell him. That was my mother's dying wish.

RAIZAN: But why was he not to be told about your existence, I wonder?

KO-FUJI: Before she died my mother gave me a letter, and in it she has written all the explanation. I have it here.
   (*Takes a letter from an amulet-case round her neck.*)

RAIZAN: May I not read it?

KO-FUJI: Yes, please do so.
   (*Hands the letter to Raizan who puts on his spectacles and reads*):
   "Since I now know that there is no hope of recovery from my illness, I shall soon have to leave this world, and so I write here something that I have so far concealed from you. That I parted from your father twenty years ago was not of my doing. It was at the confidential request of your father's elder brother who urged that duty to the family required it. But though for the sake of this obligation I brought myself to put on an indifference I did not feel, so that he might give me up, yet the love I had then for him is still unchanged. And when I think that after I am dead you will have none to care for you or look after you, and that your future will be all uncertain, my feelings almost overcome me and I can hardly bear not to let your father know of your existence. But that would be to break the promise I gave to your father's brother, and, moreover, it would be painful to me to think of your father being troubled thus all his life, far better for him to remain in ignorance. And so I have decided to say nothing. And after I am dead I beg of you, out of respect for my feelings, to take the greatest care that what is in

this letter is not revealed. This request is all I have to bequeath.
  Excuse this poor writing.
  Respectfully."
  (*Repeatedly wiping his eyes he reads to the end.*)

RAIZAN: Ah, then it was because you were afraid of giving me pain that you did not let me know when this girl was born! And I never knew it, but only thought of you with dislike as a cold and wayward girl, and all I can do now is to feel ashamed of myself!

KO-FUJI: Can it be that you are my father? Else why do you weep as you read the letter.

RAIZAN: Oh yes, I am indeed your father.
  (*They sit gazing at each other.*)

KO-FUJI: Oh, father!
  (*Getting up.*)

RAIZAN: Ah, come to me. How like your mother you are!
  (*They take each other's hands and stand in tears. Seibei comes in from the house followed by Chuēmon.*)

SEIBEI: If I can believe my ears and things are really so, then Ko-fuji must be my own cousin!

RAIZAN: I never dreamed till a moment ago that I had a daughter like this. Well, well, this is what comes of youthful indiscretions. Now, Chuēmon, don't laugh at me.

CHUĒMON: Laugh? This is a thing to rejoice about. Now that we know Ko-fuji's pedigree there can be no difficulty about her marrying the young master. It will be a happy family reunion, won't it? And this time I shall ask you to consent to it.

RAIZAN: I am very grateful to you for your kind thoughtfulness, and I may seem to you rather arbitrary and self-willed, perhaps, but I cannot receive Ko-fuji into the family.

CHUĒMON: Please do grant me this one favor, master, and I'll never ask you another. And there is no kind of service that I will not do for you in return.

RAIZAN: No. Whatever you say, I can't give my consent.
   (*Meanwhile the samurai Arimura has entered from the left and has been standing by the gate listening. At this point he enters.*)

ARIMURA: Yah! Look here! Suppose I adopt Ko-fuji as my younger sister and then marry her to Seibei, how will that do? You'll consent then, won't you?

RAIZAN: "Why surely it is the samurai who came before.

KO-FUJI: And how differently he speaks now.

ARIMURA: You may well think it strange, but I quite realize now that my conduct of a while ago was really outrageous. And if Raizan Dono had not been so kind as to stop me I should have certainly cut Ko-fuji down and then had to expiate it by cutting myself open. The life of a samurai is not his own. He must be ready at any moment to sacrifice it for his lord if the need arises. So I cannot be sufficiently grateful to Raizan Dono that he prevented me from wasting mine on a woman. A thousand thanks! (*Bows very courteously.*) I could not go back to my province without coming to pay my respects and thank you, and now, quite unexpectedly, I find an opportunity of repaying your kindness in a more substantial way. If I adopt Ko-fuji as my sister, it will be a slight return courtesy, for then, since she will be of samurai rank she can marry anyone.

SEIBEI: You were my rival in love affairs, but none can rival you in generosity. If you deign to adopt Ko-fuji and give her to me, we shall both be everlastingly indebted to you. You will have saved us both from wretchedness.

CHUĒMON: I am delighted to make your acquaintance, most honored samurai. You have indeed deigned to arrive at a most opportune moment. A thousand thanks indeed. Now the master will no doubt consent.

RAIZAN: As the sister of Arimura Dono, it will be an honor to receive her into our family.

ARIMURA: So, then you agree?

CHUĒMON: And my request is granted. How can I thank you?

RAIZAN: Arimura Dono. Up till today I thought all women were cold-hearted creatures, but I was mistaken. Their delicate forms hide a splendid spirit. Look at this letter.
(*Holds it out to him.*)

ARIMURA: And who wrote this letter?

RAIZAN: It is the last will of Ko-fuji's mother.
(*Arimura reads it.*)

ARIMURA: But what a letter! Why every character is a tear!

CHUĒMON: But for these two, tears of joy.

RAIZAN
    On the sleeve
    How can the tears
    Dry in two colors?
Seibei!

SEIBEI: Yes, father!

RAIZAN: That is a living woman. I am but a painted clay doll. Ah! These dreams of this fleeting world—(*the clappers are tapped slightly*)—have a piquant flavor after all!
(*Stands gazing at the clay doll. Seibei and Ko-fuji gaze at each other joyously. Chuēmon's face wears an expression of content. Arimura stands scanning the letter again and again.*)

CURTAIN